And It Came To Pass

And It Came To Pass

A History Of Northeast Texas And Its Families— Lewis, Martin, Norris, Perry, Sims, Walton, Weaver

2nd Edition

Greta McKelvey

Private Publishing
Sunnyvale, Texas

Published 2022, Limited, Second Edition
Manufactured in the United States of America
22 21 20 19 18 17 16 15 14 13 12 11 10 09 08 07 06   1 2 3 4 5
ISBN 0977852407
Original Cataloging Data (OCD)
McKelvey, Greta, [date].
        And It Came To Pass A History Of Northeast Texas And Its Families—Lewis, Martin,
    Norris, Perry, Sims, Walton, Weaver, Limited, Second Edition.
        p. cm.
Includes chronology, bibliography, and index.
    ISBN 0977852407 (alk. Paper)
    1. Genealogy—Texas—History—19th century. 2. Genealogy—Texas—History—20th
    century. 3. Afro-American—Texas—History—19th century. 4. Afro-American—Texas—
    History—20th century. 5. Slavery—Texas—History—19th century. 6. Texas—Race
    relations. 7. Lewis Family—Southern States—Genealogy. 8. Martin Family—Southern
    States—Genealogy. 9. Norris Family—Southern States—Genealogy. 10. Perry Family—
    Southern States—Genealogy. 11. Sims Family—Southern States—Genealogy. 12.
    Walton Family—Southern States—Genealogy. 13. Weaver Family—Southern States—
    Genealogy.
    I. Title.
Library of Congress Call Number: CS71.xxxx   2006, 2022
Dewey Decimal Call Number: 929.2—dc21   06-xxxxx
                                                                    OCD
Outsourced Commercial Printing and Binding

CAVEAT—DISCLAIMER, NOTE:
        Notice to publish has been set forth. All documents and discussions were freely
given and/or inherited; and permissions to print have been implied and/or expressively
given to the book author, complier, and/or editor. The intended purposes for all
discussions, documents, and photography received, retained, and used were to further the
ideas of family history research, review, documentation, publication, preservation, and/or
for educational purposes. References to historical events set forth in the chronology are
factual information of public record and are attainable from multiple sources and/or
within Fair Use parameters. Biblical and Christian references are with the public domain
and/or Fair Use parameters. All mistakes and/or omissions are purely accidental,
unintentional, and without malice a forethought. The author, compiler, and/or editor are
not liable for damages, even if negligent. The authors and publishers specifically and
generally disclaim all responsibility for any loss, risk, or damage, personal or otherwise,
which is incurred as a consequence, directly or indirectly, from the use, application,
enjoyment, and/or reading of any of the contents of this book.

∞ The paper used in this publication meets the minimum requirements of the American
National Standard for Information Sciences—Permanence of Paper for Printed Library
Materials, ANSI Z39.48-1992.

Where applicable, print book, printed on acid-free paper.

iii

ACKNOWLEDGMENT and DEDICATION

In memory of C. J. Weaver Sims, writer.

Glory to God! And It Came To Pass is written and published. Those who supported me and prayed with me, they know they have my undying gratitude.

EPIGRAPH

Even the mystery which hath been hid from ages and from generations, but now is made manifest to his saints:

Colossians 1:26 KJV

CONTENTS

ABBREVIATIONS

A.B.	Artium Baccalaureus (Bachelor of Arts)
aka	also known as
B.D.	Bachelor of Divinity
B.S.	Bachelor of Science
CC Camps	Civilian Conservation Corps
CD-ROM	compact disc read only memory
CME	Christian (Colored) Methodist Church
CPL	corporal—U.S. military rank/title
D.C.	Washington, D.C., District of Columbia
DIV	division
DNA	deoxyribonucleic acid
Dr.	doctor
ED	enumeration district
EEOC	Equal Employment Opportunity Commission
et al.	et alii (or et alia), and others
etc.	et cetera, and so forth
FH	funeral home
GBNF	gone but not forgotten
i.e.	id est, that is
Inc.	incorporated
INF	infantry—military division
Jr.	junior
KJV	King James Version of the Bible
LL. D.	Legum Doctor (Doctor of Laws)
MC	Methodist Church
MEC	Methodist Episcopal Church
OES	Order of the Eastern Star
PO Box	post office box
PTA	parent teacher association
PVT	private—U.S. military rank/title
Rev.	reverend
Sr.	senior
U.S.	United States of America
U.S.C.I.	United States Colored Infantry
U.S.C.T.	United States Colored Troops
UCSD	University of California, San Diego
UMC	United Methodist Church
USS	United States ship
VA	Veterans Administration
vs.	versus
WSCS	Women Society of Christian Service
WWI	World War One
WWII	World War Two

Tell ye your children of it, and let your children tell their children, and their children another generation.

Joel 1:3 KJV

PREFACE

SOME ATTRIBUTED THE POPULARITY OF GENEALOGY OR the study of family history to the book and movie miniseries *Roots*, but the quest to know and understand one's past has biblical roots. In recent years, some have linked genealogy's surge to the Internet.

While *Roots* sparked curiosity, the Internet provided accessibility to online databases and prompted curators to make depositories readily available. Year after year, more and more people began the task of interviewing loved ones, researching public records, and writing their own family's history. Newcomers sought professional credentials by accreditation or certification from various organizations. Professionals and seasoned, self-taught family historians were digging for silver and gold across the globe. Genealogists found help within genealogy groups or associations and within the self-help books, which lined the bookshelves at local libraries and bookstores. Those how-to books offered advice on genealogy topics from interviewing techniques to resource depositories to publishing options to copyright and privacy issues.

As genealogy peaked, identity theft and privacy issues mounted, prompting local and state government officials across the United States (U.S.) to restrict public record access. Identity theft and privacy issues also tamped down the open-air sharing among genealogists that was widespread in the early 1980s. The closing of public records made capturing oral history more important and begged the question: Absent DNA studies or historical archeology analysis, what source is available to the researcher and writer under a closed public records atmosphere?

DNA technology answered the question and provided the go-to source now available to genealogists and family historians where the open records atmosphere closed and when the paper trail vanished. DNA has helped the historian write a richer story.

Blue-collar wisdom once shouted, "If it is not written, it did not happen." This simply spoken adage underlines the importance of preserving family history. This book is an effort toward preservation, for the sake of strengthening and encouraging all generations.

The following record is not a how-to book nor a fictionalized family history but rather a written narration of stories, memories, interviews, personal papers, and public record documentation, absent DNA. Each brief biography portrays an image of a deceased family member who shares a bloodline and fits within four or five generations from the progenitors, forward. These approximately 250 one line mentions or sketches represent a bloodline member who is named in this genealogy book; who are now deceased, and who on average lived to reach septuagenarian or octogenarian status.

The surviving fragmented diary and journal entries written during the 1950s and 1960s by Carrie Jane Weaver Sims influenced this monumental task. Carrie's sporadic writings are specifically detailed under her section heading within the text. Given Carrie's writings, oral history, and limited surviving papers, the book author began the quest to document the family history. The result is all the documentation this writer could unearth, codified into the following chapters.

Additionally, this compilation includes a historical text chronology, juxtaposing every-day-life events with current events; for example, the reader will find a striking parallel between lynchings and births as well as parallels between racial violence and marriages. The reader may find a tendency for milestones to occur during January as opposed to September or may note repetitive naming patterns. As well, a finding aid, an every place index and an every name index are included, at the rear of the book.

May these words be written and remembered for these seven interwoven Northeast Texas families: Lewis, Martin, Norris, Perry, Sims, Walton, and Weaver, as they came to pass.

And my God put it into mine heart to gather together . . . the people, that they might be reckoned by genealogy. And I found a register of the genealogy of them which came up at the first, and found written therein.

Nehemiah 7:5 KJV

INTRODUCTION

PERHAPS A FEW NORTHEAST TEXAS ANCESTORS WERE freed persons of color. Some ancestors were chattel, imaginably torn from their families by coffle lines and chains. Progenitors were victims of the U.S. slave trade at its origins in Virginia or later ports of entry at Charleston, Natchez, New Orleans, or Galveston. Where one generation survived slavery and the Civil War, the next generation rapidly matured and stayed alive under Reconstruction, Black Codes, lynchings, and postwar racial discord. Later generations endured the Great Depression, pronounced poverty, WWI, Pearl Harbor, and WWII. Still more faced other foreign conflicts—Korea, Vietnam, and the end of the cold war. Forebears persevered day-by-day during a climate of assassinations, discrimination, and segregation, at home. Some survived the socioeconomic hardships only to succumb to death through preventable pneumonia or poisoning. Generation after generation persisted in a land wrought with inhuman treatment, unfairness, and inequality—in a land where socioeconomic justice did not realistically prevail for all. Eventually, government policies prescribed relief in the form of integration, Civil Rights, Women's Rights, and Voting Rights.

In Texas, the early ancestors found flowing water streams, abundant earth, fertile soil, and virgin forests of loblolly pine, oak, and cypress trees. Eagles and storks nestled among the treetops, alligators ruled the swamps, and wolves roamed the grassland. Sidestepping snakes and ignoring insects, the ancestors worked the land with worn hands and sore feet. With aching backs and blistering skin they worked, clearing, building, fencing, planting, and harvesting, in hope and faith. They converted all useable resources into food, clothing, and shelter. Most eventually became landowners and farmers. Later generations gained power through education to move beyond their sheer, meager beginning. Primarily they used their grit, ingenuity, and generosity to generationally move from mere subsistence and survival to health, wealth, and prosperity.

This family history book brings to life the story of seven interwoven families who came to a place the Europeans called *Texas*. The Mexicans called it *Tejauno*, and the Spaniards and Caddos called *Tejas*—the land of many friends. Barbara Jordan once described Texas as above and beyond a place of soil but rather a spiritual frame of mind that spurs rugged individualism, invincibility, and boundless achievements. The ancestors came to a place as spacious as the sapphire sky and captured its soil and soul. These seven families came to places they called Lodi, Lewis Chapel, Bear Bottom, Valley Plain, Kellyville, and Union, where they fed one another's stomach and spirit with love.

The land surveyors, the settlers, and slaveholders came—the carpetbaggers, creditors, and capitalists came— some escaping, some exploring, but all interfacing with the enslaved to begin anew in the land of cattle, cotton, and oil. The Anglo immigrants listed here in this family history book were primarily Southerns and to a lesser degree Northerns who migrated into Northeast Texas, leaving behind the environs of coal, indigo, rice, salt, tobacco, and water-based economies but bringing their slave economy and beliefs.

Sisters Ann and Minerva came. Ann became the wife of Robert "Bob" Weaver. Minerva became Minerva Lewis. Minerva was the mother of Felix. Ann was the mother of Grandison. Grandison married Richard "Dick" Norris' daughter, Malinda. Grandison and Malinda were the parents of Carrie Jane. Carrie Jane married Charley Edward, son of Berry and Rebecca (Walton) Sims. Berry and Milus lived as brothers, and Peter Perry kept Berry and Milus as children. Squire and Sarah (Sallie) Walton were the parents of Rebecca and Mary. Mary married Solomon, son of Thomas "Tom" and Sarah Martin.

Turn the pages and recapture the lives and times of the Lewis, Martin, Norris, Perry, Sims, Walton, and Weaver families of Northeast Texas. Turn the pages and find familiar family folklore—stories about military spies or stories about Anglo slaveholders—some of whom were progenitors of mixed-race children and some of whom crossed the Mississippi River, bringing their slaves to Texas. However, folktales about Native American ancestry or ex-slaves escaping to freedom in Canada are absent from the stories surrounding these seven interwoven Northeast Texas families. See how they lived; notice their migration—their longevity—their service to church, community, and country. Turn the pages of *And It Came To Past* and receive inspiration from cultural stories about consummate survivors. Their stories may not contain all answers but may suggest pathways to find answers to the most pressing who, what, when, where, and why questions. Their stories are now their records for their descendants.

Oh, the depth of the riches both of the wisdom and knowledge of God! how unreachable his judgments, and his ways past finding out!

Romans 11:33 KJV

TIME and EVENT CHART

c1790   Lettie Lee born.

1792   Approximately 450 free people of color existed in Texas.

1793   Eli Whitney invented the cotton gin, a machine that separated the seed from its fiber.

c1810   Squire Walton born.

1812   Robert "Bob" Weaver born, 1812 or 1823.

c1815   Thomas "Tom" Martin, Sr. born.

1819-1820   Cherokees forced into East Texas.

1821   Mexico won its independence from Spain, and Texas became a part of Mexico.

1822   First cottonseed brought into Texas.

1822   Stephen Fuller Austin and Anglo Americans settled in Mexico's East Texas near the lower Brazos and Colorado rivers.

1823 Robert "Bob" Weaver born, 1812 or 1823.

1824 Mexico became a republic.

c1825 Sarah (Sallie) Walton born.

1825-1835   Minerva Lewis born, May.

1829-1830   Recalcitrant Mexican government officials
             passed legislation to stem the current of
             settlers from the United States (U.S.).
             Officials banned immigration, freed the
             slaves, and levied an import tax on U.S.
             goods.

1830s Peter Martin was a Black Texas cowboy, cattle owner,
       and landlord.

1832-1833   Recoiling from pressure, Mexican
             government officials opened their boundaries
             to settlers and their slaves, permitted resident
             Anglos to keep their bondsmen, and
             promised to reconsider the import tax, but
             officials stood firm on Texas statehood.
             The threat of anarchy (friction) rapidly
             increased between Mexicans and Texans
             despite conciliatory concessions.

1834 Texas population numbered approximately 9,000,
      including 2,000 Black people.

c1835 When Rebecca McIntosh Hawkins Hagerty came to
       Texas circa 1835, she and her slaves possibly used
       the Texas Road, an early passageway between

Oklahoma and Texas.

c1835 Sarah Martin born.

1835 Caddos signed a treaty with the U.S., 01 July.

1835 Texas Revolutionary War began, 02 October.

1835 Texas Navy created.

c1836 Texas Rangers organized in Waco, McLennan County, Texas with the intention of protecting frontier settlers from hostiles.

1836 Texans won their independence from Mexico, and Texas became a republic.

1836 Texas population included 30,000 Anglo-Americans, 14,500 Indians, 5,000 Negroes, 3,470 Mexicans, and 150 free people of color.

1836 Richard "Dick" Norris born, 1836 or 1844.

1837-1841 Spurring development, Texas government officials promised land to soldiers and settlers. Government representatives continued forcibly removing Native Americans and gave away more than one million acres of land.

1839 Texas government officials passed the first homestead legislation. The law ensured that an original homestead (homes, farms, ranches, etc.) would never be seized for debt payments.

1839   Reese Hughes, a slaveholder and founder of Hughes Springs, Texas used Trammel's Trace, a north-south wagon road, when he and his slave came to Texas during the spring of 1839 from Tennessee.

1839   The Cherokee War began.

1839   Lone Star flag officially selected.

1840   Austin designated as capital of Texas.

1840   Will (Willie) Ann Perry born.

1840   Texas populated with 40,000, including slaves.

1840   Willis Whitaker, Sr. and his slaves (including old man Phil Ross) came to the Piney Woods of East Texas from South Carolina, possibly using the east-west corridor—Shreveport Trail/Road.

1841   Texas legislative act granted 640 acres to heads of families and 320 acres to single men, to attract Anglo settlers.

c1842   Georgia Ann Norris born.

1842   U.S. Supreme Court proclaimed in *Prigg vs. Pennsylvania* that state laws, which interfered with the enforcement of the Fugitive Slave Act of 1793, were unconstitutional.

1842   Captain William Perry, a northerner with rebel sentiments, came to Texas from New Hampshire.

1843   The city of Jefferson, Texas established and named in honor of Thomas Jefferson.

c1844 Ann Weaver born.

1844   Richard "Dick" Norris born, 1836 or 1844.

c1845 Peter Perry born.

c1845 A steamboat named the *Llama* (*Lama*) landed at Jefferson with W. W. Withenberry (Withenbury) as captain. Llama's owners included Thomas Muir and Captain William Perry.

1845   Abolitionists objected, but the U.S. Congress admitted Texas as the twenty-eighth state and star on the American flag.

1845   Texas populated with 100,000 Anglo settlers and 35,000 slaves, 29 December.

1845   At the beginning of the Jefferson MC, at least three slaves were recorded as members. A number of slaves helped build the church, including a slave belonging to Aaron Duke Tullis. Tullis came to Texas from either South Carolina, Georgia, or Alabama circa 1858. By 1860, Tullis as agent for his wife Martha Jane Johnson, owned two slaves: one male (age thirty) and one female (age forty). During 1867, Tullis, a Confederate veteran, registered to vote.

1846   War between U.S. and Mexico began as Texas joined the Union.

1847   Texas populated with 102,961 Anglos, 38,753 slaves, and 295 free people of color.

1847   Jefferson, Texas had sixty houses, a mill, several stores, and a warehouse.

1847   The first Jefferson newspaper began publishing as the *Democrat*.

1848-1857   Illinois, Indiana, Iowa, and Oregon passed immigration constitutional provisions, which denied free Black people the right to migrate into those states.

1849   Father and son, Trenton Alexander Pattillo and Frank Jones Pattillo, launched the first Harrison County, Texas newspaper, the *Texas Republican*, March. Robert W. Loughery joined the firm several months later. Besides being newspapermen, Trenton was a Harrison County, Texas judge, and Frank was a Methodist minister and schoolteacher. Trenton and Frank were scions of George Pattillo of Scotland.

1849   William M. Freeman and his slaves came to Texas from Georgia. Freeman owned thirteen slaves, eight of whom were part of the same family; another slave set included a mother (age sixty-five) and her son (age sixteen). The three remaining slaves showed no blood relations.

1849-1855   Felix Lewis, Sr. born.

1850   Congress passed a new Fugitive Slave Act, which prohibited the testimony of runaway slaves and denied their rights to a jury trial.

1850   Present Texas boundary lines were drawn at the Compromise of 1850.

1850   Texas population included 154,034 Anglos, 58,161 slaves, and 397 free people of color.

1850   Approximately 12,200 Texas plantations existed with 2,262 devoted to cotton and 165 to sugar.

1850   William M. Freeman along with his slaves began building the Freeman Plantation (Freeman House). Among the many manual labor-intensive tasks, slaves made bricks, cleared the woodland, and shaped the lumber with hacksaws. The home remained standing in modern day Jefferson.

1850   The first stagecoach arrived at Marshall, Harrison County, Texas from neighboring Shreveport, Caddo Parish, Louisiana.

c1851   Milus Sims born, June.

1851   Thomas Sims, a fugitive slave, was recaptured and arrested in Boston, Massachusetts. Sims was held for trial; returned to slavery in Savannah, Georgia; and dragged through the streets as an example, April.

1852-1853   Berry Sims born.

1853   Preventing slave labor competition was the motivation behind the beginnings of the Marshall, Texas, Mechanics Association.

1853   Solomon "Sol" Martin, Sr. born, 1853 or 1862.

1854   Telegraph line established, connecting users in Marshall, Shreveport, and New Orleans, 14 February.

1854   Captain William Perry built the Excelsior Hotel in Jefferson. Registered hotel guests have included notables such as former Presidents Ulysses S. Grant and Rutherford B. Hayes.

1855-1867   Monroe Lewis born.

c1856   Rebecca (Becky) Walton Sims born, 22 December.

1856   Post Office established in Jefferson, Cass County, Texas.

1856   Harrison County, Texas Anglo citizens reported that the slaves were freely talking of their hopes and expectations of freedom, if Republican presidential candidate, John C. Fremont, was elected.

c1857   Frances Lewis Wiggins born.

1857   U.S. Supreme Court ruled in *Dred Scott vs. Sanford* that Black people were not citizens, could not become citizens, and were not counted or considered at the formation of the Constitution; therefore, they had no rights and were not entitled to sue.

1857   In an oxbow and horseshoe pattern, the Butterfield
       Overland Mail Express crossed Texas.

1857   The *Jefferson Gazette* began printing operation with J.
       W. Nimmo.

1857   Sam Houston stopped and spoke in Jefferson on his
       campaign trail for Texas governor, 13 June.

c1858 Albert Norris born.

1858   Daily stagecoach service was available between
       Jefferson and Marshall.

1859   The federal government settled the Caddos on a
       reservation in present-day Caddo County,
       Oklahoma. Other Native Americans such as the
       Cherokees, Choctaws, and Comanches were
       removed from Texas to Oklahoma, between Texas
       statehood and Reconstruction.

1859   Reese Hughes and more than 140 of his slaves
       harvested 2,000 bushels of wheat in Cass County,
       Texas.

1859   William Thomas Scott of Harrison County, Texas
       owned more than 100 slaves who produced 356
       bales of cotton. Scott, born in Mississippi, came to
       Texas circa 1840.

1859   Willis Whitaker, Sr. and more than 140 of his slaves
       produced 500 bushels of rye in Bowie and Cass
       counties of Texas.

1859-1861   Sam Houston served as Texas governor.

1859-1868   Helon Lewis, Sr. born.

1860   Texas population included 412,294 Anglos, 182,566 slaves, 355 free people of color, and 3,533,767 cattle.

1860   Marion County, Texas created 08 February and organized 15 March.

1860   Marion County, Texas populated with 3,977 people, including 1,960 Anglos and 2,017 slaves.

1860   Jefferson disputably populated with 988 citizens, including 266 Black people.

1860   Marshall, Harrison County, Texas populated with 2,000 people.

1860   William M. Freeman as agent for his wife Drucilla Olivia Bowdre (Bowdrei) owned eight slaves and paid taxes on six. The three male slaves were ages: forty-five, thirty-three, and twenty-three; the five female slaves were ages: forty-three, thirty-two, twenty, fourteen, and twelve—all of whom existed in two slave houses. Their six Black slaves were valued at $5,000.00 at the Marion County property tax rolls.

1860   Rebecca McIntosh Hawkins Hagerty owned more than 150 slaves in Marion and Harrison counties of Texas. In Marion County, fifty males and fifty-three females existed within twenty-two slave quarters and worked on 3,296 acres. Though she owned over 100 slaves in Marion County, she only paid 1860 Marion County property taxes on seventy-two slaves who were valued at $36,000.00. Rebecca's 3,296 acres were valued at $9,000.00. She owned twenty-eight horses valued at $2,800.00; 120 cattle valued at $720.00; and miscellaneous property valued at $1,000.00 for a $49,520.00 total 1860 Marion County property value. However, Rebecca reported to the 1860 Marion County, Texas census takers that her real estate property value was $35,000.00 and her personal estate value was $85,000.00, totaling $115,000.00.

1860   John M. Jones, formerly of Guilford County, North Carolina, owned fifty-six slaves: twenty-six males and thirty females. The ages for the male slaves ranged from fifty to five, and the age span for the females spread from seventy to six. The slaves existed in ten slave houses on 1,600 acres of land, in Marion County. Jones, his wife Mariah E. Wood, and their children of Stewart County, Georgia came to Texas circa 1851.

1860   Elizabeth (Eliza) Ellen Sharp Matthews was a forty-two-year-old widow, planter from Georgia, slaveholding in Jefferson. The twenty-five slaves (nine males and sixteen females) that Eliza owned existed in six slave houses. The male slaves ranged in ages from fifty-one to ten, and the females were ages, fifty-two to seven.

1860   Lewis Alexander Pattillo, a North Carolina native, owned ten slaves: seven males and three females—all of whom existed in three slave houses in Marion

County. The male slaves were ages: twenty-eight, fourteen, ten, four, and two; the female slaves were ages: thirty-three, twenty-eight, fourteen, and eight. Pattillo came to Texas circa 1848 via Missouri.

1860   Marion DeKalb Taylor owned seventeen slaves (ten males and seven females) who existed in six slave houses, in Jefferson. The male slaves ranged in ages from forty to five, and the females were ages, to forty to seven. Some of the Taylor family slaves were buried outside the north fence of the Taylor family main cemetery. Marion's father was Ward Taylor, Sr., and his mother was Nancy Anne Matthews. Marion's first wife was Elizabeth Sarah. Marion and Elizabeth were parents of ten children, and Marion was known to have fathered Black children. Marion was a slaveholder, country doctor, and legislator, originally from Georgia.

1860   Peter W. Walton owned two slaves: one male named Landry, age forty-five and one female named Mary, age sixteen. Peter also worked as an overseer for another slaveholder and widow, Susan Ann Cocke Smith.

1860   Fires across Northeast Texas (including Jefferson) were attributed to abolitionists and slave insurrections, July.

1860   Abraham Lincoln elected as the sixteenth president of the U.S., 06 November.

1860s Edmonia Lewis became first acclaimed Black American sculptress; her father was a full-blooded African and her mother a full-blooded Chippewa.

1860 Ann (Anna) Lewis Berry born, 1860 or 1861.

1860-1866 Grandison W. Weaver born, July.

c1861 Edmund Norris born, 15 July.

1861 Texas population included more than 430,000 Anglos, and the slaves numbered between 182,000 and 275,000.

1861 Texas seceded from the Union, 05 March.

1861 The war of wills and words erupted. Some Southerners described it as the War Between the States; whereas, Northerners preferred, the War of the Rebellion.

1861 Wes Pattillo, slave of Lewis Alexander Pattillo, witnessed Albert A. Wilson with a club in his hand on the day Albert allegedly bludgeoned Lewis in the tanning yard, 25 July.

1861 Ann (Anna) Lewis Berry born, 1860 or 1861.

1861-1865 Several thousand Texans signed up for the Union—2,132 Anglo and forty-seven Black Americans. Collectively, 10 regiments of loyal Texans joined the Confederate ranks.

1861-1865 Throughout the war between the North and the South, slaves were allowed to join the Jefferson Methodist Church.

1862 Mississippi River blockade stalled cotton shipments and cattle drives as well disrupted the trade market. Under the circumstances, some planters seeded corn, sugar, various vegetables, and wheat for personal consumption or local profit. Some bred cattle for the same reasons.

1862 The two slaves (Landry and Mary) that Peter W. Walton owned were offered for hiring out at the Marion County Courthouse door, 09 January.

1862 Solomon "Sol" Martin, Sr. born, 1853 or 1862.

1862 Margaret Jane Norris born, 1862 or 1863.

1863 Emancipation Proclamation became effective when the U.S. Congress passed the Thirteenth Amendment, abolishing slavery in the U.S., 31 January.

1863 Margaret Jane Norris born, 1862 or 1863.

1864 Confederate forces defeated Union forces at the Battle of Mansfield, De Soto Parish, Louisiana, saving Northeast Texas homes and plantations from battleground destruction, 08 April.

1865 U.S. Congress established the Bureau of Refugees, Freedmen, and Abandoned Lands (Freedmen's Bureau), 03 March.

1865   John Wilkes Booth attempted to assassinate President Abraham Lincoln at Ford's Theatre in Washington, D.C., 14 April.

1865   President Lincoln died, 15 April.

1865   The Confederacy defeated the Union at the last battle of the Civil War. The Sixty-second U.S.C.T. (a Black American regiment) helped deliver the victory at Palmito Ranch (near White's Ranch) in the Rio Grande Valley, 13 May.

1865   General Gordon Granger came to Galveston, Texas and brought news of freedom for all Texas slaves and federal military rule for all Texans. Juneteenth celebration commemorates Emancipation, 19 June.

1865   Texas populated with 400,000 Black Americans.

1865   Freedmen's Bureau was established in Texas and tasked with daunting responsibilities: helping the newly freed adjust to freedom; providing food and clothing; overseeing labor contracts; organizing schools; protecting freedmen against violence; and settling land affairs, 05 September.

1865   Captain Stanton W. Weaver, originally of the Sixty-second U.S.C.I., was briefly assigned to Jefferson as a subassistant bureau commissioner. In derision, he was termed most enduring, and in favor, he was characterized as endearing and fair toward the newly freed.

1865   Freedmen's Bureau office opened in Marshall, Texas. The bureau chief chided the freedmen among other things to not gather within the city or camps; to obtain freedom of movement passes from their employers or risk arrest and punishment; and to work to eat, as a means to survive, November.

1865   *The Jefferson Jimplecute* began. Management suspended publication during 1872 and started publishing the newspaper again during 1874. Ward Taylor, Jr., founder, editor, and Confederate veteran, was born in Alabama.

1865   Jefferson farmers and planters exported 25,000 bales of cotton.

Post-1865   The Caddos agreed to scout for the U.S. Army during the Plains Indian wars.

1865-1867   Sanford Norris born, June or July.

1865-1870   Sallie (Sarah) Weaver White Vaughn born, 06 July.

1865-1870   More than 6,460 freedmen entered into labor contracts in the Texas counties of Harrison and Marion. With the disappointing news that 40 acres and a mule would not be a Christmas gift, some astute newly freed negotiated for land in lieu of wages, where allowed.

1865-1870   Reconstruction in Texas.

1865-1881   The U.S. Army and Indians in the West clashed 846 times.

Late 1860s   After Emancipation, a Jefferson Episcopal Church allowed freedmen to attend Sunday school. However, Black membership declined as the newly freed began building their own churches, moving to find family and to establish their economic footing.

c1866   Mary Walton Martin Lucky born.

1866   U.S. Congress authorized Black troops, respectfully called the Buffalo Soldiers.

1866   Black members of the First Baptist Church asked permission to build their own church, two years after the First Baptist Church of Jefferson was built during 1864. Slaveholder William M. Freeman was a First Baptist Church charter member.

1866   Texas legislators enacted the *Black Codes*, political dogma designed to regulate the newly freed.

1866   U.S. Congress enacted the 1866 Civil Rights Act, 09 April.

1866   Epidemic outbreak of Cholera.

1866-1867   Freedmen established five schools in Marshall, Texas even under violence and school burnings, practically unaided by bureau personnel.

1867 1885   Herdsmen drove Texas cattle nearly due north on the dirt and sand-packed Chisholm Trail.

1867   Epidemic outbreak of Yellow Fever.

1867   A Jefferson gas plant produced gas lampposts, using pine knots fuel. As water accumulated in the hollow posts, Black labor removed troubling water with a hand pump, making the posts ready for the night lighted Jefferson streets.

1867   Congress passed Reconstruction Acts including one requiring Texas to register the adult male population and permit eligible Black people and Anglos to vote, March.

1867   An Anglo protest mob of Marshall, Texas citizens attacked the home of Freedmen's Bureau schoolteacher Owen F. Baker, by breaking the windows and riddling the house with bullets.

1867   Albert Kines was one of the hundreds of Black men living in Marion County who registered to vote between 1867 and 1869. Kines came to Texas circa 1863 from Virginia. Jefferson schoolteachers Thomas Cooper and Thomas E. Younger also registered to vote, as did a few freedmen who afterward lost their lives, such as Albert Browning and Richard Stewart.

1867   Thomas Jefferson Rogers claimed to be a Union man when he registered to vote in Marion County during 1867, and he only owned one male slave (age ten) at the 1860 Slave Schedule. Rogers came to Texas circa 1847. Rogers operated a mercantile business; married Emily Mayberry (Teresa Cocke Mayberry's sister-in-law); practiced law; registered to vote again, omitting the Union descriptor; served in the Confederate army as a captain; registered to vote again, omitting the Union descriptor; promoted and held office for a railroad line; owned a cotton oil mill, all before becoming a banker during 1896.

1867   Walter P. Schluter, a Confederate veteran, a Jefferson dry goods merchant, and banker, registered to vote, corroborating the census report that he was from Kentucky, 24 August. Schluter came to Texas circa 1846.

1867   Marion Try Slaughter shot at or shot two freedmen—Albert and Cornelius Roseborough—near Jefferson, 14 February. Slaughter almost always either evaded government arrest or if apprehended waved his get-out-of-jail card—a written bond, promising appearance in next court session. Although Slaughter constantly found himself above the law during Reconstruction, he became deputy sheriff during the 1880s in Jefferson. Slaughter came to Texas from North Carolina during the 1840s. He married Mrs. Eveline J. Crutcher during 1860 and served as his wife's agent for her seventeen slaves—seven males and ten females. Slaughter was a Confederate veteran and uncle to Marion Try Slaughter II (country-western singer—a.k.a. Vernon Dalhart).

1868   Thomas E. Younger came to Texas from Alabama.
        He almost single handily setup a school for the newly
        freed in the vicinity of Jefferson. Locating an old
        building, Younger paid the owner the value of one
        month's rent. He made the necessary school
        furniture (benches, tables) and used his personal
        money to purchase needed school supplies. With
        the facility converted and cleaned, he opened the
        school. Only nineteen enrolled.

1868   U.S. Congress ratified the Fourteenth Amendment,
        guaranteeing the rights of citizenship and equal
        protection of the law.

1868   Patsey Norris Smith born, 1868 or 1869.

1868   Some of Jefferson's business district burned in a fire.

1868   Marshall Anglo citizens refused to hire Black citizens
        for jobs without Black Americans providing *proof of
        political cleanliness*—a certification document from the
        Anglo Democratic Party, May.

1868   Texas constitutional convention assembled in Austin
        with nine Black Americans and eighty-one Anglo
        state legislators, 01 June.

1868   Anglo citizens broke up the two Freedmen schools in
        Jefferson and sent the bureau schoolteachers fleeing
        for their lives, July.

1868   A broadcloth mob took Albert Browning from his
        bed, wife, and child. Jefferson Anglo citizens led
        Browning a distance away from his home, and then

they took his money, belongings, and life, 26 August. Browning was from Alabama.

1868   Freedmen Bureau office opened in Jefferson, October.

1868   Armed and angry Anglos of Caddo Parish, Louisiana apprehended five Black men from their work site (Tom Johnson's brickyard). The mob tied the Black workers' hands and paraded them through the plantation of Reuben White, on the way to the Red River. Positioned at the riverbank, the mob riddled the Black workers' bodies with bullets, 12 October.

1868   Anglo men of Caddo Parish, Louisiana killed Robert Gray, the Justice of the Peace, and killed James Watson because of his voting record. This Anglo mob went to every Black man's house, taking away their guns, rifles, and ammunition, 14 October.

1868   Freedmen Bureaus closed in Texas, December.

1868-1869   Marshall, Texas school facilities were considered the best in North Texas.

1869   Attributable to the poor school facility, a Jefferson African Methodist Church school attendance dropped.

1869   George Addison Kelly began publishing *The Home Advocate*, a newspaper that Frank Jones Pattillo, later continued. Kelly came to Texas circa 1852. During 1860, Kelly owned one forty-year-old female slave valued at $600.00, but he claimed to have been a

Union man from Tennessee at the 1867 registration of eligible voters. Kelly successfully created and sold a steel soil plow, lightweight and effective enough to be pulled by horses as opposed to oxen.

1869   Captain William Perry was murdered on the streets of Jefferson, 02 January.

1869   Passengers and crewmembers lost their lives when the steamboat *Mittie Stephens* sank on Caddo Lake from a hay fire, as it was steaming from Shreveport to Jefferson, 12 February.

1869   The Stockade Case. Some of Jefferson's finest Anglo residents were charged with the murder of an Anglo Republican and Union soldier George Washington Smith and two freedmen—Lewis Grant and Richard Stewart. Until trial, the accused, prominent townsmen were held at the stockade (jail) as were three accused freemen: John Brooks, Richard Davis, and Nathaniel McCoy. Smith, a New Yorker, was number two in line at the voter registration during 1867, and Stewart, a Virginian, was number twenty. One of their accused murders, McCoy, was from Louisiana; he too registered to vote albeit during 1869.

1869   Patsey Norris Smith born, 1868 or 1869.

1869-1874   Richard Weaver, Sr. born, 12 July.

1870   Sawmill and lumber industry took shape in the Piney Woods of Northeast Texas.

1870   The *Arrow Line* steamboat landed at Jefferson with immigrants.

1870   Texas legislators ratified the Thirteenth, Fourteenth, and Fifteenth Amendments to the U.S. Constitution; President Ulysses S. Grant declared Reconstruction in Texas at an end; and the U.S. Congress readmitted Texas to the Union, 30 March.

1870   Texas populated with 818,579 people.

1870   Jefferson populated with 4,190, including 1,825 Black Americans.

1870   Texas women who earned income worked in varied occupations. Collectively, 14,031 worked as farm laborers/ranch hands; 10,603 as domestics; 1,017 as laundresses. By the hundreds, women became planters (851); seamstresses (454); teachers (431); milliners (167); carpet makers (122). Smaller numbers of women worked as nurses; and midwives, 59 and 30 respectively. The majority of domestic workers and laundresses were Black American.

1870   Marion County was home to at least twenty-four Black American women labeled as laundresses at the census. Women referred to as washwomen were not included in the laundress count.

1870   Farmers numbered 186 in Marion County.

1870   Marion County census report included two Black American schoolteachers: Thomas Cooper who was twenty-four years of age and from Mississippi and

Coleman Clark who was forty years old and from Alabama. Uncommonly, Clark had a property value of $200.00.

1870 Not all of the Black American children at the Marion County census were laborers, nurse maids, or servants; for example, multiple children from these families were listed as attending school: Hoddin, Johnson, M<u>c</u>Coy, Powell, and Roberts.

1870 Malinda Norris Weaver born, 10 January.

1870 Willy Sims, jockey and two-time Kentucky Derby winner, was born in Augusta, Georgia, 11 January.

1870 Jefferson Insurance Savings and Exchange Company chartered, 13 August.

1870s The Old Jefferson Courthouse used as a school for Black American students.

1870s Meshack Roberts, an ex-slave, was beaten and left for dead, but he survived to later represent Harrison County, Texas for three terms in the state legislature. Roberts was also a blacksmith and Methodist Church lay leader.

1871 National Bank of Jefferson chartered, 28 January.

1871 Citizens Savings Bank of Jefferson chartered with stockholder John V. Ford, 21 March.

1871 Jefferson Real Estate Trust and Dollar Savings Company chartered, 01 December.

1871   Railroad expansion across Texas precluded the end of the Chisholm Trail cattle drives.

1872   Jefferson farmers, ranchers, and lumbermen exported 76,328 bales of cotton, 84,762 dry hides, 5,381 cattle, 121,000 feet of lumber, and 226 steamboats arrived at its port.

c1873 Another Jefferson first—refrigeration, albeit artificially with ammonia.

c1873 With its headquarters in Marshall, Texas, the Texas and Pacific Railroad laid tracks and became operational through Jefferson.

c1873 Thanksgiving Day, the U.S. Army Corps of Engineers finally cleared a downriver raft on the Red River, near Shreveport, blasting the bulk of the raft with dynamite and nitroglycerine, November. The clearing of the raft decreased water levels upstream at Jefferson on the Cypress Bayou, making steamboat travel uncertain and eventually impossible, as bayou water levels continued to recede.

1873   Wiley College, located in Marshall, Texas, founded during 1873 by the Freedmen's Aid Society of the Methodist Episcopal Church and chartered, 1882.

1873   Greatest annual rainfall ever recorded in Texas (109.38) fell in Clarksville, Red River County, Texas.

1873   Epidemic outbreak of Yellow Fever.

1873   Felix Lewis, Sr. married Emaline (Emiline) Spencer Lewis, 25 January.

1873-1879   Dr. Charles Monroe Lewis, Sr. born, April.

1874   Armed and determined Democrats took Texas government by force, stopping Radical Reconstruction in Texas, 17 January.

1874   Milus Sims married Angeline (Angelina) Love Sims, 04 February.

1874   Harrison County, Texas citizens elected three Black Americans as state legislators: David Abner, Sr., Ed Brown, and Meshack Roberts. Marion County, Texas acquired an accession of acreage supposedly during the legislative tenures of one of these three men, being duly convinced by a senior senator from Marion County.

1874   At county elections, four Black Americans earned enough votes to win appointments as Justices of the Peace. However, none could secure the required financial backing (bonds) to take office, in Marion County.

1874-1880   Hezekiah Johnson, Sr. born, February.

1875   Oliver Lewis, a Black American jockey, won the first Kentucky Derby.

1875   Marion County Democratic Party denied Black Americans the right to vote for convention delegates.

1875   Anglo mechanics blamed Black American mechanics for job losses, complaining that Black Americans worked for less pay in Marshall, Texas.

1875   Ada Lewis Dixon Davis born, 01 January.

1875   With the aid of Albert Kines, Peter Perry purchased 150 acres of land from Elizabeth (Eliza) Ellen Sharp Matthews, 01 January.

1875   Frances Lewis Wiggins married Green Wiggins, 29 May.

1875   Adaline (Ada, Addie) M. Weaver Norris born, October.

1875   Berry Sims and Rebecca (Becky) Walton Sims married, 29 December.

1876   Marion County had three Black American county commissioners.

1876   Railroad companies were operating in Northeast Texas, at full steam, transporting crops, hides, lumber, and goods to any U.S. market.

1876   Frank Jones Pattillo and W. Z. Leader, publishers of the *Evening Reflector* newspaper, competed with Ward Taylor, Jr., editor and founder of the *Jefferson Jimplecute*. With weapons at hand, a cowhide and a pistol, they settled their rivalry in the streets of Jefferson, where Taylor shot and killed Pattillo.

1877   Black American laundresses in Galveston went on strike for higher wages.

1877   Diamond Bessie Moore was murdered in Jefferson. A Black American woman named Sarah King discovered Bessie's body in the woods while gathering firewood.

1877   Peter Perry paid Elizabeth (Eliza) Ellen Sharp Matthews $200.00 for 50 acres of land on the waters of Kitchens Creek, as part of the Cadenhead Survey, 16 August.

1877   Lewis Chapel Methodist Episcopal Church was established and originally located between the present-day church and the Lewis Chapel Cemetery, 19 September.

1878   The land deal between Peter Perry and Elizabeth (Eliza) Ellen Sharp Matthews, which supplied Peter with 26 acres and the church with 2 acres, were a part of the Charles Grayson League Survey and cost Peter $117.00 at 10 percent interest rate, 01 January.

1878   Nancy Sims Sharp Bryant born, 1878 or 1879.

1878-1887   After a combined campaign involving the Buffalo Soldiers, U.S. troops, and Mexican forces, all Native American warfare ended in Texas.

1878   First telephone call was made in Texas between a home and a business.

1878   Matt Perduy elected as a Jefferson alderman for the first ward.

1878   More than 500 Black American residents of Marion County, petitioned Texas Governor, Richard B. Hubbard, to prevent the Texas and Pacific Railroad from replacing them with convicts.

1878   Jake Weaver born, April.

1879   American Colonization Society sponsored twelve Black Americans who wanted to leave Marshall, Texas and make Liberia their homeland.

1879   Nancy Sims Sharp Bryant born, 1878 or 1879.

1879   Georgia Ann Norris died, December.

1880   Ann (Anna) Lewis Berry married Aaron Berry, 26 February.

1880   Corporal Asa Weaver, Buffalo Solider, discovered and chased the elusive Victoria, an Apache Chief, in a fifteen-mile running fight near Alamo Springs, 03 August.

1880s   Jim Perry, a Black American Texas cowboy, cook, fiddler, rider, roper, worked on the XIT ranch.

1880s   Texas farmers planted, grew, and harvested more cotton than any other state.

1880s   Texas farmers began using machines in growing cotton. However, harvesting remained hands on until the 1950s.

1880s Jefferson's cultural development thrived with theatrical plays, musicals, and operas at the Taylor Opera House and other social centers.

1880 Farmers numbered 1,063 in Marion County.

1880 Texas populated with 1,591,749 people.

1880 Jefferson populated with 3,260 people.

1880 Moses "M. K." Crawford was elected as tax assessor of Marion County, but he failed to qualify because of inability to post surety bond. However, the 1880 census labeled him as a constable. Crawford, formerly of Virginia, promptly registered to vote during 1867 and 1869, and given the opportunity, he remained politically active.

1880 Jefferson authorities charged sixty-five citizens with interfering with voting rights by intimidation, fraud, and violence against Black American voters. The federal court called approximately 3,000 witnesses. However, only forty-five of the sixty-five charged received indictments. All indicted plead guilty, and the court assessed a one dollar fine, plus court costs.

1880 Unprecedented, two Black Americans of Marion County served as jurors on the Diamond Bessie Moore murder trial, December.

1881 Berry Sims entered into a sharecropping agreement with Frederica Hoeffner Fox; Berry farmed land at a location referred to as the Ford Plantation, 14 May. Frederica Fox owned a vast amount of land, in her own right; she married Hugo V. Fox, originally of New Orleans and a manufacturer of confections and sweet meats.

1881   Charley Edward Sims, Sr. born, 03 March 1881 or 1882.

1881   Oscar Perry, Sr. born, 14 November 1881 or 1882.

1881-1885   Isaac Lewis born.

1882   Charley Edward Sims, Sr. born, 03 March 1881 or 1882.

1882   Steamboat, the *Lessie B.*, sank on Cypress Bayou after cotton onboard caught fire as it was steaming from Jefferson to Shreveport, 21 March.

1882   Oscar Perry, Sr. born, 14 November 1881 or 1882.

1883   Hattie Mae Sims Hodge born, 13 March.

c1883   Marion Try Slaughter II, country-western singer, known as Vernon Dalhart, born near Jefferson, 06 April.

1884   Benjamin F. Orr and Whitmill "Whit" Phillips owned and operated a sawmill in Kellyville and a lumber facility in Lassater; both towns were located in Marion County. Whit Phillips, a Confederate veteran, came to Texas from Georgia circa 1851.

1884   Mary Walton Martin Lucky and Solomon "Sol" Martin, Sr. married, 19 July.

1885   John Wesley Martin, Sr. born, January.

1885   Sallie (Sarah) Weaver White Vaughn married Sydney J. White, 31 December.

1885-1888   Edward Norris born, 29 January or 29 March.

1885-1890   Sallie B. Lewis Cole Stevenson born, June.

1886   The Texas State Fair began.

1886   Edmund Norris married Emma Smith Norris, 11 February.

1886   Ward Taylor, Sr., et al. sold Minerva Lewis and her son, Monroe Lewis, 44 acres of land, as part of the Joseph Watkins Head Right Survey, 08 November. Minerva and her son later sold this same land to Walter P. Schluter.

c1887   Helon Lewis, Sr. married Elizabeth (Lizzie) C. Moore Lewis (daughter of Marion DeKalb Taylor and Sallie Sims).

1887   Texas Baseball League organized.

1887   Richard "Dick" Norris bought 60 acres from Benjamin F. Orr and Whitmill "Whit" Phillips, 01 January.

1887   Grandison W. Weaver and Malinda Norris Weaver married, 03 February.

1887   Carrie Jane Weaver Sims born, 10 December.

1887-1891   Felix Lewis, Jr. born, 08 April.

1888   Solomon "Sonny" Martin, Jr. born, January.

1888   Monroe Lewis married Adeline (Addie) King Lewis, 28 February.

1888   Berry Sims purchased his first 100 acres of land from a Confederate veteran, Ambrose Fitzgerald, 27 October. Fitzgerald came to Texas circa 1846 from Tennessee.

1888   Felix Lewis, Sr. bought 97 acres from neighbor Marion DeKalb Taylor, 26 December.

1888   Samuel Norris born, 30 November 1888 or 1889.

1889   Minerva and her son, Monroe, sold 44 acres of land for $160.00 to Walter P. Schluter, 26 February.

1889   Patsey Norris Smith married Joseph "Joe" Smith, 07 March.

1889   Henry Lee Weaver born, 30 October.

1889   Samuel Norris born, 30 November 1888 or 1889.

c1890   Huddie William Ledbetter (aka Leadbelly–folk musician) and his parents came to Harrison County,

Texas from Caddo Parish, Louisiana. Years later, the U.S. Postal Service issued a .32 cents stamp honoring Leadbelly.

1890 Alex "Alec" Norris born, 1890 or 1891.

1890 Texas populated with 2,235,527 people.

1890 Farmers and laborers cultivated 32,000 acres with 18,000 acres devoted to cotton in Marion County. Though 567 farms existed, not everyone owned their farms. Some 764 worked on rented farmland, and another 484 worked for hire. Merely, ten sawmills operated within the county.

1890 John Coleman of Shreveport, Caddo Parish, Louisiana lynched, 29 June.

1890 Sherman Anti-Trust Act established.

1890s The Episcopal Church established a mission in Marshall, Texas.

1891 Alex "Alec" Norris born, 1890 or 1891.

1891 Babe Lewis married Ida Peppers Lewis, 15 January.

1891 William Hartfield and Munn Sheppard of Cass County, Texas lynched, 28 June.

1891 Richard "Dick" Norris sold crops to G. M. Jones (agent), which were harvested from land worked by he and Wes Pattillo, 29 August. Mrs. G. M. Jones was the daughter of Thomas L. and Sallie Christian

Lyon. The Lyon family came to Jefferson during the summer of 1867 and soon purchased a home, which years later their daughter still occupied. Captain Lyon jointly owned and operated a business on Dallas Street, involving cotton and general mercantile and named Mooring and Lyon.

1891   Leo Green of Linden, Cass County, Texas lynched, 26 October.

1891   Richard "Dick" Norris and wife Sarah sold 60 acres to Harrison Williams; Joe Smith; and Edmund Norris, 11 November.

c1892 Ada Lewis Dixon Davis married John Dixon.

1892   Nathan Andrews of Caddo Parish, Louisiana lynched, 09 January.

1892   Rev. Richard McCallihan Weaver born, 20 January.

1892   Adene Dixon Graham Rose born, 09 September.

1892   William Martin Dunn, Martin Homer Wurtsbaugh, and Edwin Jacob Rand sold Berry Sims 98 ½ acres, from the land surveyed by land mogul, Charles Grayson, 26 November. Peter Perry's property was a part of this same survey.

1892   Helon Lewis, Sr. and wife Elizabeth C. Moore Lewis purchased 44 acres of land from Marion DeKalb Taylor, 30 November, paying $200.00, $40.00 more than the amount Walter P. Schluter paid for the same land during 1889 when he acquired it from Minerva Lewis and son, Monroe.

1892-1894   Mary Norris Brown born, July.

1893   Long-distance telephone calls were made possible between Houston and Galveston.

1893   Stock market crash.

1893   Berry Sims sold his horse called Billy, and mule called Kit, to Max Simmons for $200.00, 17 February.

1893   Sarah Norris bought land from Benjamin F. Orr and Whitmill "Whit" Phillips, 21 February.

1893   Pauline Dixon Cooper born, November.

1893-1907   William Martin Dunn, Martin Homer Wurtsbaugh, and Edwin Jacob Rand owned and operated the Lodi Lumber Company, north of Jefferson. The company cut 50,000 feet of lumber daily, logging on 2,000 acres of land. William Martin Dunn was also a Confederate veteran and the son of Samuel Dunn and Esther Sims of Georgia.

1894   Oil discovered in Corsicana, Navarro County, Texas.

1894   Grant W. Weaver, Jr. born, 15 January.

1894   Henry Scott of Jefferson, Marion County lynched, 17 May.

1895   Mattie Sims Crawford Jordan Heard Taylor born, 18 May.

1895   Richard Weaver, Sr. married Mary Lee Etta Williams Weaver, 19 December.

1895-1897   Inez Weaver Reeves born, 30 October.

c1896   Booker T. Washington visited Houston, Harris County, Texas.

c1896   Lucille Ophelia Vaughn Jenkins Galbreath born.

1896   Milton Weaver born, 22 January.

1896   Isaac Pizer of Shreveport, Caddo Parish, Louisiana lynched, 23 March.

1896   U.S. Supreme Court endorsed the separate but equal doctrine in *Plessy vs. Ferguson*, 18 May.

1896   Will Norris born, 29 August.

1896-1901   Ruby Lee Sharp Thompson born.

1897   Rev. Joseph Sims born, 22 February.

1897   Robert Brown, Hal Wright, and Russell Wright of Harrison County, Texas lynched, 27 April.

1897   Bessie Mae Martin Williams Rhynes born, 19 September 1897 or 1898.

1897   Sanford Norris married Adaline (Ada, Addie) M.

Weaver Norris, 29 December.

1897   Lela Viola Dixon High born, 1897 or 1898.

1897-1899   Ben Louis Norris born, 18 October or 18 November.

1898   Spanish-American War.

1898   Lela Viola Dixon High born, 1897 or 1898.

1898   Eula V. Weaver Rice born, 15 February.

1898   Bessie Mae Martin Williams Rhynes born, 19 September 1897 or 1898.

1898   Asa "Acie" Weaver born, 15 or 16 October 1898 or 1899.

1898-1899   Texas experienced its coldest winter of record with twenty- three degrees below zero, establishing the statewide record.

1899   *Imperium in Iimperio* published by Arno Press and written by Sutton Elbert Griggs, a Texas Black American author.

1899   Texas legislature discontinued giving away 160 acres of land to homesteaders who lived on their claimed land three years.

1899   Robert William Norris born, 14 May 1899 or 1900.

1899   Asa "Acie" Weaver born, 15 or 16 October 1898 or

1899.

1899   Grandison W. Weaver purchased 61 acres of land that were part of the William K. Allen Head Right Survey from the heirs of Ann Virginia Allen Ward Bynum with Sylvanus Grady Echols as agent, 20 October.

1900   Texas populated with 3,048,710 people.

1900   Marion County populated with 10,754 people.

1900   With 10,000 existing miles of railroad tracks, the Texas legislature gave away 32 million more acres for railroad development, selling nearby land at $1.50 per acre.

1900   Only 470 Indians remained in Texas, according to U.S. census enumerators.

1900   Using farm machinery, Texas farmers cultivated 5 million acres of corn.

1900   Farmers numbered 1,260 in Marion County.

1900   A hurricane struck Galveston, Texas, killing thousands; thousands more were injured. Property damage assessed in the millions.

1900   Nancy Sims Sharp Bryant married John Henry Sharp, 02 March.

1900   Robert William Norris born, 14 May 1899 or 1900.

1900   Ada Sharp Calhoun born, 03 October.

1900   Three Black American men: Lige Miles, Jim Shaw, and Freeman Terhune were accused of attempted murder of Dr. Thomas Hardin Stallcup and lynched in Jefferson. Their bodies were hanged at the Texas and Pacific Railroad Company bridge, 15 November.

1900   Felix Lewis, Sr. bought 86 acres from Joe D. Mercer and wife Sallie Liverman, 22 November.

c1901   Annie Lee Weaver Rebecca Vaughn Gilham Allen Bell born, 10 or 15 September.

c1901   Hezekiah Johnson, Sr. married Erbie (Irby) Williams Johnson.

c1901   June Weaver born.

1901   Bluebonnet designated as the state flower.

1901   Spindletop oil (black gold) field discovered, near Beaumont, Jefferson County, Texas.

1901   Sarah Norris sold Betty Pattillo the wife of Wes Pattillo 10 acres, the same 10 acres that Sarah purchased from Orr and Phillips, 27 July.

1901   Professor John C. Pitts began his fifty-nine-year career at Central—a school for Black Americans in Marion County.

1901   Frank Thompson of Shreveport, Caddo Parish, Louisiana lynched, 24 November.

1901   Charley "Jim Bo" Henry Sharp born, 31 December 1901 or 1902.

1902   Texas Library Association established.

1902   A poll tax required for voting.

1902   *Unfettered* published by AMS Press and written by Sutton Elbert Griggs, a Texas Black American author.

1902   Rev. Curtis Shedwell Weaver born, 20 September.

1902   Charley "Jim Bo" Henry Sharp born, 31 December 1901 or 1902.

1903   Oscar Perry, Sr. married Addie Houston Perry, 05 January.

1903-1906   Rev. Sanford Norris born, 24 or 26 April.

1903   Dr. Charles Monroe Lewis, Sr. married Birdie Mae Washington Lewis, 24 June.

1903   Jennie Steers of Shreveport, Caddo Parish, Louisiana lynched, 27 July.

1903   Walker Davis of Marshall, Harrison County, Texas lynched, 01 October.

1904   T. J. Rogers and Sons (Thomas Jefferson Rogers) reflected its national bank status with a name change to, Rogers National Bank of Jefferson. Through mergers and name changes, Rogers' bank became the modern-day First National Bank of Jefferson. Second generation, Black American farmers such as Charley Edward Sims, Sr. and Grandison W. Weaver found that they could bank with T. J. Rogers and Sons in the early 1900s.

1904 Felix Lewis, Sr. bought land from Enoch Love and wife Jennie, setting aside 1 acre for a family cemetery which became Union Chapel Cemetery, 01 January.

1904 Isaac "Ike" Gilham Weaver born, 11 January.

1904 Richard Weaver, Jr. born, 02 November.

1904 Dr. Roscoe Conklin Lewis born, 21 December.

c1905 C. W. Perry, a Black American skilled laborer living in Harrison County, Texas, with a highly envied and competitive railroad job and established home, left Marshall, Texas for Boley, Okfuskee County, Oklahoma, a Black American town.

1905 The Lone Star state led the way in railroad development with approximately 12,000 miles of tracks.

1905 The *Anna Tardy* made the last commercial steamboat plyings at Jefferson.

1905 Texas Association (Federation) of Colored Women's Clubs organized.

1905 Isaac Lewis married Mary Lou Jackson Lewis, 25 November.

1906   Moscoe Dixon born, 27 March or 05 May.

1906   Annie Myrtle Norris Glover Schuford born, 06 July.

1906   In retaliation for racial insults, Black American
        soldiers stationed near Brownsville, Cameron
        County, allegedly raided the Texas town, resulting in
        the death of one man and two other injury reports,
        13 August.

1906   Charley Edward Sims, Sr. and Carrie Jane Weaver
        Sims married, 31 October.

1906   President Theodore Roosevelt responded to the
        Brownsville Raid by ordering discharges for three
        companies (167 soldiers) of 25th Infantry, 1st
        Battalion Regiment, 06 November.

c1907   Sallie B. Lewis Cole Stevenson married Aboliva
        Cole.

1907   Andrew Carnegie's grant funded Jefferson's Carnegie
        Library construction. A doll collection remained on
        permanent display on the main level and an opera
        house on the second floor.

1907   Tom Belcher sold Berry Sims 39 ½ acres and a second
        tract of 50 acres, totaling 89 ½ acres more or less, 25
        January.

1907   Berry and Rebecca Sims sold M. M. Fitzgerald the
        same 106 acres that they initially bought during
        1888 from Ambrose Fitzgerald. M. M. Fitzgerald was
        the administrator of Ambrose's estate, 16 February

1907   S. B. Bryant born, 18 April 1907 or 1908.

1907   Ima Viola Sims Jefferson born, 25 October.

1907   John Wesley Martin, Sr. married Mary Exter Moon Martin Hawkins Rockwell Davis, 22 December.

1907-1909   Charles Monroe Lewis, Jr. born.

1907-1909   Adaline (Ada, Addie) M. Weaver Norris died.

c1908   Eula V. Weaver Rice married Edgar Lorenzo "Love" Rice, Jr.

1908   *Pointing The Way* published by AMS Press and written by Sutton Elbert Griggs, a Texas Black American author.

1908   Jack Johnson of Galveston, Texas won the world boxing championship.

1908   S. B. Bryant born, 18 April 1907 or 1908.

1908   Jasper Douglas of Atlanta, Cass County, Texas lynched, 19 April.

1908   Heavy rain during a three-day period stranded trains and hundreds of passengers in Jefferson, as bridges and trestles were washed away in the wind and rain. Passengers took their meals at area hotels, and passenger train cars served as lodging, May.

1908   Edward Norris married Addie Lee Smith Norris, 17 June.

1908   Hattie Mae Sims Hodge married Isom Hodge, Jr., 22 June.

1908   Solomon "Sol" Martin, Sr. died, 03 August.

1908   John Wesley Martin, Jr. born, 21 November.

1908   Felix Lewis, Jr. married Mabel Moore Lewis Isaac, 25 November.

1908   Spencer Weaver born, 19, 20, or 29 November.

1908   Eleanor Dixon Hodge born, 10 December.

1909   Henry Ford began assembly line automobile manufacturing.

1909   Rebecca Bryant Ball Lawson Eaton born, 19 March.

1909   James Hodges of Marshall, Harrison County, Texas lynched, 27 April.

1909   Matthew Chase, Mose Creole, and Pie Hill of Marshall, Harrison County, Texas lynched, 30 April.

1909   Howard Cleveland Sims born, 01 October.

1909   Marie Lewis Windom born, 18 October.

1909   Henry Rachel of Shreveport, Caddo Parish, Louisiana lynched, 27 November.

1910   Zettie Mae Hodge born, 16 or 17 February 1910 or 1911.

1910   Morris Wellington Weaver born, 03 April 1910 or 1915.

1910   Sanford Norris married Luella (Ella) Gallou Norris, 06 April.

1910   Zena (Zennie) Arvesta Lewis Williams born, 26 October or 20 November 1910 or 1912.

1910   Texas population included 3,896,542 people.

1910   Marion County populated with 10,472 people.

1910   Jefferson populated with 2,515 people.

1910   Approximately 1,345 Marion County farmers ginned 4,900 bales of cotton.

1910   Oil well drilled in Marion County.

1910   Clyde E. Lewis born.

1910-1914   Sallie Gray Weaver Green Hill born, 24 July.

1911   Martin Homer Wurtsbaugh, his wife Sallie Irby Stallup, and family moved from Jefferson to Shreveport. Branching out from William Martin Dunn and Edwin Jacob Rand, Wurtsbaugh started another lumber company during 1907, operating mills in Cass and Marion counties of Texas as well in Louisiana.

1911   Zettie Mae Hodge born, 16 or 17 February 1910 or 1911.

1911   Mary Lou Bryant White born, 19 February.

1911   Texas Pacific Railroad hired Black American firefighters, and Anglo railroad firefighters struck in protest, 09 March.

1911   Prohibition rally was held Tuesday night at Saint Paul Methodist Episcopal Church, Jefferson, June.

1911   Juneteenth celebration was held in Marion County either Saturday, the 17th or Monday, the 19th of June.

1911   Black American citizens celebrated the Fourth with a barbecue and picnic at Lover's Leap, west of Jefferson. A large crowd attended and enjoyed the holiday celebration, which lasted into the evening, 04 July.

1911   Rev. Ernest Sims born, 09 September.

1912   Johnny Wesley (Love) Sims born, 19 January.

1912   Mary Jackson and George Saunders of Marshall, Harrison County, Texas lynched, 13 February.

1912   Thomas Miles of Shreveport, Caddo Parish, Louisiana lynched, 09 April.

1912   Bertran A. Lewis born, 13 May 1912 or 1913.

1912   Clarence Hodge born, 23 August.

1912   Zena (Zennie) Arvesta Lewis Williams born, 26 October or 20 November 1910 or 1912.

1913   Soror Myra Lillian Davis Hemmings, a Texas native, was one of the charter members of Delta Sigma Theta Sorority, Inc., as founded at Howard University, Washington, D.C., 13 January.

1913   Nancy Sims Sharp Bryant married Rev. James "Jim" Bryant, 24 January.

1913   Robert Perry of Karnack, Harrison County, Texas lynched, 25 February.

1913   Ann Weaver died, 04 March.

1913   Bertran A. Lewis born, 13 May 1912 or 1913.

1913   Maggie Martin Fitzpatrick born, 17 May.

1913   Grandison W. Weaver and his brother Richard Weaver, Sr. purchased 40 acres of land from Walter P. Schluter, 17 May.

1913   Malinda Elizabeth Sims born, 04 July.

1913   Berry Sims and wife Rebecca Walton Sims paid vendor's lien notes held by J. H. Matthews, initially executed by Tom Belcher, 11 August.

1913   Peter Perry died, 22 October.

1913   Alma Lee Lewis Tindall born, 10 November.

1913   Erma Lewis McAlister Frierson born, 13 June or 16/17 July 1913 or 1914.

1914   David Lee of Jefferson, Marion County lynched for shooting and wounding Sheriff Billy Taylor. Lee's body hanged at a bridge crossing the Black Cypress, 08 January.

1914   Edward Hamilton of Shreveport, Caddo Parish, Louisiana lynched, 12 May.

1914   Erma Lewis McAlister Frierson born, 13 June or 16/17 July 1913 or 1914.

1914   Bread Henderson and Charles Washington of Mooringsport, Caddo Parish, Louisiana lynched, 11 December.

1914   Watkins Lewis of Shreveport, Caddo Parish, Louisiana lynched, 12 December.

1914-1918   Will Norris, Milton Weaver, Rev. Richard McCallihan Weaver, and Sydney White, Jr. served their country with honor, integrity, and bravery during WWI (The Great War).

1915   Morris Wellington Weaver born, 03 April 1910 or 1915.

1915   Milus Sims died, 07 May 1915.

1915   Charley Edward Sims, Jr. born, 10 June.

1915   U.S. Supreme Court determined in *Guinn vs. United States* that voter eligibility based on grandfather clauses violated the Fifteenth Amendment, 21 June.

1915   Corrine Laverne Lewis Jackson born, 10 October 1915 or 1917.

1916   Henry Lee Weaver married Edith Smith Weaver, 20 December.

1917   The State Highway Department (Texas Department of Transportation) established.

1917   Mary Norris Brown married Ranie Brown, 28 January.

1917   Henry Brooks of Shreveport, Caddo Parish, Louisiana lynched, 11 May.

1917   Loyd Edward Sims born, 14 July 1917 or 1918.

1917   Charles Jones of Marshall, Harrison County, Texas lynched, 22 August.

1917   Houston, Texas race riot between Black American soldiers of the 24th Infantry Regiment and the Anglo populist resulted in the deaths of two Blacks, seventeen Whites, and the subsequent hangings of thirteen soldiers. Officials declared martial law, 23 August.

1917   Grandison W. and Malinda Norris Weaver signed a partition deed, separating their 20 acres of land from Richard Weaver's 20 acres of land, 06 October.

1917   Corrine Laverne Lewis Jackson born, 10 October 1915 or 1917.

1918   Epidemic outbreak of Influenza.

1918   *Reminiscences* written by Rev. J. H. McLean, printing by Smith and Lamar Publishing House.

1918   Loyd Edward Sims born, 14 July 1917 or 1918.

1918   Ben Louis Norris married Frances Jane Royal Norris, 17 November.

1918   Carl Lee Lewis born, 03 December.

1919   Women won the right to vote in Texas.

1919   Gertie Mae Hodge Singleton born, 11 or 12 January.

1919   Irene Mabel Lewis Dilliard born, 08 April.

1919   Ivory Pearl Hodge Sims Whaley born, 10 April.

1919   Racial violence and rioting erupted in Longview, Gregg County, Texas. Martial law in effect, 13-18 July.

1919   Milton Weaver married Bessie Dixon Weaver, 25 August.

1919   Ada Sharp Calhoun married Oscar Calhoun, 27 September.

1919   Hattie Mae Sims Tyson born, 09 October.

1920   Nineteenth Amendment to the U.S. Constitution granted suffrage to women, nationwide.

1920   Texas population included 4,663,228 people.

1920   Marion County populated with 10,886 people.

1920   Jefferson populated with 2,549 people.

1920   More than 23,500 Black Americans owned farms in Texas.

1920   Marion County burst with sixty new businesses.

1920s   Charley Young's Barber Shop opened to Jefferson's elite business class from ten o'clock in the morning until four o'clock in the evening, six days a week. Haircuts at Young's shop cost $1.00 (.75 cents more than customary).

1920   Rev. Richard McCallihan Weaver married Verna Burns Weaver, 01 January.

1920   Felix Lewis, Sr. married Eliza (Liza) Luster Lewis, 04 January.

1920   Robert William Norris married Mattie Lee Pitts Norris, 01 February.

1920   Rev. Joseph Sims married Willie B. Crawford Sims, 01 June.

1920   Henry Lee Weaver married Betty Smith Weaver, July.

1921   Mary Walton Martin Lucky married Chappell "J. C." or "Chap" Lucky, 25 March.

1921   Oscar Douglas Hodge born, 04 April.

1921   The tornado of twenty-one touched down in Marion County, 15 April.

1921   Bessie Coleman, born in Atlanta, Cass County, Texas, received her aviation license from a school in France, 15 June. Bessie returned to the U.S. during September, becoming the first Black American female licensed pilot. During 1995 the U.S. Postal Service honored Coleman with a postal stamp.

1921   Milton Sims born, 09, 13, or 14 September.

1921   Milton Weaver died, 06 November.

1921   Felix Lewis, Jr. died, 19 December.

1922   J. T. Walton was a Black American cast member of *The Wife Hunters*, which was a 1922 film produced by a Texas-based Black American film company.

1922   Charley "Jim Bo" Henry Sharp married Lillie B. Freeman Sharp, 28 June.

1922   Verna Mae Rice Sedberry Warren born, 01 September.

1922   Helon Lewis, Sr. died, 1922 or 1925.

1923   Odelle Hodge Allen born, 05 January.

1923   Clinton Sims born, 08 or 09 June.

1923   Will Norris married Wilhelmina Hawkins Norris, 19 August.

1923   S. B. Bryant married Ethel Proctor Bryant, 23 August.

1924   Grant W. Weaver, Jr. married Olivia (Doll) Ross Weaver, 09 January.

1925   Helon Lewis, Sr. died, 1922 or 1925.

1925   Dorothy Scarborough's *The Wind* published.

1925   Texaco filling station opened for business in Jefferson with a sign of the times—three restrooms: one for men, one for women, and one for Black Americans.

1925   Novelle Hodge Richardson Jackson born, 21 or 29 June.

1925   Grandison W. Weaver and wife Malinda Norris Weaver entered into an oil and gas lease with George S. Niedermeir, granting drilling rights in exchange for money, 01 August.

1926   Annie Lee Weaver Rebecca Vaughn Gilham Allen Bell married Frank Gilham.

1926   Mattie Sims Crawford Jordan Heard Taylor married James "Jim" Heard, 21 January.

1926   Rev. Curtis Shedwell Weaver married Patsey Charleston Jones Weaver, 02 February 1926 or 1927.

1926   Marion County farmers produced 9,638 bales of cotton and 57,000 bushels of corn.

1926-1928   Curtis Martin Weaver, Jr. born, 08 June.

c1927   Felix Lewis, Sr. died.

c1927   Moscoe Dixon married Bessie Riser Dixon.

c1927   The Berry Sims Family Reunion began the third Sunday in August with Rebecca Walton Sims.

c1927   The antibiotic, penicillin, discovered.

1927   Rev. Curtis Shedwell Weaver married Patsey Charleston Jones Weaver, 02 February 1926 or 1927.

1927   Jesse Weaver died, 07 February.

1927   In *Nixon vs. Herndon*, the U.S. Supreme Court overruled Texas law that excluded Black Americans from state Democratic primaries, 07 March.

1927   James Vaughn Gilham born, 21 June.

1927   Ester Weaver Sims Cole Hawkins born, 06 September.

1927   Berry Sims died, 27 September.

1927   Nancy Sims Sharp Bryant died, 30 October.

c1928   Gulf Gas Station opened in Jefferson.

1929   Stock market crash.

1929   Marion County farmers and laborers milked 1,672 cows.

1929   John H. Martin, son of Marie Lewis Windom, born, 24 March.

1929   Clyde E. Lewis died, 25 June.

1929   Ruby Lee Sharp Thompson married W. B. Thompson, 20 July.

1929   Mary Walton Martin Lucky died, 04 August.

1930s   Marie Lewis Windom married.

1930s   The Civilian Conservation Corps was one of the many governmental agencies that began under President Franklin D. Roosevelt's New Deal and a group that Milton Sims joined during the early 1940s in Texas.

1930   Texas native Jessie Daniel Ames organized the Association of Southern Women for the Prevention of Lynching.

1930   Texas populated with 5,824,715 people.

1930   Texas population included 854,964 Black Americans.

1930   Marion County populated with 10,371 people.

1930   Jefferson populated with 2,329 people.

1930 Harrison County, Texas housed eight, one-room schools for Black Americans.

1930 Jefferson streets, homes, and businesses flood, May.

1930 Mattie Sims Crawford Jordan Heard Taylor married Rev. Theodore "Ted" R. Taylor, 02 June.

1930 Grandison W. Weaver and wife Malinda Norris Weaver entered into an oil and gas lease with J. M. Singleton, granting drilling rights in exchange for money, 07 October.

1931 Oil field discovered in Gregg County, Texas.

1931 A. B. MacDonald of the Kansas City, Missouri *Star* won a Pulitzer for the reporting of a murder in Amarillo, Randall County, Texas.

1931 Howard Cleveland Sims married Corrie Lee Moss Sims Manuel, 25 September.

1932 Annie Lee Weaver Rebecca Vaughn Gilham Allen Bell married Edgar "Tige" Allen.

1932 Spencer Weaver married Murrie Greenwood Weaver, 23 November.

1933 *Negrito, Negro Dialect Poems of the Southwest* published by Books for Libraries Press and written by John Mason Brewer, a Texas Black American author.

1933 Eleanor Dixon Hodge married Willy L. Hodge, 17 June.

1933   Rev. Ernest Sims married Ollie Mae Bennett Perry Sims, 30 September.

1933   Alex "Alec" Norris died, 06 December.

1934   Edmund Norris died, 16 August.

1934   John Wesley Martin, Jr. married Willie Mae Mathis Criss Martin Reed, 1934 or 1935.

1935   Approximately 1,600 Marion County farmers worked more than 34,000 acres of land, growing and harvesting crops. Farmers and laborers milked more than 2,400 cows and managed more than 6,000 cattle.

1935   With seventy years post-Emancipation of Texas slaves and Juneteenth celebration, only 21,938 Black American agriculturalists owned their farms. A smaller number (5,427) owned a portion of the land they farmed. The majority were tenant farmers (50,921) or sharecroppers (23,688). Merely 246 managed farms.

1935   John Wesley Martin, Jr. married Willie Mae Mathis Criss Martin Reed, 1934 or 1935.

1935   Bruce Edward Martin born, 07 March 1935 or 22 March 1936.

1935   Arzel "Z. Z." Hill, blues artist, born near Cass County, Texas, 30 September.

1936   Dr. Charles Monroe Lewis, Sr. died, 06 March.

1936   Bruce Edward Martin born, 07 March 1935 or 22 March 1936.

1936   Gertie Mae Hodge Singleton married Lester B. Singleton, 12 May.

1936   Annie Myrtle Norris Glover Schuford died, 29 July.

1936   Dr. Roscoe Conklin Lewis married Era Elizabeth Robinson Lewis, 19 September.

1936   Richard Weaver, Jr. died, 24 October.

1936   Texas Highway 8 plaited through Jefferson and designated as U.S. Highway 59.

1937   Rhodessa (Rodessa) Oil Field was discovered. This Louisiana oil field influenced landowners in Cass and Marion counties of Texas as lease hounds began scouting and hounding land owners into selling oil, gas, and/or mineral leases.

1937   Malinda Norris Weaver died, 12 February.

1937   Johnny Wesley (Love) Sims married Annie Mae Ruffin Sims, 18 April.

c1938   Erma Lewis McAlister Frierson married Bonnie Ray McAlister.

1938   Texas had the majority of high schools among the southern states. The Southern Association of Colleges and Secondary Schools awarded sixty-two schools with full accreditation and eleven high schools with a Class A rating. Marshall, Texas was home to one of those eleven Class A high schools.

1938   School-age Black Americans students living in the Lewis Chapel community attended a three-room, t-structured, schoolhouse that accommodated 106 students and three teachers. Ms. Norman and Ms. Annie Jackson were two of the schoolteachers in the Lodi community during the 1930s.

1938   The Union Chapel School continued serving children in the Union community, and Lewis and Weaver children were among the forty-six students taught by one primary teacher. During the early 1930s Anna Smith was a schoolteacher at the Union Chapel School.

1938   Grandison W. Weaver died, 1938 or 1939.

1939   Grandison W. Weaver died, 1938 or 1939.

1940   Texas populated with 6,414,824 people.

1940   Marion County populated with 11,457 people and only seven manufacturing firms existed.

1940   Jefferson populated with 2,797 or by another account 3,800 people and 150 businesses.

1940   Rebecca (Becky) Walton Sims died, 22 July.

1940   Novelle Hodge Richardson Jackson married Oscar Richardson, 27 July.

1940   Samuel Norris died, 28 December.

1941-1945   Hezekiah Johnson, Jr., Carl Lee Lewis, Charles Monroe Lewis, Jr., Clinton Sims, Milton Sims, Morris Wellington Weaver participated with others from Northeast Texas in WWII (Allies vs. Axis).

1941-1945   Brothers, Ben and Sam Norris, had sons to participate in WWII. Unfortunately, Benny Norris, Jr. did not survive. Sam's son, Edmond, returned home alive.

1941   *Hold Autumn in Your Hand* published by Viking, written by George Sessions Perry, and earned the National Book Award and the Texas Institute of Letters award.

1941   Ada Sharp Calhoun died, 10 May.

1941   Loyd Edward Sims married, 04 October.

1941   Messman Dorie Miller of Waco, Texas, awarded the Navy Cross for his actions and bravery on the USS *Arizona* during the Pearl Harbor attack, 07 December.

1942   Sallie B. Lewis Cole Stevenson married Dan Stevenson, 20 January.

1942   Sanford Norris died, 01 May.

1943   Odelle Hodge Allen married George Edward Allen, 22 May.

1943   Reportedly, two deaths attributed to racial violence and rioting in Beaumont, Texas, 16 June.

1943   Zettie Mae Hodge died, 07 September.

1944   Deluxe Barber Shop, a Black American establishment, opened for business in Jefferson.

1944   Maggie Martin Fitzpatrick married Samuel Fitzpatrick, 10 June.

1944   Hilda Simms starred in the play *Anna Lucasta*, which opened on Broadway, New York, August.

1944   Benny Norris Jr. died, 02 September.

1944   Richard Weaver, Sr. died, 13 September.

1945   John Wesley Martin, Jr. died.

1945   Jefferson streets flood Easter Sunday, 01 April.

1945   Moscoe Dixon died, 20 August.

1946   Johnny Wesley (Love) Sims married Lula Harris Sims.

1946   Milton Sims married.

1946   Black American citizens held their ground, demanding voting participation in Democratic primary, in the face of Marshall National Guard resistance.

1946   Nathaniel L. Sims died, August.

1947   Curtis Martin Weaver, Jr. married, June.

1948   International Paper Company began their pulpwood and shipping business in Marion County.

1948   *High John the Conqueror* published by MacMillan Company and written by John Walter Wilson.

1948   Sallie (Sarah) Weaver White Vaughn died, 19 December.

1949   Verna Mae Rice Sedberry Warren married Henry Arthur Warren, 12 May.

1949-1957   Allan Shivers served as Texas governor.

1950-1953   John H. Martin, a Marine and son of Marie Lewis Windom, was killed in action during the Korean War. Bruce Edward Martin, presumably joined the navy during this period, and Curtis Martin Weaver, Jr., the army.

1950   Texas populated with 7,711,194 people.

1950   Marion County populated with 10,172 people.

1950   Jefferson populated with 3,164 people.

1951   Federal courts began denouncing the exclusions of Black Americans from local party primaries.

1951   Ruby Lee Sharp Thompson died, 21 June.

1951   Isaac Lewis died, 13 October.

1952   Lucille Ophelia Vaughn Jenkins Galbreath died, December.

1953   Annie Lee Weaver Rebecca Vaughn Gilham Allen Bell married Theodore Bell.

1953   *The Word on the Brazos* published by University of Texas Press and written by John Mason Brewer, a Texas Black American author.

1953   Willie Mims Dean's *Jefferson, Texas: Queen of the Cypress* published.

1954   Robert William Norris died, 21 January.

1954   Hezekiah Johnson, Sr. died, 12 May.

1954   U.S. Supreme Court decided on *Brown vs. Board of Education of Topeka, Kansas*, overruling the separate but equal doctrine and making way for integration of public schools. The Court unanimously ruled that segregation in public school was unconstitutional and a protected right provided by the Fourteenth Amendment, 17 May.

1954   Mary Lou Bryant White married Leslie White, 21 June.

1954   Charley Edward Sims, Sr. died, 21 September.

1955   The *Diamond Bessie Murder Trial* play or re-enactment began, in Jefferson.

1955 *With all deliberate speed*, were the marching orders from the U.S. Supreme Court to the nation, regarding implementing school integration, 31 May.

1955 The Jefferson Independent School District absorbed the Lewis Chapel School for Black Americans. The Lewis Chapel School was located where the Lewis Chapel UMC structure is now situated.

1956 Federal Aid Highway Act of 1956, creating the Interstate System.

1956 Demonstrators circled Mansfield High School in Mansfield, Tarrant County, Texas to prevent Black American students from enrolling, 30 August.

1956 Lewis Chapel MC destroyed by fire, 06 May. Prior to the fire, someone lifted the brass bell, which rang at the hands of Tom Cooper on Sunday mornings or when a community member passed away. Allowing for the age differences, this Tom Cooper who rang the church bell was obviously a different person from Thomas Cooper, the 1870 Jefferson schoolteacher. Church services were held at the old Lewis Chapel School building until a new church structure was built.

1956 Various Felix Lewis heirs were plaintiffs in a boundary case involving acres of land as part of the Clark Simmons Survey in Marion County, 08 November.

1956 Rev. Ernest Sims married Leola White Sims, 21 December.

1957-1963   Price Daniel served as Texas governor.

1957   Rev. Ernest Sims died, 18 February.

1957   Novelle Hodge Richardson Jackson married Elvis Jackson, 26 June.

1958   *Dog Ghosts, and Other Texas Negro Folktales* published by University of Texas Press and written by John Mason Brewer, a Texas Black American author.

1959   Elithe Hamilton Kirkland's *Love is a Wild Assault*, a novel based on the life of Harriet Moore Page Potter Ames is published.

1960   Texas populated with 9,579,677 people.

1960   Marion County populated with 8,049 people.

1960   Residents integrated lunch counters in San Antonio, Bexar County, Texas, 16 March.

1960s   Citizens still practice manipulative politics in East Texas counties such as Marion and Upshur.

1960s   Black American agriculturalists in Marion County received only 15 percent of government aid for farm conservation programs. However, their numbers equaled 46 percent of the countywide industry group.

1960s   Louis E. Martin selected to rally the Black American vote in favor of Senator John Fitzgerald Kennedy during Kennedy's campaign for president of the U.S.

Kennedy received 86 percent of the Black American vote.

1961   *Black Like Me* published by Houghton Mifflin and written by John Howard Griffin.

1961   Record-setting tornado traveled through Marion County, causing $250,000.00 in property damage, 27 April.

1961   Rev. Richard McCallihan Weaver died, 08 or 09 July.

1961-1973   Northeast Texas American soldiers (including a Weaver descendant) involved in the Vietnam War, Southeast Asia.

1962   Bessie Mae Martin Williams Rhynes married Jimmy Rhynes, 01 June.

1963   President John Fitzgerald Kennedy assassinated in Dallas, Dallas County, Texas, 22 November.

1963   Lyndon Baines Johnson became thirty-sixth president of the U.S., 22 November. President Johnson married Claudia (Lady Bird) Alta Taylor, a scion of George Pattillo of Scotland. Lady Bird was born in Karnack; lived in Jefferson; and attended high school in Marshall, Texas.

1963-1969   John Connally served as Texas governor.

1964   Tornado twists through Marion County, causing $3,000.00 in property damage, 25 April.

1964   Sallie B. Lewis Cole Stevenson died, 06 July.

1964   Robert H. Jackson of the *Dallas Times Herald* won a
Pulitzer for photography of the Lee Harvey Oswald
murder, by Jack Ruby, a Dallas nightclub owner.

1964   Civil Rights Act.

1964   Louis E. Martin credited as the campaign leader
responsible for President Johnson receiving more
than 90 percent of the Black American vote.

1965   Voting Rights Act.

1966   Amendment to the Texas Constitution eliminated
poll tax payments as a prerequisite to voting in
Texas.

1966   Harold R. Perry appointed Roman Catholic bishop.

1966   *Jefferson on the Bayou: Glamorous Cultural City of Stern-
wheelers and Wagon Trains* written by Rebecca M.
Cameron and Ruth Lester published.

1966   *Port Caddo A Vanished Village and Vignettes of Harrison
County* written by V. H. Hackney published Marshall
National Bank.

1966   Edward Norris died, 13 January.

1966   Bruce Edward Martin married.

1967   Rev. Joseph Sims married Nellie Martin Brown Sims.

1967   Erma Lewis McAlister Frierson died, 16 February.

1967   A Texas federal court found Muhammad Ali guilty
of violating the Selective Service Act; the court
imposed a $10,000.00 fine and a five-year prison
sentence. Ali opposed the Vietnam War and
objected to military service on the grounds of
Muslim religious edicts, 20 June.

1967   Sanford Norris, III died, 26 June.

1968   Staff Sergeant Clifford C. Sims posthumously
received the Congressional Medal of Honor. On
patrol near Hue, Vietnam, Sergeant Sims shielded
his men from a bomb blast with his body.

1968   *American Negro Folklore* published by Quadrangle
Books and written by John Mason Brewer, a Texas
Black American author.

1968   Grant W. Weaver, Jr. died, November.

1968   Rev. Joseph Sims died, 04 December.

1968   Tornado touched down in Marion County, causing
$3,000.00 in property damage, 27 December.

1969-1973   Preston Smith served as Texas governor.

1969   *The Hindered Hand* published by Mnemosyne
Publishing and written by Sutton Elbert Griggs, a
Texas Black American author.

1969   Much of the Brooks House destroyed in a Jefferson

fire.

1969 *No Quittin' Sense* published by University of Texas Press, told by C. C. White, and written by A. Morehead Holland.

1969 Oscar Perry, Sr. died.

1969 *Soul Sister* published by World Publishing Company and written by Grace Halsell.

1969 Henry Lee Weaver died, February.

1969 *Apollo 11* spacecraft lands on the Moon, July.

1969 Howard Cleveland Sims died, 08 December.

1970 Texas populated with more than 11,195,000 people.

1970 Marion County populated with 8,517 people; Anglos became the majority of the populist.

1970 Jefferson populated with more than 3,000 people.

1970 The majority of the remaining 223 Marion County farms were devoted to cattle, rather than cotton or corn, and a scant (twenty-six) manufacturing firms existed.

1970 Black American playwright, Ted Shines' play entitled *Shoes* premiered.

1970   *The Brownsville Raid The Story of America's Black Dreyfus Affair*, written by John Downing Weaver published.

1970   Carrie Jane Weaver Sims died, 08 April.

1970   Eva E. Sims died, May.

1970   Maceo Leonard Norris died, 03 August.

1971   The Strand Theater in Jefferson burned.

1971   *Overshadowed* published by Books for Libraries Press and written by Sutton Elbert Griggs, a Texas Black American author.

1971   Russell Traylor's *The Diamond Bessie Murder and Rothchild Trials* published.

1971   Lela Viola Dixon High died, 09 March.

1971   Charley "Jim Bo" Henry Sharp died, 11 March.

1971   Eula V. Weaver Rice died, 27 April.

1971   The U.S. Supreme Court overruled the lower court's decision, finding Muhammad Ali not guilty of violating the Selective Service Act, 28 June.

1972   Dr. Roscoe Conklin Lewis died, 26 May.

1972   Military records of Brownsville soldiers cleared; surviving soldier(s) and widows received monetary compensation and reference books.

1972   Barbara Charline Jordan, a Black American Texas Senator and U.S. House of Representative Congresswoman, served as Texas governor for a day.

1973   Watergate Investigation.

1973   Mattie Sims Crawford Jordan Heard Taylor died, 28 October.

1973-1979   Dolph Briscoe served as Texas governor.

1974   *Caddo Lake: Mysterious Swampland* written by Mildred Mays McClung published.

1974   Mary Lou Bryant White died, 23 March.

1974   Barbara Charline Jordan served on the Watergate investigation committee, 09 May.

1974   Isaac "Ike" Gilham Weaver married Etta Mae McKie Yeldell Weaver, 31 August.

1975   Ben Louis Norris died, 06 January.

1975   Lowell W. Perry chosen as EEOC chairperson, 21 May.

1975   Robert Thomas Norris died, 24 November.

1976   Pauline Dixon Cooper died, 04 February.

1976   S. B. Bryant died, 10 April.

1976   Scott Joplin, born 1868 near Linden, Cass County, Texas, won a Pulitzer for the first large-scale production of an opera by a Black American. A Pulitzer was posthumously bestowed upon the Ragtime musician for *Treemonisha*.

1977   Alex Haley's Pulitzer Prize-winning *Roots* premiered on U.S. television as a movie miniseries, establishing television audience records, 23-30 January.

1978   Curtis Martin Weaver, Jr. died, January.

1978   Morris Wellington Weaver died, 26 January.

1978   Loyd Edward Sims crouched behind the furniture he was delivering when a shoot-out occurred in a Caddo, Bryan County, Oklahoma neighborhood between escaped convicts and police. Those killed included escapees, troopers, and other officials, May.

1979   Record-breaking Marion County area tornado caused $2.5 million in property damage and one reported injury, 01 April.

1979-1983   William P. Clements served as Texas governor.

1980   Texas populated with more than 14,225,000 people.

1980   Marion County populated with 10,360 people.

1980   Rev. Sanford Norris died, February.

1980   Charles Edward Tibbs died, August.

1980 Asa "Acie" Weaver died, 19 November.

1980 Erwin H. Hagler of the *Dallas Times Herald* won a Pulitzer for feature photography in a western cowboy series.

1981 *Ramona and Her Father* by Beverly Cleary received the Texas Bluebonnet Award, a children's book award.

1981 Larry C. Price of the Fort Worth, Texas *Star Telegram* won a Pulitzer for spot news photography of slayings in Liberia.

1982 Bessie Mae Martin Williams Rhynes died, 11 January.

1982 Adene Dixon Graham Rose died, 15 April.

1982 Will Norris died, 21 September.

1983 The majority of Marion County citizens found employment within the retail and service sectors as opposed to agricultural farming.

1983 U.S. Marines killed during barracks bombing in Beirut, Lebanon, October.

1983 U.S. military invaded Grenada, Caribbean Islands, West Indies, October.

1983 Eddie Mae Foxx died, October.

1983 Equal rights amendment failed.

1983-1987   Mark White served as Texas governor.

1983-1988   Iran Contra Affair.

1984   *Racehoss Big Emma's Boy* published by Eakin Press and written by Albert Race Sample.

1984   Arzel "Z. Z." Hill, blues artist, died in Dallas County, Texas, 27 April.

1984   Carl Lewis won four gold medals in the track and field events at the Olympic Games in Los Angeles, California, August.

1984   Miller Norris died, 03 November.

1985   *Skinnybones* by Barbara Park received the Texas Bluebonnet Award, a children's book award.

1985   Maurice Leon Norris died, 13 June.

1985   Nancy Mae Sims Black died, 19 August.

1985   Inez Weaver Reeves died, 05 September.

1986   Craig Flournoy and George Rodrigue (*Dallas Morning News* journalists) won a Pulitzer for their investigation and national reporting of the East Texas subsidized housing scandal.

1986   The Space Shuttle *Challenger* disaster, January.

1986   Zena (Zennie) Arvesta Lewis Williams died, May.

1986　Melvin Calhoun and Ada Calhoun descendants sold their undivided interest in the Berry Sims Estate (98 ½ acres and the 39 ½ acres of land) to the Brooks Farms, a partnership to include the Estate of Rebecca Willis Brooks, deceased, 18 August.

1986　Raymond Calhoun sold his undivided interest in the Berry Sims Estate (98 ½ acres and the 39 ½ acres of land) to the Brooks Farms, a partnership to include the Estate of Rebecca Willis Brooks, deceased, 01 October.

1986　Ada Calhoun descendant sold an undivided interest in the Berry Sims Estate (98 ½ acres and the 39 ½ acres of land) to the Brooks Farms, a partnership to include the Estate of Rebecca Willis Brooks, deceased, 05 December.

1986　Nancy Sims Sharp Bryant descendant sold an undivided interest in the Berry Sims Estate (98 ½ acres and the 39 ½ acres of land) to the Brooks Farms, a partnership to include the Estate of Rebecca Willis Brooks, deceased, 21 December.

1987　Eleanor Dixon Hodge died, 10 August.

1987　Black Monday, the largest one-day decline in recorded stock market history, 19 October.

1987-1991　William P. Clements served as Texas governor.

1988   Scott Shaw of the Odessa, Ector County, Texas *American* won a Pulitzer for spot news photography, capturing a small girl being rescued from a well.

1988   Hattie Mae Sims Hodge died, 15 or 16 February.

1988   Thelma Lois Norris Jones died, 03 June.

1988   Bertran A. Lewis died, 12 September.

1988   Clifton Earl Sims died, October

1988   Raymond Calhoun died, October.

1988   Alvert Norris died, 16 or 18 November.

1989   Edmond Norris died, 24 February.

1989   Milton Sims died, February or March.

1989   Sallie Gray Weaver Green Hill married Willy C. Hill, 21 March.

1989   Mamie Lee Norris Nelson Jones died, 25 March.

1989   Spencer Weaver died, 27 July.

1989   U.S. military invaded Panama, Central America, December.

1990   Texas populated with approximately 17 million people.

1990   Marion County populated with 9,984 people:

4,915 men and 5,069 women.

1990   Jefferson, Texas populated with 2,199 people.

1990   Johnson's Clean Air Act revised.

1990   *There's a Boy in the Girl's Bathroom* by Louis Sachar received the Texas Bluebonnet Award.

1990   Helen Marie Norris Hodge died, 12 August.

1991-1995   Ann Willis Richards (Dorothy Ann Willis) served as Texas governor.

1991   Persian Gulf War.

1991   Ivory Pearl Hodge Sims Whaley died, 05/06 June or 04 July.

1991   Ruby Lee Norris Davis died, 13 November.

1991   Annie Lee Weaver Rebecca Vaughn Gilham Allen Bell died, 05 December.

1992   Alfred L. Norris appointed bishop in the majority Anglo Texas Methodist Church conference.

1992   Terry Norris, of Lubbock, Lubbock County, Texas, won the super welterweight boxing title.

1992   *The Kind of Light That Shines on Texas* published by Little, Brown and written by Reginald McKnight, a Texas Black American author.

1992   Cold War officially ended.

1992   Melvin Calhoun died, April.

1992   Rev. Curtis Shedwell Weaver died, 17 May.

1992   Charley Edward Sims, Jr. died, 19 September.

1993   Jefferson won the bid for construction of an International Paper Company plant.

1993   Ken Geiger and William Snyder of the *Dallas Morning News* won the Pulitzer Prize for their spot news photography, covering the Barcelona, Spain Summer Olympic Games during 1992.

1993   World Trade Center terrorist bombing, New York.

1993   Branch Davidian compound episode, near Waco, McLennan County, Texas, 28 February – 19 April.

1993   Sallie Gray Weaver Green Hill died, 23 March.

1993   Maggie Martin Fitzpatrick died, 24 March.

1993   Hail caused $50,000.00 in property damage, Jefferson, 09 May.

1993   Valerie Sims Richardson died, 27 May.

1993   Corine Lois Norris Evans died 05 July.

1993   Thunderstorm and strong wind caused $10,000.00

in property damage for Kellyville and Jefferson, 02-03 August.

1993   Marie Lewis Windom died, 1993 or 1994.

1994   Ice storm for Marion County area caused $50,000.00 in property damage, 09 February.

1994   U.S. military invaded Haiti, Caribbean Island, West Indies19 September.

1994   *Shiloh* by Phyllis Reynolds Naylor received the Texas Bluebonnet Award, a children's book award.

1994   Marie Lewis Windom died, 1993 or 1994.

1995-2000   George W. Bush served as Texas governor.

1995   Lonny Norris died, January.

1995   James Edward Jefferson died, 21 January.

1995   Bombing of federal building in the city, county, and state of Oklahoma, April.

1995   Isaac "Ike" Gilham Weaver died, 18 June.

1995   Verna Mae Rice Sedberry Warren died, 04 July.

1996   Bruce Edward Martin died, 26 January.

1996   Khobar Towers bombing in Saudi Arabia killed nineteen U.S. military personnel and injured more than 500 people.

1996   Gertie Mae Hodge Singleton died, 25 August.

1996   Novelle Hodge Richardson Jackson died, 31 October.

1996   Malinda Elizabeth Sims died, 20 November.

1996   Veria Mae Jefferson Benson died, 26 December.

1996   Dr. Lonnie H. Norris, a Texas native, appointed
        dean of the School of Dental Medicine at Tuffs
        University in Boston, Massachusetts.

1997   The Marshall, Texas Public Library won an award
        grant from the Texas Book Festival.

1997   Texas Legislature named Jefferson the Bed and
        Breakfast Capital of Texas, 29 January.

1997   Oscar Douglas Hodge died, 18 February.

1997   Flooding throughout Harrison and Marion counties
        of Texas created $100,000.00 in property damage,
        01-09 May.

1998   Texas cattlemen lose defamation lawsuit against
        Oprah Winfrey in Amarillo, Randall County, Texas.
        Oprah responded with a free speech retort and a
        raised fist.

1998   Tornado by Betsy Byars received the Texas
        Bluebonnet Award, a children's book award.

1998   Marion County, Texas Veterans Memorial
        Dedication held in Jefferson. Granite slate panels

list known military service members involved in all conflicts from the Spanish-American War to present-day conflicts, 30 May.

1998   Clarence Otis Norris died, 03 July.

1998   Alma Lee Lewis Tindall died, 04 July.

1998   William Lee Norris died, 21 August.

1998   Willy Taylor Sims, Sr. died, 06 December.

1999   Last East Texas home of the Caddos discovered in Marion County, February.

1999   Louella Beasley Ray died, February.

1999   Deluxe Barber Shop, a Black American establishment, closed after fifty-five years of business in Jefferson, March.

1999   Joe "Smokey" Williams was born Seguin, Guadalupe County, Texas. As a Black American baseball pitcher in the Negro Leagues, he was posthumously inducted into the Baseball Hall of Fame, July.

1999   Corrine Laverne Lewis Jackson died, August.

1999   *Verdi* by Janell Cannon received the Texas Bluebonnet Award, a children's book award.

1999   For the category, young people's literature, *When Zachary Beaver Came to Town* by Kimberly Willis Holt, received the National Book Award, from the National Book Foundation.

2000   Texas populated with 20,851,820 Texans.

2000   Marion County populated with 10,941 citizens.

2000   Jefferson populated with 2,024 residents.

2000-2014   James Richard Perry served as Texas governor.

2000   USS *Cole* (navy ship) attacked in Port of Aden, Yemen, October.

2000   Ice storm created $123 million in property damage for Marion and other Northeast Texas counties, 12 December.

2000   Convicts (the Texas Seven) escaped from the John Connally Unit in Kenedy, Karnes County, Texas, southeast of San Antonio, Texas, 13 December.

2000   Another area ice storm caused more than $31 million in property damage for Marion and surrounding counties, on Christmas Eve.

2001   Rev. Oris Luther High died, 12 February.

2001   Major flood for Harrison and Marion counties of Texas produced $425,000.00 in property damage for residents, 17-28 February.

2001   Terrorists hijacked U.S. passenger airplanes, crashing the planes into the World Trade Center, New York, the Pentagon, and a wooden area in Somerset County, Pennsylvania, 11 September.

2001   *Cock-A-Doodle-Doo!* by Janet Stevens and Susan Stevens Crummel won the Texas Bluebonnet Award.

2002   More than 200 human cases of West Nile Virus found in Texas.

2002   Strong winds settled on the Berea community in Jefferson, leaving $25,000.00 in property damage, 07 April.

2003   Persian Gulf War.

2003   *The Dawn at My Back Memoir of a Black Texas Upbringing* published by University of Texas Press and written by Black American Texas filmmaker, Carroll Parrott Blue.

2003   Johnny Wesley (Love) Sims died, 15 January.

2003   Pieces of debris from the Space Shuttle *Columbia* fell over Texas, February.

2003   Clinton Sims died, 19 April.

2003   Charles Edward Sims died, 05 June.

2003   Approximately 360 human cases of West Nile Virus found in Texas.

2004   Dr. Spencer Wells, geneticist, published *The Journey of Man A Genetic Odyssey.*

2004   Loyd Edward Sims died, 03 March.

2004   Newly minted Texas quarter made available to the
        general public, 10 June.

2004   An army of Methodist youth came to Jefferson ready
        to tackle their mission—helping Jefferson's senior
        citizens with minor home repairs, 21-25 June.

2004   Chester Sims died, 25 June.

2004   Denzel Washington visited Jefferson and Wiley
        College in Marshall, Texas, September. Washington
        was touring the area, in preparation for a film about
        the top-notch 1935 Wiley College debate team.

2004   Clarence Hodge died, 23 September.

2004   Civilian Conservation Corps veterans held reunion at
        Caddo Lake State Park, 24-25 September.

2004   George W. Bush garnered enough political capital for
        another four-year term at the presidential election.

2004   Cullen Baker County Fair was held in Cass County,
        Texas, 06 November. Annual fair was named in
        honor of Texas Confederate soldier and notorious
        outlaw who would kill a freedman for a fist few of
        dollars. Baker was buried in a Jefferson

2004   Carl Lee Lewis died, 05 December.

2005   Freddy Norris died, 08 September.

2005   Shirley C. Sims Reeder died, 30 December.

2006   And It Came To Pass, 1st edition is published by author and family historian Greta McKelvey.

2006   Curtis Norris, Rev. died, 26 February.

2006   Rebecca Bryant Ball Lawson Eaton died, 01 May.

2006   William Charles Norris, Jr. died, 29 June.

2007   Genevieve "Jennie V." Calhoun Beard died, May.

2007   Charley Berry Calhoun died, October.

2007   Ima Viola Sims Jefferson died, 29 October.

2008   Mary Lou Wilson Kado died, February.

2008   Ethel L. Norris died, 24 February.

2008   Frank Faulkner Jr., Rev. died, August.

2008   Allan Calhoun died, 02 October.

2008   Hattie Mae Sims Tyson died, 31 December.

2009   Mass shooting at Fort Hood, Texas, 05 November.

2010   James Vaughn Gilham died, January.

2010   Alma Marie Sharp Merriweather died, August.

2011   Charley Ray Sims died, 22 April.

2011   Irene Mabel Lewis Dilliard died, 21 July.

2013   Edgar Lorenzo Rice, III died, 08 April.

2014   Oscar Calhoun, Jr. died, June.

2014   Queen Ester Norris Brown died, 30 July.

2015   Ethel Raye Weaver Davis died, May.

2015   Clarence Sims died, 18 June.

2016   Ester Weaver Sims Cole Hawkins died, 14 December.

2017   Tornado tear through the Dallas, Texas area, April.

2017   Hurricane Harvey hits Houston, Texas, August.

2018   Global COVID-19 Pandemic.

2018   Mae Dean Norris Newton died, 03 October.

2018   Odelle Hodge Allen died, 05 December.

2019   Mattie D. Sims Armstrong died, May.

2019   Joshua Norris died, 12 July.

2021   North Texas Deep Winter Freeze and Blackout, February.

2021   Gertrude Elizabeth Norris Sowels Canada died, 05 December.

the righteous shall inherit the land, and dwell therein for ever.

Psalm 37:29 KJV

BRANCH ONE

. . . .

THE LEWIS FAMILY TREE

Minerva Lewis

THE MATRIARCH MINERVA LEWIS WAS
BORN INTO slavery between 1825 and 1835 during the
month of May. Minerva could have been born in any
southern state such as Alabama, Arkansas, or Georgia. None
of the examined census records reconciled her birthplace, and
state boundary lines have changed over the years. However,
oral and printed history established that Minerva Lewis and
Ann Weaver were sisters who lived and died in Texas.
Minerva and Ann's parents were born in either Georgia or
Virginia. Only one document referred to Minerva as a widow.
None of the documents considered and none of the
interviewees provided an inkling as to who fathered Minerva's
children. Looking at the photograph of Minerva's eldest son
Felix Lewis, Sr., one could possibly presume Felix, Sr. was the
product of a master and slave relationship.

According to oral history, three of Minerva's children:
Felix, Sr., Helon, and Monroe Lewis traveled from Poplar
Bluff, Butler County, Missouri onto Texarkana, Bowie
County, Texas before settling down in Jefferson, Marion
County, Texas. If a Lewis village existed in Missouri as

suggested, perhaps some of Minerva's twelve children stayed there. Similarly, one of Minerva's sons made a life for himself in Texarkana.

This oral account of the family's migration and settlement is not necessarily contrary to Carrie's written notes, which depicted Minerva as the Lewis matriarch. Minerva and her family came to Texas, together or separate—slave or free—walked or by wagon train. If they were in fact three brothers and two sisters as the early census records indicated, the size of the family could imply that the family traveled together into Texas as free people of color. On the other hand, Minerva and her five children could have migrated to Texas in a coffle line, considering scores of slaveholders removed their bondsmen *en masse* to the unscarred Texas frontier, trying to save their property and fortunes from wartime destruction.

Regarding Minerva's early Texas life, conversations and existing documents provided an image of Minerva keeping a wooden, narrow shotgun house throughout 1870 yet astutely buying and selling land with one of her sons during 1886 and 1889. Interesting enough to note, these 44 acres of land that Minerva bought from Ward Taylor, Sr., et al. were a part of the Joseph Watkins Head Right Survey that she later sold to Walter P. Schluter.

Carrie's journal presented Minerva Lewis as the mother of Felix Lewis, and early census records established Felix's brothers as Monroe and Helon and his sisters as Frances and Ann (Anna). A later census record provided Minerva Lewis as the mother of twelve children, but only three enumerated with Minerva at 1900. Although Felix and Minerva Lewis were in the same family group at the 1870 census, this cohabitation does not necessarily support the common misconception of marriage, especially in light of Carrie's journal entry. Sensibly, the Lewis family established itself just after slavery, and Mother Minerva kept house as her eldest son Felix and other children began their new lives.

Either the census takers missed enumerating Minerva Lewis at the 1910, 1920, and 1930 census records, or perhaps by this time, Minerva had reached the end of her fate and passed away, leaving few memories and children:

- Felix Lewis, Sr.
- Monroe Lewis
- Helon Lewis, Sr.
- Frances Lewis Wiggins
- Ann (Anna) Lewis Berry

Felix Lewis, Sr.

Minerva's son Felix Lewis, Sr. was born during slavery in Georgia between 1849 and 1855. In Marion County, Texas, the Mulatto Felix married twice; on both occasions, he wed at the start of the New Year. At first, Felix married Emaline (Emiline) Spencer during 1873, and their marriage lasted forty-five years. During 1920, two years after Emaline's death, Felix married Eliza (Liza) Luster with Rev. James "J. P." Patrick performing the nuptials.

At the early census records, Felix was a laborer who became a farmer as his land acquisitions increased. Felix also worked as a blacksmith and carpenter at his workshop located behind his home; he reportedly operated a syrup mill 'sugar house' on his property, as well. Felix epitomized the men of his time—Felix had attitude, skill, and drive.

A bit of oral history traveled the generations, claiming Felix Lewis was not a Texas slave but rather a Civil War spy who traded secrets for land. Felix's large farmhouse sat on a hill, overlooking approximately 200 acres of land in the Union community.

Interesting enough to note, throughout 1880 Felix lived among scions of former slaveholding families such as the Brooks, Veal, and Taylor. However, Felix's real property records began during 1888 or 1889 with his initial deed of record. At this transaction Felix purchased 97 acres of land, a mere fraction of the Henry L. Lightfoot Head Right Survey from neighbor Marion DeKalb Taylor. The land deal cost $110.00, an additional two promissory notes, each for $201.98 at 12 percent interest. Felix had paid off this particular note by November 1899.

From around 1872 forward, Felix paid property taxes on farm machinery, tools, and animals necessary to cultivate the land. Felix's tax receipt, number 141 shows that he paid $236.00 in property taxes during 1888. As the years progressed, Felix purchased more land; as he added more acreage, land value appreciated, and property taxes continually increased. For example, during 1889, Felix paid $433.00 (receipt number 1750), and during 1896, he paid $568.00 (receipt number 894, abstract number 256).

During November of 1900, Felix purchased 86 acres, a section of the Clark Simmons Head Right Survey from Joe D. Mercer and his wife Sallie for $300.00. Felix bought his next property four years later from Enoch Love and wife Jennie for $150.00 at 10 percent interest. These 32 acres represented another snippet of the Clark Simmons Head Right Survey, and Felix reserved one acre for a Union Chapel Cemetery. By 22 March 1909, Felix had paid off this particular Love note.

Supposedly of all Felix's children his out-of-wedlock son Hezekiah Johnson, Sr. favored him the most. Felix's other children included:

- Ada Lewis Dixon Davis
- Charles Monroe Lewis, Sr., Dr.
- Isaac Lewis

- Sallie B. Lewis Cole Stevenson
- Felix Lewis, Jr.
- Babe Lewis (a male)
- Isora (Izora) Lewis

While Felix's children were growing up, there was never any talk about not attending church or not rising above expectations. A few of Felix's sons or daughters became farmers; some moved away from the homestead and established lives elsewhere. However, Felix did not sever ties with the children who relocated but continued to care and communicate. For example, Felix, Sr. supported his widowed daughter-in-law and his grandchildren after Felix, Jr. died. Son Charles' heart was open to communicate, considering Charles and his family visited the homestead and corresponded via post cards and pictures.

Felix Lewis, Sr. was virile, tall, lean, yet heavy as a man. A surviving photograph of Felix depicted him in a hat, three-piece suit, displaying a Mason medallion on the lapel. He had a full mustache, a square chin, broad-shoulders, and steely, piercing, gray-green eyes.

Felix Lewis, Sr. passed during the late 1920s. Though his name carried weight, the very community cemetery that Felix purchased, as stipulated in land deed of 1904, does not hold a headstone for him nor his second wife. Perhaps their headstones have been lost to weather or vandalism.

Ada Lewis Dixon Davis

Felix's first born happened to be a girl born on the first day of the New Year (1875) in Marion County. Around age 17, Ada married John Dixon, and by 1900, the couple had been married for eight years. Ada and John conceived eight children, and of the eight, four preceded Ada in death. Ada and John's children included:

- Adene (Addline) (Addine) Dixon Graham Rose
- Pauline Dixon Cooper
- Lela Viola Dixon High
- Moscoe Dixon
- Eleanor Dixon Hodge

After the lynching of first husband John Dixon, Ada married Tobe Davis.

Ada's skin was a dark chocolate color that she did not try to protect by wearing straw hats. Instead, Ada commonly wore a handkerchief *bandana* on her head and near-floor length dresses or skirts and aprons. Ada was prudent and competent in all things, which is why both the community and her family religiously depended on her as a midwife. However, Ada was understandably and periodically unavailable as a midwife when her daughter Eleanor required assistance, during Eleanor's visits to doctors in Dallas, Dallas County, Texas.

At a young age, Ada united with Union Chapel MC. Later in life, she united with Logan Chapel MC. Ada served Logan Chapel as a faithful member until poor health prevented her from attending and actively participating. Ada lived, married, and died in Marion County.

Adene (Addline) (Addine) Dixon Graham Rose

Ada's eldest daughter Adene was born during Ada's first year of marriage (1892) in Jefferson. Adene married Jim Graham, and they conceived three children:

- Zuma Graham François Brown Hawkins

- James Graham
- Robert Louis Graham

Later in life, Adene married Ellis Rose. Adene and Ellis did not conceive any children together.

Community folks described Adene as pleasant and attentive. She worked inside the home as a homemaker and outside in the yard as a landscape artist. She kept a pristine yard of dirt, not grass, which she meticulously swept with a handmade broom. She loved flowers especially petunias and honeysuckle.

After dipping snuff, Adene picked her teeth with twigs and such. Adene cooked from the fireplace and later her wood burning stove, reportedly making the strongest black coffee, best syrup bread pudding, and sweet potatoes in the community. Adene generously shared with whoever knocked and asked.

Adene applied for a Social Security number during 1955 at age 62, and she lived for approximately another thirty years on Route 1 in Jefferson, surviving three children.

At age 90 Adene reached the end of her fate and passed away.

Pauline Dixon Cooper

Ada's daughter Pauline was born circa 1893 in Jefferson and attended school at Union Chapel. Around age 20, Pauline gave birth to James "Jack" Calvin Cole who was named and raised by Pauline's aunt Sallie. Malachi Johnson was Jack's biological father. Later, Pauline married and divorced M. T. Cooper.

Pauline moved from Jefferson during the 1940s, bound for Alvarado, Johnson County, Texas. Perhaps a mixture of personal and economic reasons drove Pauline to

Alvarado. Regardless of the reasons why, Pauline settled in Alvarado. There, she found employment and a peaceful place, retreating to an apartment next door to her last employer. She worked effortlessly as a domestic for an influential lawyer, as a source of income, and she wrote poetry, as a pastime.

Through the years, Pauline kept in touch with at least one niece, sending the niece care packages and poems.

At age 82 Pauline reached the end of her fate and passed away during 1976 in Alvarado.

Lela Viola Dixon High

Ada's daughter Lela Viola was born during 1897 or 1898. Lela married John High; the couple conceived at least eleven children and raised three grandchildren. Lela doled out kindness and strictness, fairly. When pressed, she spared not the rod—she spanked the grandchildren with a switch. Leal was a Christian who ensured her children and grandchildren in her care were fed, safe, and attended their church in Marshall, Harrison County, Texas. Primarily, Lela was a homemaker who occasionally helped others with surfacing cleaning.

Around age 73 Lela reached the end of her fate just before the spring of 1971 in Harrison County and passed away, leaving children:

- Edward High
- Oris Luther High, Rev.
- Kelly High
- Floyd High
- Melba Constance High

Moscoe Dixon

Ada's son Moscoe Dixon was born during 1906; lived in the Union community; attended the early Union Chapel School; and married Bessie Riser around 1927. Moscoe and Bessie conceived at least five children, one dying at birth being premature.

Eventually, Moscoe and his family moved to Houston, Harris County, Texas, where he worked as a laborer at the Dixon Gun Plant. Moscoe and the family resided on Jensen Drive when on 18 August, Moscoe and his wife argued, which resulted in Moscoe stabbing his wife and poisoning himself with lye.

A few days later, at age 39 Moscoe reached the end of his fate and passed away at Jefferson Davis Hospital from alkali poisoning.

Eleanor Dixon Hodge

Ada's daughter Eleanor was born in Jefferson during the 1908 Christmas season. She attended the early Union Chapel School and Central High School in Jefferson. Eleanor became a dazzling June bride, marrying Willy L. Hodge in 1933. Eleanor and Willy conceived six children.

Eleanor did not work outside the home partly because of her heart problems. However, she faithfully participated in church activities in Jefferson and Dallas, playing the piano for the local Baptist and Methodist churches. Eleanor's heart ailment and related issues caused she and her husband to make recurrent trips to various doctors in Dallas. Eventually, Eleanor rented an apartment for use during her frequent medical trips, to Dallas.

After a brief illness, at age 78 Eleanor reached the end of her fate and passed away during 1987 in San Antonio,

Bexar County, Texas. The family laid Eleanor to rest at Logan's Chapel Cemetery, Jefferson.

Dr. Charles Monroe Lewis, Sr.

Felix's first son Dr. Charles Monroe Lewis, Sr. was born in Jefferson circa1876. By enrolling at Wiley College in Marshall, Charles was the first in his family to attend undergraduate college. Quite possibly, Charles also studied at Morehouse College in Atlanta, Fulton County, Georgia before finishing medical school during 1905 at Meharry Medical College, Nashville, Davidson County, Tennessee.

During 1903, Charles married Birdie Mae Washington in Marion County. Between 1904 and 1909, Charles and his family relocated to Hope, Hempstead County, Arkansas, where Charles practiced medicine. Charles and Birdie conceived three sons:

- Roscoe Conklin Lewis, Dr.
- Charles Monroe Lewis, Jr.
- Bertran A. Lewis

Throughout the early 1900s, Charles and Birdie opened their home to relatives, friends, or other renters. Feasibly some renters, in exchange for lodging, helped with domestic chores at the house or administrative tasks at the medical clinic.

At age 60 Dr. Charles Monroe Lewis, Sr. reached the end of his fate and passed away from cerebral apoplexy during 1936 in Hope.

Dr. Roscoe Conklin Lewis

Dr. Roscoe Conklin Lewis was born during the 1904 Christmas season in Jefferson. He obtained his early education in Hempstead County but returned to Texas for undergraduate college, graduating from Wiley College during 1926 or 1927. Again emulating his father, Roscoe graduated from Meharry Medical College during 1931.

In Hope, Roscoe married Era Elizabeth Robinson during the Depression era. Roscoe practiced medicine for forty years, maintaining medical offices in Hempstead and Ouachita counties of Arkansas. By 1961, Roscoe and family were living in Camden, Ouachita County.

Regarding Roscoe's health, Roscoe contracted Rheumatic fever. Later, he was diagnosed with a defective aorta valve. During 1972, he traveled to Houston for a heart valve replacement surgery. However, Roscoe never fully recovered.

At age 69 Dr. Roscoe Conklin Lewis reached the end of his fate and passed away from congestive heart failure in Camden. The family laid Roscoe to rest at Scott Memorial Garden in Hope.

Charles Monroe Lewis, Jr.

Charles Monroe Lewis, Jr. was born circa 1908 in Hope. He too attended grammar school in Hempstead County but later returned to Texas, graduating from Wiley College on 03 June 1930. Charles, Jr. became a postal employee, married, and joined the U.S. Army during WWII. Charles, Jr. previously lived in Little Rock and Los Angeles and passed away perhaps in Richmond, Virginia.

Bertran A. Lewis

Bertran A. Lewis was born during 1912 or 1913 in Hempstead County, Arkansas, later attending school in the same county. Bertran married at least four times. Bertran lived in Little Rock for a phase.

At age 75 or 76 Bertran reached the end of his fate and passed away during 1988 in Oakland, Alameda County, California. His body was cremated.

Isaac Lewis

Felix's son Isaac Lewis was born in Texas between 1881 and 1885. Isaac stayed in the Union community and became a farmer, blacksmith, and carpenter, like his father. Isaac married Mary Lou Jackson (the sister to his brother's wife) around Thanksgiving of 1905 in Marion County, with Rev. D. C. Hailey performing the nuptials. Isaac and Mary Lou conceived five children:

- LaRue Lewis
- Clyde E. Lewis
- Carl Lee Lewis
- Erma Lewis McAlister Frierson
- Zena (Zennie) Arvesta Lewis Williams

Isaac supposedly suffered from an undiagnosed cancer, but he died at his Jefferson home. At age 69 Isaac reached the end of his fate and passed away from pneumonia during October of 1951.

Clyde E. Lewis

Isaac's son Clyde E. was born circa 1910 in Texas. Certainly, Clyde attended school between ages seven and nine. Legions of little boys grow up to become men, marry, father children, and provide for their families. Clyde never had the opportunity; his life ended early. Clyde passed during 1929 from dysentery as diagnosed by Dr. Felix Peebles. Family and friends gathered from near and far to express condolences at Clyde's funeral and burial on 19 May 1929 at Union Chapel Cemetery.

Zena (Zennie) Arvesta Lewis Williams

Isaac's daughter Zena (Zennie) Arvesta was born during October or November of 1910 or 1912 in Jefferson. She attended elementary school throughout 1919. As a young person, Zennie moved to Hot Springs, Garland County, Arkansas. Not yet married by 1939, Zennie worked for H. H. Harper. Eventually, Zennie married twice while living in Arkansas. The name of her first spouse is unknown; her second husband's surname was Williams. Zennie did not have children.

At age 74 or 76 Zennie reached the end of her fate and passed away during May of 1986 in Arkansas.

Erma Lewis McAlister Frierson

Isaac's daughter Erma was born in June or July between 1913 and 1914, during a spell of documented lynchings in Texas. She too attended school in Jefferson. Erma married Bonnie Ray McAlister in Marion County around 1938. Later, Erma along with her second husband Lee W. Frierson followed Erma's relatives to Arkansas. Erma and her husband lived in Hempstead County for several years before eventually relocating to the city and county of San Francisco, California. Erma did not have any children.

At age 53 or 54 Erma reached the end of her fate and passed away from cancer during 1967.

LaRue Lewis

Isaac's son LaRue was born in Marion County and passed during 1917 at age one or two.

Carl Lee Lewis

Carl Lee Lewis was the last son born to Isaac and Mary and their last child to pass away. Cast in the image of his father and paternal grandfather, Carl Lee was born during 1918 in Jefferson, where he worked the land, paid the property taxes, and lived his entire life except for a short military tour of duty during WWII.

Young Carl Lee fell in love with Verna Mae, his cousin with the big, beautiful eyes, but the prospective mother-in-law forbade Carl Lee to marry his cousin Verna Mae. Instead, just before reporting to wartime military duty, Carl Lee married Lillian Delia McAlister.

Unfortunately during retirement, Carl Lee suffered from several debilitating strokes. Never fully recovering, Carl Lee passed in Jefferson as the 2004 Christmas season approached. Just two days after his 86th birthday, Carl reached the end of his fate and passed away. The family laid Carl to rest at Union Chapel Cemetery.

Interesting enough to note, Carl Lee served as a pallbearer at the funeral of both Weaver cousins: Verna Burns Weaver and Verna Mae Rice Sedberry Warren. Incidentally in the early, small, rural communities, family and friends fulfilled some of the duties of the undertakers, i.e., community folks washed and dressed the body for burial, dug the grave, and served as pallbearers.

Sallie B. Lewis Cole Stevenson

Felix's daughter Sallie B. was born in Texas during 1885. As expected, Sallie attended the early Union Chapel School in Jefferson. Around 1907, Sallie married Aboliva Cole in Marion County, and the couple lived in the Union settlement where Sallie attended the Union Chapel MC.

Sallie became known as a giving and hospitable neighbor with open arms and doors. Sallie worked inside the home always helping anybody and any stray animal. Early in Sallie's marriage, Marshall Watkins stayed with Sallie and Aboliva. Later, they named and raised great nephew James "Jack" Calvin Cole. Others such as nephew Troy Cole stayed with Sallie and Aboliva, as well. Sallie bore no natural children of her own, so the list of those she helped is lengthy. For some she cooked. For others she shared crops, which she cultivated from the family (communal) farmland. The community grew to depend on the generous, heavy woman with brown skin, beautiful hair, and who loved to cook.

Later in life, Sallie met Dan Stevenson. During the January cold of 1942, Sallie married Dan with Rev. A. Perkins performing their nuptials. The couple moved to the Kellyville community of Marion County. There, Sallie became known as the woman with the oldest pipe organ in her home. Coincidentally, Sallie shared at least one business connection with Carrie Jane Weaver Sims; on 06 January 1959, Carrie sold Sallie one bushel of sweet potatoes for $2.00.

Prior to Sallie's 1964 death she had been hospitalized at Dr. Douglas' clinic in Jefferson. Around age 79 Sallie reached the end of her fate and passed away. The family laid

Sallie to rest at Union Chapel Cemetery. However, her headstone has been lost to weather or vandalism.

Felix, Lewis, Jr.

Some family members affectionately nicknamed Felix, Jr., "Uncle Buddy." Felix, Jr. was born in Texas circa 1888, and he attended the Union Chapel School, as a young boy. By the time Felix, Jr. reached the age of majority, he had married Charlie Mabel Moore Lewis Isaac. They wed around Thanksgiving in Marion County. There, Felix, Jr. and his growing family stayed with his parents, at the start of their marriage.

As a maturing adult, Felix, Jr. knew he did not want to farm the land. His pioneering spirit led him to assert his own way of providing for his family. Purposefully, Felix, Jr., his wife, and five children settled in Marshall where Felix, Jr. made locomotive engines for the Texas and Pacific Railroad.

Regarding their children, an infant son born at fourteen pounds during 1921 or 1922, did not survive. However, Felix's other children survived to maturity:

- Marie Lewis Windom
- Alma Lee Lewis Tindall
- Corrine Laverne Lewis Jackson
- Irene Mabel Lewis Dilliard

Throughout his life, Felix, Jr. maintained almost perfect health, except for the illness that caused his death during the 1921 Christmas season. At his death, either no one notified a physician, or the physician was unavailable. Around age 33 Felix, Jr. reached the end of his fate and passed away from pneumonia.

Marie Lewis Windom

Marie was born during 1909 in Jefferson. As a child, she attended the Lewis Chapel School. After Marie's father (Felix, Jr.) died during December of 1921, the family moved from Marshall to Henderson, Rusk County, Texas.

Marie married during the Depression era. Around age 20, Marie gave birth to a son who she named John H. Martin. John grew into a soldier and courageously lost his life serving his country during the Korean War. John's body was interred at Lewis Chapel Cemetery.

Though Marie married and lived in Rusk County for a time, this branch of the family eventually moved to Houston. Marie was sociable and compassionate—demonstrating great concern for other people—people from all walks-of-life.

At age 84 or 85 Marie reached the end of her fate and passed away in Houston from cancer during 1993 or 1994. The family held Marie's funeral at Mount Vernon UMC and laid her to rest at Veterans Cemetery in Houston.

Alma Lee Lewis Tindall

Alma Lee was born circa 1913 in Jefferson and named in honor of Emaline (Emiline) Spencer Lewis (Felix, Jr.'s mother). Alma attended school in Marshall. Growing up, she worked as a maid for the Ledbetters at the Houston Medical Arts Hospital during the Depression era. Houston remained Alma's home, where she married and conceived three children.

At age 84 Alma reached the end of her fate and passed away during the record-setting Texas heat of July 1998 after suffering from a stroke.

Corrine Laverne Lewis Jackson

Corrine Laverne was born in Jefferson during 1915 or
1917. Corrine attended school in Marshall but finished high
school at Phyllis Wheatley during 1935 in Houston. Corrine
married in Houston and was a homemaker. Later in life, the
family relocated to California.

At age 82 or 84 Corrine reached the end of her fate
and passed away during 1999 in the city and county of Los
Angeles.

Irene Mabel Lewis Dilliard

Baby Irene grew up in a loving home despite early
hardships from the sudden death of her father and infant
brother. As the family relocated to Marshall and eventually
Houston, Irene graduated from the Phyllis Wheatley School in
May of 1937. As a young adult she worked as a seamstress
who loved styling and storytelling. She kept family history
alive, annually attending reunions and sharing folklore in the
oral tradition.

At age 92 Irene Mabel reached the end of her fate and
passed away. The family laid Irene Mabel to rest at Paradise
North Cemetery, Houston, Harris County, Texas.

Babe Lewis

Babe Lewis was the other son born to Felix, Sr. Babe
married Ida Peppers during January of 1891. This line
remains obscured.

Hezekiah Johnson, Sr.

Hezekiah Johnson, Sr. was born between 1874 and 1880 in Texas. Around 1901, Hezekiah, Sr. married Erbie (Irby) Williams, and they conceived at least three children. Of the children, two were named: Winnie and Hezekiah. Winnie V. Johnson passed during 1994, and Hezekiah, Jr. settled in Houston, served in WWII (army), and passed during 1986.

Hezekiah, Sr. embodied the character and image of his biological father, Felix Lewis, Sr., except for their varying complexions. Apparently, dark brown in complexion, Hezekiah, Sr. stood stalwart, approximately six feet one inch tall, with his strength, bravery, and steadfastness never in question. Even Hezekiah's walk resembled his father's stride.

Around age 78 Hezekiah, Sr. reached the end of his fate and passed away during 1954.

Monroe Lewis

Minerva's son Monroe was born between 1855 and 1867 in either Georgia or Texas. Throughout 1880, Monroe worked as a laborer; during 1888, he married Adeline (Addie) King in Marion County. They conceived seven children, naming them:

- Frances
- Another daughter
- Eva
- Ruby
- William "Willy"
- Charles B. "C. B."
- Charles L. "C. L."

Minerva bought 40 acres of land with her son Monroe and his wife Adeline during 1886 for $160.00; they sold the identical acreage tract for the same price three years later during 1889. Though Addie was a widow during 1920, she had owned her home by this time.

Helon Lewis, Sr.

Minerva's son Helon was born between 1859 and 1868 in either Arkansas or Texas. Helon married Elizabeth (Lizzie) C. Moore around 1887. They conceived eleven or twelve children including possibly one unnamed son and:

- Colonel Luther
- Governor Edward
- Ross E.
- Valentine
- Lizzie
- George
- Helon, Jr., Rev.
- Alvin
- Alzadie (Alzadia) Zadie (Zadia)
- Ada
- Bennett

Dr. Fred Edward Lewis (descendant of Helon Lewis, Sr.) along with others have researched and produced a written genealogy of the Helon Lewis, Sr. branch of the family. A few notable mentions from Helon's branch include the following: Helon's wife, Elizabeth, and her Anglo father. One oral story corroborated courthouse records, supporting his name as Marion DeKalb Taylor who was a slaveholder, country doctor, and legislator. Elizabeth's mother name was recorded as Sallie Sims.

During 1892, Helon and Elizabeth purchased 44 acres of land from Marion DeKalb Taylor, paying $200.00. Helon and Elizabeth paid $40.00 more than the amount Walter P. Schluter paid for the same land during 1889 when he acquired it from Minerva and Monroe. Helon and his wife owned their home by 1920. Helon suffered for a stretch after an injury from a horse; consequently, he passed during the 1920s from the fall and injury.

A few of the Lewises from the Helon Lewis branch married into the Marion County, Texas Rand and Douglas families. Another of Helon Lewis' sons became a minister and established his ministry and home in Texarkana.

Helon's son George was another Lewis heir who maintained relations with the Weavers besides Helon's brother, Felix, Sr. George was a logger. As a logger, he moved often, following the sawmill towns, such as Smithville, Bastrop County, Texas and Huntsville, Walker County, Texas. June Weaver, Carrie's brother who later disappeared, chopped cotton for Cousin George and Mattie Lewis when they lived in Marshall.

Frances Lewis Wiggins

Minerva's daughter Frances was born circa 1857 perhaps in Texas. Frances married Green Wiggins during 1875 in Marion County. Just five years later, Green appeared at the 1880 census as husband to Lula. Perhaps Frances died, or she and Green divorced. This family line remains obscure.

Ann (Anna) Lewis Berry

Minerva's daughter Ann (Anna) was born during 1860 or 1861 perhaps in Texas; she and Aaron Berry married during 1880 in Marion County. By 1880, Ann Berry was age

20, keeping house, and enumerated just next door to Minerva Lewis (her mother).

End note: Hopefully another family historian will research the Marion County, Texas Wiggins and Berry families, discovering more details regarding a possible connection to the Lewis lineage.

THIS IS AN ACCOUNT OF THE LEWIS FAMILY.
MAY THEIR STORIES BE REMEMBERED AND
SPIRITS HONORED.

The face of the Lord is against them that do evil, to cut off the remembrance of them from the earth.

Psalm 34:16 KJV

BRANCH TWO

. . . .

THE MARTIN FAMILY TREE

Thomas "Tom" Martin, Sr. and Sarah Martin

BY 1880 IN MARION COUNTY, TEXAS, THOMAS "Tom" and Sarah Martin had fostered a family of fourteen children:

- Alfred
- Lee Ann
- Liza
- Rhoda (Rody)
- Lucy
- Ann
- Foster
- Solomon "Sol"
- Simon,
- Jane
- Thomas, Jr.
- Felix
- Millie
- Mary

Thomas, a farmer, was age 65 and born in Tennessee. Thomas' wife Sarah was age 45 and born in Alabama. Judging their ages, both Tom and Sarah were born during slavery. Oral history tells the story of Tom Martin, Sr. coming to Texas as a member of a wagon train from Virginia. Without documentation corroborating their migration, the oral history remains unsupported.

From the census, birth, and marriage records, Tom, Sr. and his ilk clearly settled and multiplied in Northeast Texas. Documented marriages for Tom and Sarah's children have provided these couplings: Alfred Martin and Hattie Taylor Johnson; marriage between Lee Ann Martin and Peter Perry; marriage between Rody Martin and Jim Suttis; marriage between Ann Martin and Warren Williams; and the union between Solomon and Mary.

Solomon "Sol" Martin, Sr.

Solomon Martin, Sr. was born during either 1853 or 1862. Throughout 1880, Solomon lived in his parents' household and worked as a laborer. During the hot July of 1884, Rev. J. Hazelwood married Solomon and Mary Walton Martin Lucky in Jefferson. Solomon and Mary tried to establish themselves, but according to Marion County property tax records, they eked out a poor existence. Between 1891 and 1893, Solomon owned insignificant miscellaneous property for which he paid minimum taxes. Unfortunately, Sol contracted Malaria and died before securing an optimistic future for his family.

Mary Walton Martin Lucky

Mary was born during slavery either 1852, according to her headstone or circa 1865, according to the 1870 and

1900 Marion County census records. Solomon and Mary conceived three children:

- John Wesley Martin, Sr.
- Solomon "Sonny" Martin, Jr.
- Bessie Martin Williams Rhynes

For thirteen years, Mary struggled alone to nurture and counsel her three children.

Exhausted yet hopeful, Mary accepted Chappell "J. C." Lucky's marriage proposal; during 1921, Rev. Armstrong Lange performed the nuptials in Marion County. Chappell was significantly older than Mary and already a retired widower. Mary, her new husband, and possibly Daughter Bessie lived within the city limits of Jefferson.

Unfortunately, Mary died eight years into her second marriage. Dr. R. L. Futrell cited chronic Bright's disease as the cause of death. Mary was buried on the same day that she died in Jefferson. Equipped or not, Mary's three children had to fend against poverty for themselves.

John Wesley Martin, Sr.

John Wesley Martin, Sr. was the first born of Solomon and Mary, arriving during the January cold. John Wesley was short in stature and cute, by all accounts. Sims descendants remembered John Wesley, and John Wesley had some knowledge of family relations, as he found pleasure in visiting his cousin Carrie on occasion.

John Wesley visibly had an unhappy and unstable existence. Grasping at normal relations, John Wesley married Mary Exter Moon during the 1907 Christmas season in Marion County. Exter was Mary's middle name, and Moon was her maiden name. Mary's married names became Martin

Hawkins, Rockwell, and Davis, as she married four times. Deeming the Martins as the eldest of Mary's children, Mary's marriage to John Wesley probably was her first marriage as well as John Wesley's first marriage. Rev. W. W. Neal performed the nuptials, for John Wesley and Mary, in Marion County. John Wesley and Mary conceived two children:

- John Wesley, Jr.
- Maggie

As an adult and at various times, John lived in steel towns, such as Ore City, Upshur County, Texas and in train towns, such as Hope, Hempstead County, Arkansas. John Wesley's body was badly burned in a house fire, from which he later died, in Hope. John Wesley's body was sent home to Jefferson in a bag on the train. There was neither a funeral nor an obituary.

John Wesley Martin, Jr.

John Wesley Martin, Jr. was born during 1908. In Marion County, John, Jr. married Willie Mae Mathis Criss Martin Reed around age 26 during the Depression era. Although, the McAlister family raised Willie Mae, Mathis was Willie Mae's maiden name. John, Jr. and Willie Mae did not have children, together. However, John, Jr. fathered a son named Bruce Edward Martin.

John, Jr. was compulsive by nature, which created keen anxiety about his wrongdoings. John, Jr. lived in Jefferson for a stint but died in Hope during 1945 (the year of the Jefferson flood). Unusually, John, Jr. died prior to his father, as he suffered from liver disease. Coincidentally, John Wesley and John, Jr. simultaneously lived in Hope with the Lewis relatives;

however, no interviewees offered any oral history addressing the question of whether they associated with one another.

Bruce Edward Martin

Bruce Edward Martin was born in Jefferson either on 07 March 1935, according to his Social Security number application or 22 March 1936, per his obituary. Bruce had a bitter life in Jefferson, so he left, never to return, bound for California. Bruce's grandmother raised him in Berkeley, Alameda County, California, where he finished his education in the public school system.

Young, inexperienced, and unsuccessful at gaining long-term employment, Bruce stayed home on Kirkham Court, Oakland, Alameda County until he joined the U.S. Navy. After military service, Bruce moved to Los Angeles during 1955. Around Thanksgiving of 1966, Bruce married in either Los Angeles or Alameda County.

At age 60 or 61 Bruce reached the end of his fate and passed away passed in Los Angeles, from emphysema during the winter of 1996. Bruce was laid to rest at Rose Hills Cemetery.

Maggie Martin Fitzpatrick

John Wesley's daughter Maggie was born during 1913, and around age 30, she married Samuel Fitzpatrick in Jefferson. Maggie and Sam ambled to the county courthouse and applied for their marriage license on the fifth of the month, and they returned five days later with a with a firm decision to jump the broom. William E. Singleton, Sr., the esteemed Marion County Justice of the Peace, pronounced them husband and wife. With big hearts and strong minds,

Maggie and Sam conceived nine children; six of whom have passed away:

- Wilburn Fitzpatrick
- Alice Faye Fitzpatrick
- Sammie Lois Fitzpatrick
- Justa Faye Fitzpatrick
- Melvin Fitzpatrick
- Clarence Arthur Fitzpatrick

At age 79 Maggie reached the end of her fate and passed away during 1993 in Marion County. The family laid Maggie to rest at Cedar Grove Cemetery, Jefferson.

Solomon "Sonny" Martin, Jr.

Solomon and Mary's second son Solomon "Sonny" Martin, Jr. was also born in Jefferson during the January cold. Unfortunately, Solomon, Jr. was another family member who disappeared, never to be heard from again. Sonny was rumored to have conceived children who lived in Shreveport, Caddo Parish, Louisiana. Without additional oral history and documentation, details of Sonny's life remain obscure. Optimistically, Sonny's life mattered enough for someone to mark the place where his body dissolved into the dirt.

Bessie Mae Martin Williams Rhynes

Lastly, Bessie Mae was born during 1897 to Solomon and Mary. Early in life, Bessie married Wash Williams. Years later (1962), facing the on-duty Marion County judge, Bessie became a dazzling June bride, marrying Jimmy Rhynes.

Bessie bore no natural children. However, Bessie led a strong and long Christian life, caring for her community and her relatives. Bessie believed Rebecca (Becky) and Carrie Jane Weaver Sims were her cousins. Bessie referred to Rebecca as Aunt Becky, and once Bessie nursed Cousin Carrie back to health. Being a member of the family-at-large, Bessie religiously attended the Sims Family Reunion.

At age 84 Bessie reached the end of her fate and passed away during the January cold of 1982 in Jefferson, where she had lived her entire life. The family laid Bessie to rest at Coverson Cemetery, Jefferson.

Lee Ann Martin Perry

Traveling in small circles, Solomon's sister, Lee Ann Martin, married Peter Perry. See their findings under the Perry Family section heading.

End note: The lives of the remaining twelve Martin children are open for discovery. However, descendant and family historian, Belzora Cheatham of Chicago, Cook County, Illinois, has researched the Alfred Martin line. Alfred was one of the remaining twelve children from the Thomas "Tom" Martin, Sr. and Sarah Martin family.

THIS IS AN ACCOUNT OF THE MARTIN FAMILY. MAY THEIR STORIES BE REMEMBERED AND SPIRITS HONORED.

That the generation to come might know them, even the children which should be born, who should arise and declare them to their children.

Psalm 78:6 KJV

BRANCH THREE

. . . .

THE NORRIS FAMILY TREE

UPON INTERVIEWING COMMUNITY ELDERS REGARDING THE NORTHEAST Texas Norris line, these senior citizens recalled the history they learned in school from the renowned and beloved Professor John C. Pitts. According to the history lesson, not all Black people who existed in Northeast Texas were slaves. Some were free people of color, having either bought their freedom; some were fugitives, having escaped slavery.

Supposedly, supporters smuggled those fleeing bondage to various waterway points and instructed the group to follow the riverbed until they reached a considerable distance from the towns. These free people of color traveled down the Red River, Caddo, and the Black Cypress riverbeds, *their underground railroad*, avoiding the plantations, populations, civilization, and re-enslavement. Supposedly, the Norris, Smith, and Williams families arrived on riverbed boats at different times.

Someone told these family heads that they could possess and own as much land as they could clear. The Norris, Smith, and Williams progenitors called their settlement area, Valley Plain, situated along the Black Cypress in Marion County. After slavery, they started documenting their land decisions with various agreements, tax payments, and deeds. These families buried their loved ones at a place called Bare Bottom, which was close to the river and near the Adventist Colony (Burna). Approximately, three miles beyond the Burna Point was Bare Bottom in Marion County.

Richard "Dick" Norris

Norris patriarch Richard "Dick" Norris' voter registration corroborated this school history lesson in so far as the migration date. When Richard "Dick" Norris registered to vote during 1867, he stated that he had been in the state of Texas for seven years, arriving circa 1860 and had been in Marion County for the same period. Another revealing fact was that Richard's voter registration record showed that he was a native of South Carolina. Unfortunately, Richard's early census records of 1870 and 1880 failed to substantiate South Carolina as Richard's birthplace. In fact, the early census records of 1870 and 1880 were inconsistent, showing Georgia and Louisiana respectively as Richard's birthplaces. Reasonably, Richard previously traveled through Georgia and Louisiana before arriving in Texas. Judging Richard's age, he was born during slavery. If Richard "Dick" Norris came to Texas, traveling as a free person of color through Georgia and Louisiana, without parents or wife or children, then he was most certainly a brave and determined young man of age 24 or 26.

Richard did have a wife. Her name was Georgia Ann Norris who presumably was born circa 1842, Georgia. They apparently lived in Louisiana a few years before crossing the border into Texas. Their eldest child was born in Louisiana circa 1858. Oddly, Richard and Georgia conceived children every few years except the period between Emancipation and Juneteenth. Perhaps at this time, Georgia Ann was consumed with keeping house and raising their children; reasonably, Georgia Ann was healing or helping Richard provide for their family. Post-Civil War, Richard was engaged in some form of work-for-hire; because, Richard and his wife filed a claim with the Freedmen's Bureau against Andrew J. Lewis for nonpayment of a labor contract.

The newly freed were not the only ones struggling to survive. Interestingly, slaveholder Andrew J. Lewis only reported five slaves to the 1860 enumerators. Only one female was over age twenty; the remaining three females were under age twenty. The one male slave was three months of age. Post-war, Lewis needed to hire laborers to help harvest his cotton crop; Richard and his wife were obviously two of those laborers employed by Andrew J. Lewis. Post-war, Lewis was imaginably one cotton sale away from a similar poverty faced by Richard and wife.

Between 1870 and 1880, life in Marion County changed quite a bit for the Mulatto Richard "Dick" Norris. At the 1870 census, Richard was coupled with wife Georgia Ann, a twenty-eight-year-old Georgia native, and five children:

- Albert
- Edmund
- Margaret Jane
- Sanford
- Patsey

Note: For an unknown reason, the October 1870 census enumerators did not include Richard and Georgia Ann Norris' last child, infant daughter Malinda

Norris Weaver, who was born during January of 1870.

The neighbors who surrounded Richard and Georgia Ann at 1870 were not the same neighbors of 1880. Throughout 1870, Richard and Georgia were enumerated near slaveholder John M. Jones and his wife Mariah E. Wood. More importantly, the census enumerators in 1880 omitted wife Georgia Ann, oldest son Albert, and youngest daughter Malinda. Perhaps wife Georgia Ann and son Albert were already deceased. Safe and secure, little ten-year-old Malinda resided a distance away as a member of the 1880 Emory household. Whereas, Richard was coupled with his second wife Sarah and his four children:

- Edmund
- Margaret Jane
- Sanford
- Patsey

Too much speculation and not enough facts make up the stories regarding what happened to Richard's first wife Georgia Ann, their oldest son Albert, and their baby daughter Malinda.

Allegedly, Albert Norris drifted, leaving Texas and winding up in Arkansas. Purportedly later in life, through an acquaintance in common, Malinda discovered the whereabouts of her older brother Albert who began visiting and supporting her.

Believingly, baby Malinda was abandoned or orphaned and raised by the Emorys. Years later, the Emorys introduced Malinda to her husband-to-be Grandison Weaver.

A truth worth unearthing is why second wife Sarah claimed entitlements as a surviving soldier's wife, as evidenced by the June 1890 census. Was Richard "Dick" Norris part of the U.S. Colored Troops, a military scout, or a spy during the Civil War; therefore entitling Sarah the surviving widow to government charity?

From 1871 forward, Richard "Dick" Norris owned personal property; paid property taxes; and worked the land as a sharecropper or tenant farmer. However, Richard was not able to purchase his initial patch of land until 1887 as evidenced by a recorded land deed. Benjamin F. Orr and Whitmill "Whit" Phillips sold Richard 60 acres of land from the John Brown Survey for $300.00 cash and two promissory notes of $150.00 each, retaining a vendor's lien until Richard paid the note, in full. It is not clear whether Richard ever actually lived on a portion of these 60 acres or whether he used the entire acreage for farming. Subsequent bill of sales, such as the one during 1891, showed Richard lived at Miss L. A. Jones' place while he and friend Wes Pattillo farmed the 60 acres. Wes and Richard cultivated cotton, corn, and potatoes, selling one-fourth to one-half of the cotton crop for $300.00 to G. M. Jones agent during 1891.

Miss L. A. Jones was Laura Ann Jones, and G. M. Jones was Granville Martin Jones. Granville and Laura's father was slaveholder John M. Jones of Guilford County, North Carolina who happened to be Richard's 1870 neighbor. Most of the Jones' children were born in Georgia.

Around 1891 the paper trail of Richard's property tax payments ceased, and he and second wife Sarah sold their 60 acres for $325.00 at 10 percent interest to Harrison Williams; son-in-law Joe Smith; and his son Edmund Norris.

Sarah purchased one-eighth of an 80-acre tract from Benjamin F. Orr and Whitmill "Whit" Phillips during February of 1893, distributed from the Andrew S. Beard Head Right Survey. Later, Sarah sold 10 of these acres to friend Betty Pattillo during July of 1901. These 10 acres were located in an area referred to as Bare Bottom or the bottom.

Evidently, these years were lean years for Sarah; because, her property tax payments were sporadic, paying only during 1896, 1897, and 1900. For example, during 1896, Sarah paid $4.91 in taxes for the 10 acres worth $25.00; one horse worth $25.00; four cattle worth $32.00; two goats/hogs worth $2.00; dogs worth $25.00; and tools valued at $15.00. Unexplainably, Sarah participated in the June 1890 census for the surviving widows. However, the 1890 property tax roll provided payments made in the name of Richard Norris.

Seemingly, around age 50 Richard reached the end of his fate and probably passed away during 1891. Likewise, around age 37 first wife and mother Georgia Ann reached the end of her fate and apparently passed away during December 1879 of pneumonia. Presumably, Georgia Ann, Richard, and second wife Sarah were buried at Bare Bottom.

Albert Norris

Richard's first born son was named Albert Norris, whose family line remains obscure.

Edmund "Ed" or "A. E." Norris

Edmund was Richard's beloved second son. Edmund purchased land from his father Richard and stepmother Sarah, and he worked the land his entire life, providing for his family and building a respectable reputation. When the local newspaper *Jefferson Jimplecute* called the Colored voters to organize a prohibition rally, Edmund and other male community leaders such as Rev. John P. Belcher, Tobe Davis, Rev. Sam Dixon, and S. W. Williams were members of the executive committee. In fondness, family and friends nicknamed Edmund, "Ed" or "A. E.", perhaps in honor of his older brother Albert.

Edmund was born during a hot July circa 1861 and believably born in Marion County. Early census records described Edmund as a Mulatto. No evidence surfaced pertaining to Edmund's formal education.

At age 24 or 26 Edmund married Emma Smith, a local midwife. Rev. Daniel Benjamin performed the nuptials, as he did a few years later for Edmund's sister Patsey when she married Emma's brother Joseph. Interestingly, Harrison Williams, who shared in land transactions with Edmund, also married Sarah Smith. Sarah was a sister to Emma and Joseph. Edmund and Emma conceived eight children—the five who survived to adulthood were named:

- Samuel "Sam"
- Alex "Alec"
- Mary Norris Brown
- Will "Willy"
- Ben "Benny" Louis

Edmund also fathered another son Edward Norris.

Around age 73 Edmund reached the end of his fate and passed away in Jefferson from chronic intestinal nephritis, as diagnosed by Dr. Felix Peebles. The family laid Edmund to rest at Valley Plain Cemetery, Jefferson.

Samuel "Sam" Norris

Edmund's son Samuel "Sam" was born during 1888 or 1889 around Thanksgiving in Marion County. Samuel worked on the railroad and eventually became a farmer. Sam married Maggie Williams in Marion County, and they conceived seven children. Samuel also fathered two other children. Their deceased children include:

- Edmond Norris
- Corine Lois Norris
- Robert Thomas Norris
- Augustus Norris (died as a teenager)
- Ethel L. Norris
- Emma Lee Norris (died as an infant)
- Lois Norris (died as a toddler)

At age 51 or 52 Samuel reached the end of his fate and passed away during the 1940 Christmas season.

Alex "Alec" Norris

Edmund's son Alex "Alec" Norris was born during 1890 or 1891 in Marion County. Fatigued or frustrated from farming as a child, Alex chose to work in the sawmills, eventually hauling logs for approximately fifteen years.

Alex married Lishie Fabb (Fobbs); they conceived three children. Lishie also conceived another child. Lishie practically raised the children alone after Alex left the family, supposedly never to return. Their deceased children included:

- William Lee Norris
- Mae Dean Norris
- Lonny Norris

Caged and disillusioned, Alex fled to work on the railroad, in later years. As the 1933 Christmas season approached, at age 42 or 43 Alex reached the end of his fate and passed away in Marion County from pneumonia, according to Dr. Felix Peebles. The family laid Alex to rest at the Valley Plain Cemetery.

Mary Norris Brown

Edmund's daughter Mary was born during a hot July in Texas circa 1893. As a young person, she too worked on the home farm as a laborer. During the January cold of 1917, Mary married Ranie Brown, facing their pastor, Rev. W. E. Hutcherson. Mary bore no natural children. However, Mary cooked as though she fed all the children in the Marion County community. She helped care for Alex's children, which involved caring, cooking, and waiting for them at the school bus stop. Mary also reminded her niece (Alex's daughter) about her father, showing pictures and telling stories.

Later in life, Mary became blind and lost her hearing. Around age 59 Mary reached the end of her fate and passed away after an unknown illness, as the 1952 Christmas season ended.

Will "Willy" Norris

Edmund's son Will "Willy" Norris was born during August of 1896 in Jefferson. He worked on the home farm before serving his country during WWI. Will was age 21, unmarried, and without children when he signed his draft registration card. Will's card described him as medium build, black eyes, and black hair. After the war Will returned home with his legs, arms, and spirit intact; he resumed life, as he knew it prior to the war, staying with his parents and working as a farmer.

During August of 1923, Will exchanged marriage vows with Wilhelmina Hawkins in Marion County. L. A.

Greenwood pronounced the couple as husband and wife. Soon, Will and Wilhelmina moved from the Kellyville area to Texarkana, Bowie County, Texas to earn better wages and to start their family. They conceived three children. Their deceased children included:

- Thelma Lois Norris
- William Charles Norris, Jr.
- Maceo Leonard Norris

During 1936, Will completed his Social Security number application, writing that he worked for Texarkana Sheet Metal Works on Front Street. Initially, Will and Wilhelmina resided at 2204 West Fifteenth Street. A few years later, during the 1940s, they moved to 1714 West Third Street. By the 1960s, the family had settled at 1524 North Street. Will's strength, practical nature, and deep, inside inertia caused him to work his entire life.

At age 86 Will reached the end of his fate and passed away at the Veterans Administration Hospital in Shreveport of complications from a stroke during September of 1982. The family laid Will to rest at Chapelwood Memorial Garden, Nash, Bowie County, Texas.

Rev. Ben "Benny" Louis Norris

Edmund's son Ben "Benny" Louis Norris was also born in Jefferson circa 1897. He too started out working on the home farm. Around the age of majority, Benny decided to marry, and he choose the 1918 Thanksgiving holiday season as the most opportune time. As autumn harvest and festivities funneled everyone's thoughts, Ben took his betrothed to the Marion County courthouse, where W. E. Hutcherson pronounced, he and Frances Jane Royal, husband and wife.

After their wedding, Ben continued farming and eventually started preaching part time at a Jefferson Methodist Church. Between farming and preaching, Ben operated a taxi service and worked for Louis Lee in Lassater, Marion County, Texas. As Ben's ministerial career advanced, he pastored several Churches of Christ congregations.

Ben and Frances conceived five children, and the family settled in the Kellyville community of Marion County, just off Avinger Highway. Their deceased children included:

- Benny Norris, Jr.
- Freddy Norris
- Mamie Lee Norris
- Clarence Otis Norris

Around age 78 Ben reached the end of his fate and passed away during the January cold of 1975 in Marion County after an illness. The family held Ben's funeral at the Church of Christ in Marshall, Harrison County, Texas, and they laid Ben to rest in his wife's home town of Hughes Springs, Cass County, Texas at Rivers Cemetery.

Edward "Ed" or "Eddy" Norris

Edmund's son Edward Norris was born in Jefferson circa 1886. Being a bit unconventional, assertive, and artistic, Ed chose a different way of life than farming. Early in life, Ed worked in sawmills established along the eastern corridor of Texas and western Louisiana; frequently moving, he followed the ebb and flow of jobs.

In Vernon Parish, Louisiana, Ed made Addie Lee Smith a dazzling June bride when he married her during 1908. They conceived four children. Their deceased children included:

- Theodore Lorenzo Norris
- Hazel Pearl Norris
- Mazel Norris
- Eddy Leon Norris

By 1920, Ed and his family were staying with the Johnsons in Neame, Vernon Parish, Louisiana. During 1926 or 1927, the family moved to Beaumont, Jefferson County, Texas, where they remained, purchasing several homes and joining a church. During the early 1930s, Ed and the family resided on Isla Avenue in Beaumont. By 1936, the family was residing on Andrus Street in Beaumont.

Ed ensured the family's well being during the Depression by working at the local wholesale grocery and earning extra income from the sale of jewelry and ironing boards that he made. During the latter 1930s, Ed worked at Tyrrell Hardware Company. Perhaps tired from heavy manual labor, Ed decided to become a professional barber. Ed began as an apprentice amid the racial violence and rioting in Beaumont during the 1940s; eventually Ed graduated from Tyler Barber College of Houston, Harris County, Texas. Later, Ed came to own a Beaumont barbershop and resided at 1057 Willow in Beaumont. Locally he was well respected, popular, and referred to as a veteran barber.

Around age 79 Ed Norris reached the end of his fate and passed away at the Martin de Porres Hospital after a brief illness. The family held his funeral on 16 January at McGovern Street Christ Sanctified and Holy Church and laid Ed to rest at Greenlawn Cemetery of Beaumont.

Margaret Jane Norris

Research revealed hardly anything regarding Richard's daughter Margaret Jane who was born during 1862 or 1863 in

Texas. Like her siblings, she worked on the farm at a young age. Matching the depiction of her siblings, Margaret Jane was described as a Mulatto at the early census records. Unless Margaret Jane is the mysterious and wealthy Cousin Jane (Janie) Ellison of El Paso, El Paso County, Texas, her life leaves the writer and reader wanting.

Sanford "Sandy" or "S. D." or "Sam D." Norris

Richard's son Sanford was affectionally nicknamed "Sandy," S. D.," and sometimes "Sam D.," for distinction. Sanford was born during either June or July circa 1866 in Texas and described as a Mulatto on early census records. He worked the land and became a farmer.

Around age 30, Sanford married Adaline M. Weaver (a distant relative by marriage) in Jefferson just after Christmas. S. E. Ewing pronounced Sandy and Addie as husband and wife. Their family increased to five children but only three survived:

- Robert William Norris
- Sanford Norris, Rev.
- Annie Myrtle Norris Glover Schuford

Adaline was a midwife in the community, and she passed between 1907 and 1909.

Sanford needed help raising the children. A few years after Adaline's death, Sanford married Luella (Ella) Gallou, facing the esteemed Marion County Justice of the Peace L. B. Todd. The 1910 census data also indicated another daughter named Ida Norris, but none of the surviving Norris descendants interviewed remembered anyone by the name of Ida. Ida possibly died prior to the next census and before memories took shape.

At age 76 Sanford reached the end of his fate and passed away during 1942 from a cerebral hemorrhage, living his entire life in Jefferson. The family laid Sanford to rest at Kellyville Cemetery.

Robert William Norris

Sanford's son Robert William Norris was born during May of 1899 or 1900 in Jefferson. During February of 1920, Robert married Mattie Lee Pitts in Marion County. At the start of their marriage, the couple lived at the home of Robert's parents, and Robert worked on the railroad. Robert and Mattie conceived twelve children with nine to survive. Their deceased children included:

- Queen Ester Norris Brown
- Ruby Lee Norris
- Curtis Norris, Rev.
- Sanford Norris, III
- Gertrude Elizabeth Norris Sowels Canada
- Alvert Norris
- Miller Norris
- Joshua Norris

By 1930, the couple had established their own home. Robert worked the land, driving mule and horse on the farm and selling wood. After cutting the trees and loading the wood in the wagon, he then drove the five miles from Kellyville to Jefferson to sell the wood. Sometimes he would not arrive home until after dark, around ten o'clock, in the evening. If any of Robert's children misbehaved in his absence, their mother told the father upon his return, as chastising was his domain.

During the 1940s and 1950s, the family moved several times. Around the late 1940s, they resided at 1217 East Second in Fort Worth, Tarrant County, Texas. The family lived in Odessa, Ector County, Texas during the 1950s.

Around age 54 Robert reached the end of his fate and passed away from asphyxiation caused by an old, faulty gas heater during the January cold of 1954. The family held Robert's funeral and burial in Fort Worth.

Rev. Sanford Norris

Sanford's son Sanford Norris was born circa 1904 in Jefferson and finished school there. As a young person, throughout the 1920s, Sanford labored on the farm. By the 1930s, he had moved to Fort Worth, residing at 1217 East Second Street and working for Oakhurst Land Company on 1341 Carnation Street. Sanford married Marzella Heath during 1939 or 1940 in a Fort Worth Methodist Church.

At some point, Sanford became a Methodist minister, and the church became his life. As such, Sanford and his family moved and traveled the church circuit. Rev. Sanford Norris served as pastor of churches in Ennis, Ellis County, Texas and in Fort Worth. He also conducted church revivals in the Plainview and Kellyville area Methodist churches during the 1950s. His preaching voice led countless souls to witness, convert, and shout in the old time traditions. On occasion, Rev. Sanford was a guest evangelist of Eastland, Eastland County, Texas for his nephew Rev. Curtis Norris' Baptist Church in Odessa, Ector County, Texas. He helped build Vincent Chapel CME Church and helped remodel Jubilee Chapel CME Church, both in Fort Worth. Rev. Sanford Norris maintained membership at the Carter Metropolitan CME Church of Fort Worth—the church where he and his wife married.

Rev. Sanford Norris and his wife conceived two children. Their deceased children include:

- Maurice Leon Norris
- Helen Marie Norris

The Reverend Sanford Norris of 815 Irma Street, Fort Worth suffered from a heart attack in the pulpit of his church, *Holy Temple CME in Ennis, Texas. Around age 75 Rev. Norris reached the end of his fate and passed away as church members rushed him to the Ennis hospital. The family laid Rev. Norris to rest at Cedar Hill Memorial Park Cemetery, Arlington, Tarrant County, Texas.

Note: *Another source recorded this CME church as Holsey Chapel.

Annie Myrtle Norris Glover Schuford

Sanford's daughter Annie Myrtle was born during July of 1906 and was probably only two years of age when her mother died in Jefferson. Early in life, Annie worked on the farm. Later in life, she became a homemaker, marrying William "Bill" Mack Glover. Annie and Bill conceived one daughter, now deceased. To sustain and maintain herself and her child, Annie worked as a domestic wherever she could. At Annie Myrtle's second marriage, she wedded William "Will" Schuford, in Fort Worth.

Around age 39 Annie Myrtle reached the end of her fate and passed away from poisoning, in Fort Worth. The family laid Annie Myrtle to rest in Jefferson.

Patsey Norris Smith

Richard's daughter Patsey was born just after of the Emancipation of enslaved Texans and during Reconstruction in Marion County. Synonymous with her siblings, Patsey was described as a Mulatto at the early census records. No information surfaced regarding her schooling. While growing up, Patsey worked on the farm, and around age 20, Patsey married Joseph "Joe" Smith in Marion County. Patsey and Joe stayed with Joe's parents in the Valley Plain community throughout 1910, alongside their adopted and only son John Patsey Smith. Patsey and Joe were small in size and short in stature. Symbolizing ordinary farmers, they rode their mule-drawn-wagon into town on Saturdays, as an outing for business and a pleasurable pastime. After Patsey's husband passed during 1947, Patsey supposedly stayed with her son in Dallas where she later passed.

Malinda Norris Weaver

See information regarding Richard and Georgia Ann's youngest daughter and last child Malinda Norris Weaver at the Weaver Family. DNA has corroborated the blood family connection between the Norris, Sims, and Weaver families of Marion County, Texas.

End note: Credentialed genealogist, Dr. Cheryl Gaines of Chicago, Cook County, Illinois has thoroughly researched and documented the Norris Family.

THIS IS AN ACCOUNT OF THE NORRIS FAMILY. MAY THEIR STORIES BE REMEMBERED AND SPIRITS HONORED.

I will make thy name to be remembered in all generations: therefore shall the people praise thee for ever and ever.

Psalm 45:17 KJV

BRANCH FOUR

. . . .

THE PERRY FAMILY TREE

SIMPLY BECAUSE PEOPLE SHARED THE SAME SURNAME, ethnicity, and were existing in the same vicinity does not necessarily prove such persons carried a blood relation. This was the situation with Harrison, Lawrence, and Peter Perry.

Peter and Lawrence lived in Texas from 1859 forward and lived in Marion County, Texas since 1863. Lawrence and Peter were around the same age, and they both bravely registered to vote as newly freed persons of color. Harrison was not shown to join Peter and Lawrence in Marion County until after 1880. Harrison Perry previously endured in Upshur County, Texas.

All three Perry men eventually and simultaneously lived in Marion County; all owned Marion County property; and paid applicable taxes. Yet there is no oral history or documentation to date connecting Harrison, Lawrence, and Peter Perry by blood.

Delving into the Anglo Perrys who settled in the tri-county area of Cass, Harrison, and Marion counties may prove fruitful, as several owned a vast number of slaves who imaginably adopted the Perry surname.

Peter Perry

Who was Peter Perry? Who were his parents and siblings? Where was Peter from, and why did he come to Texas? Was Peter born in Georgia as his peer Lawrence, or was he born in Alabama like Harrison? The questions are perpetual.

The earliest evidence that provided a glimpse of Peter's beginnings was his voter registration record. According to Peter's voter registration, he was born in Georgia. Contrastingly, the 1870 census indicated Alabama as Peter's birthplace. Substantiating the registration, the 1880 census showed Georgia as Peter's birth state.

Judging Peter's age, he was born a slave. Was Peter in Caddo Parish, Louisiana prior to 1859? Where in Texas was Peter between 1859 and 1863? Was Peter existing and working in Upshur County like Harrison before moving to Marion County? Was Peter's move to Marion County haphazard or purposeful and calculated? How are Peter's origins of impact to future generations? Peter's beginnings are important; because, Peter is the earliest documented connection to the Sims' patriarch Berry Sims.

At the 1870 Marion County census, Berry and his brother Milus were enumerated with Peter in the Perry household; Berry and Milus theoretically had been staying with Peter the entire five years period, between Emancipation and the 1870 census.

Also residing in the Peter Perry household was a woman named Will (Willie) Ann, presumably Berry's mother. Peter is presumably Berry and Milus' uncle or surrogate father. Peter and Will Ann were still living together ten years later during 1880. Interestingly, Will Ann is labeled as a Mulatto at both the 1870 and 1880 census. Supposedly, she too was born in Georgia circa 1840.

Analogous to the other newly freed upon Emancipation, Peter worked as a sharecropper, tenant farmer, hired hand, or on the railroad. Apparently, Peter saved his income; because, he soon started buying property. Throughout 1870, Peter had one horse to his name, worth $30.00. He acquired four cattle and a mule during 1872, valued at $60.00. By 1874, he had purchased a few more cattle and mules. He added dogs, goats, tools, and farm equipment.

By 1875, both Milus and Berry had married and on their own. Peter began paying property taxes during 1876, managing 75 acres valued at $150.00, a sliver of the Charles Grayson Survey (abstract 164). During 1877, Peter picked up a wagon and another 100 acres worth $200.00, as part of the Antonio de los Santos Coy Survey. The next year, Peter added another 100 acres worth $200.00 from the S. P. Cadenhead Survey.

While Peter continued farming throughout 1880, Will Ann perhaps continued housekeeping and mothering adults Berry and Milus nearby. Peter's property value continually increased. From the farming proceeds, Peter was able to pay his property taxes. At some point after the 1880 census, Will (Willie) Ann Perry probably died.

By 1881 or 1882, Peter had fathered a son Oscar with his new wife Lee Ann Martin. Peter and Lee Ann conceived three other children:

- Briggs
- Minnie
- Susie

Of these four children, Oscar was the only one to reach adulthood.

After Lee Ann passed around 1890, Peter married a third time. Community members gossiped about Peter's choice for a wife; the sentiment spread that Winnie Kines would mistreat the children. Winnie was from Tennessee and comparative in age to Peter, and Winnie was the former Mrs. Albert Kines.

Were it not for Albert Kines' kindness, Peter would not have been able to purchase his initial real property. Obviously, Peter did not listen to the talk; he married Winnie anyway. By 1910, Peter and Winnie were senior citizens, living just a few doors down the road from Oscar.

On 22 October 1913 both Peter and Winnie reached the end of their respective fate and passed away. The family laid them to rest in Jefferson at Lewis Chapel Cemetery.

Oscar Perry, Sr.

A few years passed and Oscar was old enough to marry. At the start of the New Year (1903), Oscar married Addie Houston, facing Elias Harper their minister. Like his father, Oscar became a father and a Marion County farmer.

On 27 April 1920, Oscar made an Affidavit of Heirship, stating he was the sole heir to all of Peter Perry's property, more than 200 acres of land in Marion County. At the uncontested affidavit, the boundary lines definitely fell in a pleasant place for Oscar.

Oscar was near adulthood when Berry purchased the contiguous land, belonging to the identical survey and abstract as Peter's land. Were neighbors and nephews Berry and Milus, not *heirs-in kind?* Oscar behaved as though he and Berry were relatives even if the affidavit implied otherwise. A few months prior to the affidavit, Oscar stood attesting to the birth of Berry's granddaughter. Such an act is typical of a trustful relative or faithful family friend. Standing attesting to the birth of a child is similar to the present-day tradition of standing in the delivery room at the birth of a baby, taking pictures or coaching. Oscar attended church with the Sims; he played baseball with the Sims. Years later, Oscar's daughter Evaline even stayed with Cousin Isaac Weaver in Fort Worth, for a stint, as a few of Berry Sims' descendants had.

One of Oscar's sons interviewed for this family history book spoke of a bloodline between the Sims and the Perrys; he remembered hearing while growing up that the Sims and Perrys were related. Decades later, the Sims descendant who married the Perry descendant even knew of the blood relation; moreover, the couple was warned, chided and teased not to marry each other because of the bloodline—because they were cousins.

Peter knew of the bloodline between the Sims and the Perrys. Peter knew and was concerned enough to complain to the Freedman's Bureau administrators during Reconstruction in 1867 that a Mr. Zackery had taken his nephew from him and placed his nephew into apprenticeship.

Oscar and Addie conceived at least twelve children, including two sets of twins. The names of their deceased issue included:

- Bessie Lee Perry Waites Darty
- Jennie A. Perry Brown Armstrong
- Viola Perry
- C. A. (Charles A.) "Buddie" Perry
- Almaline Perry King Dearborne Lewis (female twin)
- Evaline Perry Taylor (female twin)
- Sallie Perry Bell
- Herschel (Hurshel) Perry (male twin)

- a male twin to Herschel (died very young)
- Addie Day Perry Williams*
- Claude Albert Perry
- Oscar Perry, Jr.
- Nathaniel Perry

*Addie Perry Jackson at 1951 death.

Mother Addie passed during 1946. Around age 88 Father Oscar reached the end of his fate and passed away during 1969.

End note: Another family historian has begun researching the Oscar Perry family tree. Their story is for another historian to record. It is interesting enough to note that the Perry family continued to intertwine with the other six families who are the subjects of this family history book. For example, Almaline Perry's third husband was Dr. Fred Lewis, a descendant of Helon Lewis, Sr.; Helon was Felix Lewis' brother. Charles A. Perry's first wife was Ollie Mae Bennett Perry Sims; Ollie Mae later became the wife of Rev. Ernest Sims.

THIS IS AN ACCOUNT OF THE PERRY FAMILY.
MAY THEIR STORIES BE REMEMBERED AND
SPIRITS HONORED.

Thy seed will I establish for ever, and build up thy throne to all generations.

Psalm 89:4 KJV

BRANCH FIVE

. . . .

THE SIMS FAMILY TREE

Berry Sims

THE ONE GREAT-GRANDSON WHO BERRY SIMS raised said his great-grandfather was from Madagascar. Madagascar, an island situated off the southeast coast of Africa, was once a French territory with slave activity. The long-standing Sims matriarch and centenarian Ima Viola Sims Jefferson told the story of Berry Sims arriving in the new world on a slave ship, where one of the Anglos on board liked Berry as a little boy and pretended to throw Berry overboard.

If Berry found favor with the slave ship's captain and crew, we will never know with certainty. If he was a little boy among the hundreds shackled and crouched in the ship's belly for the five to eight weeks journey to the new world, the grace of God saved Berry, not necessarily man's favor. If Berry Sims made such a perilous, brutal, and diseased journey as millions of others, God certainly had a purpose and plan for his life. Countless captives died along the way to a new world, and their bodies were presumably thrown overboard into the ocean.

153

All but one of the applicable census records listed Berry Sims as a Georgia native. Great-granddaughter Ima Viola Sims Jefferson also told the story of Berry Sims coming to Northeast Texas alongside his mother from Mooringsport, Caddo Parish, Louisiana.

Another great-grandson described Berry Sims' ancestry and appearance as a Black Frenchman with rich, creamy, smooth, chocolate-colored skin that rarely needed shaving. Berry had wavy, smooth, soft, salt and pepper hair. Though Berry's height was short, he stood with a dignified stature. Elder Hattie Wallace Brown described the similarity between Berry Sims and his allegedly half brother Phil Ross, Sr. as both being of a short height and shady hue.

Judging the age of Berry Sims, he was a child slave. Research was inconclusive as to whether Berry was a child slave in Georgia, Louisiana, or Texas. Several elder Sims descendants recalled one story of Berry Sims as a child during slavery. "The boss man told Berry to churn. He asked him, 'is the churn good enough.' The boss man told him, 'no churn some more.' Berry asked him again, and the boss man said, 'churn some more.' Berry Sims kept churning until all the butter had churned away."

After Emancipation, some of the newly freed fled bondage in search of lost loved ones. Understandably groupings banded together as families out of necessity in order to survive—others banded together as they were blood relations. Possibly owing to the enumerator's error Peter Perry, Will (Willie) Ann, Berry, and Milus were grouped as a family at the 1870 census, perhaps living together at least five more years until Berry and Milus' respective marriages in 1875. Will (Willie) Ann may have been Berry and Milus' biological or surrogate mother, and Peter behaved as their uncle or surrogate father. As adults, Berry and Milus dropped the surname Perry and adopted Sims as their last name.

Berry Sims married Rebecca (Becky) Walton just after Christmas during 1875. Their names were their credentials. Their residence was a grand wooden house, at least adequate in size and features to accommodate boarding for themselves; their families; and boarders such as local teachers (Professor Beal and his wife and later, Ms. Kelly).

Berry knew how to read and write. He often read the newspaper on the front porch, and on rainy days, he read by the fireplace. Berry's surviving Methodist Church Discipline provided his handwriting sample and proof of his church affiliation. Berry's surviving ritual and degree book placed him as a member of an early fraternal organization, the United Brothers of Friendship.

Berry was a skilled artisan—blacksmith, cook, and farmer. His two eldest great-grandchildren followed him around all-day while he worked. According to his great-grandchild, Ima Viola Sims Jefferson, "Honey he could plow two mules to cultivate. He would 'ha and gee', twist with lines around his waist, and get the horses on the right path. He could plow and comb a row up so pretty of cotton or whatever crop." Berry was even nimble at tooth extractions. His blacksmith shop was located across the road from his home where he made shoes for horses/mules; repaired wagons/buggies; and fashioned farm tools.

The year of Berry's marriage, he owned a horse or mule; three cattle; and three hogs or goats, paying taxes on the same. Throughout 1878, Berry owned a carriage or buggy, mules, horses, cattle, nine hogs, and the necessary implements to farm the land. He cultivated 36 acres to make a corn and cotton crop while sharecropping at the Ford Plantation, throughout 1881.

Saving enough money, Berry paid taxes on his initial patch of land (25 acres) around 1886. After arranging financing during 1888, Berry bought 106 acres from Ambrose Fitzgerald at an exorbitant 10 percent annual interest rate. That was the year Berry had difficulty paying his property tax and Berry's brother paid on his behalf, not his 'uncle' Peter. These 106 acres were from the Stephen Peters Survey, and the lien was released on 09 August 1907. Berry later sold this identical parcel back to the Fitzgerald family.

During November of 1892, Berry purchased the contiguous land, belonging to the identical survey (Charles Grayson) and abstract (164) as Peter's land. Lumbermen William Martin Dunn, Martin Homer Wurtsbaugh, and Edwin Jacob Rand sold Berry Sims the 98 ½ acres of land, Amazingly for almost a century, the Sims Family remained the sole owner of this tract of land—a statistic that kept the family in the one-time 10 percent estimate of Black Americans who still owned their ancestral land.

The next February, Berry Sims sold his mare mule or sorrel called Kit and his dark bay horse called Billy to Max Simmons for $200.00. Land deals continued cropping up, for example during 1907 and 1913. During January of 1907, Tom Belcher offered Berry a warranty deed on two tracts of land: 39 ½ acres and 50 acres. During August of 1913, Berry retained the 39 ½ acre tract and sold the 50 acres to J. H. Matthews. Young strapping men, Berry's son Charley; his grandson Joseph; his great-grandson Johnny joined him in farming the land as a means to survive and provide.

Torpidly, Berry was working in his blacksmith shop when he became sick, confining him for two years with anguish. His youngest daughter told her father's remarks from his deathbed, "I don't mind dying if death was all."

Berry Sims received rest and peace during the autumn of 1927 when at age 74 or 75 he reached the end of his fate and passed away. The family laid Berry to rest at Lewis Chapel Cemetery.

Rebecca (Becky) Walton Sims

How heart wrenching it must have been for Becky to lose her husband and eldest daughter within one month of each other. Gratefully, Becky was not alone. Nearby Becky had her son Charley, a newborn granddaughter Ester, and great-grandson Johnny. Assuredly, Becky found comfort in her memories, the Sims Family Reunions, and acres of land, which allowed her to survive and to support the family. With several descendants living on the property and working the land, one could characterize the Sims property as the Sims Estate.

In the community, Berry and Becky were highly regarded and lived high. Becky almost always wore an apron with a pocket full of money around her waist, though she rarely worked outside the home. Occasionally, Becky kept newborn babies for Anglo families during the first few weeks of life. Primarily, Becky raised her children and grandchildren as well as managed her house and farm. Farm life was hard work, yet she remained generous and content throughout her life.

Becky was a short woman, approximately 160-175 pounds—not too stout—not too plump; perhaps she managed to be uniquely small but heavy simultaneously. People in the community often referred to Rebecca as Aunt Becky. Becky had smooth, brown skin and pretty, soft, wavy black hair that she let her granddaughter Ester comb and plait into numerous individual braids. As Becky aged, her hair turned silver grey.

She wore ankle-high, button and lace up shoes that resembled short boots.

Becky had an angelic way of calling for her great-grandson Johnny, sweetening her melody when she wanted him to appear. Though Becky spoiled Johnny, he pounced upon opportunities to play pranks such as when Becky had arranged to ride into town with the neighbor Mr. Ford. As the Fords approached the house, Johnny yelled, "She's not going." Mr. Ford replied, "That's exactly what I said." The Fords traveled to town without Becky, that day.

Farming, cooking, and canning were necessary tasks, but fishing and quilting were Becky's pleasurable pastimes. Large, beautiful patchwork quilts covered Becky's fluffy feather mattress atop her large brass or iron bed. Becky dipped snuff too and could fall asleep in seconds—ofttimes exhaustion overcame her while sitting in her favorite chair on the front porch. If Johnny found Becky asleep on the porch, he would tie her to the chair using twine and enjoy watching Becky struggle to free herself. Becky was strong in all respects—physically, mentally, and spiritually. Leisurely, Becky sat on the porch with a toothpick, twig, snuff, or food in her mouth. Depending on a silver moon and Becky's mood, she ate her catch of fish in the dark, from the front porch.

For the times, Berry and Becky's home was big and beautiful. Becky and Carrie's homes were in hollering distance from each other, and the responsibility of running errands between the two houses always fell to the youngest granddaughter Ester. Running this short distance between the two houses, often led to the reward of spending the night with Becky.

If anyone arrived, one would only have to look through the window pane of the single front door to ascertain whether somebody was home. The long, broad center hall in Becky's home allowed sight from front to back and divided the house in halve. To the left was a living room, guest bedroom, dining room, and Johnny's room. To the right was a huge first bedroom, the long kitchen, and the back porch off from the kitchen. The back porch was for shelling peas or making ice cream. In their one-story home, country living extended to the back and front porch, bringing the inside, outside.

The Sims Family Reunion in the old days took place at Berry and Becky's home. There, a low front porch stretched across the width of the house. A large walnut tree stood behind the house, and sycamore trees were scattered around. With one small step into their dirt-filled front yard or even at the scent of her spring flowers or the smell of a roaring fireplace, their home captured country living at its core, welcoming family and friends.

The Sims Family Reunion began in the 1920s and were held annually for over a century. During those early years, everyone came—family and friends. All were welcomed on the third Sunday in August. Everyone started baking days ahead but did not crank up the old-fashioned ice cream freezer until Sunday morning. Some of Nancy's children and grandchildren traveled from Shreveport. Hattie and her family who lived in Linden also joined the festive reunion. The Martins and Weavers came too. Family from Fort Worth, Houston, and California came—sometimes even some of the Norris relatives attended.

Later in life, Becky became ill. Her condition persisted from at least March to July and gradually worsened until her last breath. At this cultural phase in the community, families alternated visits to the dying person. By taking turns, the families maintained a steady presence, praying, fanning, or damp wiping as comforts to the dying person. When the Calhoun family members participated in the fanning of Becky, Mrs. Calhoun sent her daughter. The young Calhoun girl recalled being afraid and hearing Becky's repeating chant:

"Take me Lord, take me." Becky's granddaughter Ester watched Becky take her last breath, looking with dismay and disbelief through the footboard of Becky's the iron or brass bed in the front room with the fireplace. Carrie and other women from the community prepared Becky's body in anticipation of the undertakers by washing her body using a shallow wash pan filled with water; afterward, they dressed Becky for burial. A physician last examined Becky alive on the eleventh.

Born during the cold December circa 1856 to parents Squire and Sarah (Sallie) Walton, Rebecca (Becky) Walton Sims passed during the agonizingly hot July of 1940 from congestive heart failure and generalized arteriosclerosis. Beyond three score and ten, Becky reached the end of her fate and passed away. The family laid Becky to rest next to Berry at Lewis Chapel Cemetery.

Berry and Rebecca (Becky) conceived four children but only three children survived to adulthood. Their second daughter Jane died soon after birth during 1880. Berry and Rebecca named their four children:

- Nancy
- Jane
- Charley
- Hattie

Nancy Sims Sharp Bryant

Berry and Becky's first daughter Nancy was born in Jefferson during 1878 or 1879. Setting the commotion, Nancy was raised on the Sims' farm. Certainly, playing with her cousins, chores, some schooling, and church covered the best of Nancy's early days.

Too soon, Berry and Becky's first born became a mother, herself. At age 16, Nancy and James "Jim" Crawford gave life to Mattie, and at age 18, Nancy and Henry Jackson conceived Joseph "Joe." Berry and Becky did what they could, practically raising the grandchildren (Mattie and Joe) themselves. The next sets of grandchildren were born from a relationship sealed with a marriage certificate. Nancy married John Henry Sharp during March of 1900 in Jefferson. After they tied the knot, three children were born during a span of three to four years: Ada Sharp Calhoun, Ruby Lee Sharp Thompson, and Charley "Jim Bo" Henry Sharp. Between 1911 and 1912, Nancy was embroiled in a bitter legal battle over the Sharp land. Nancy waited thirteen years to marry again and conceived three more children. This time, Nancy married Rev. James "Jim" Bryant, and they conceived three children: S. B. Bryant (a boy), Rebecca Bryant, and Mary Lou Bryant.

Around 1913, Nancy, her children, and second husband moved to Shreveport, Caddo Parish, Louisiana to make a new start, a new life, with reasons similar to present-day motivation for relocating. In a turnabout, Nancy's migration mimicked her eldest daughter's movement. Once Nancy and her family relocated to Shreveport, they moved several places before settling into their home house. Nancy's children were raised in their permanent residence on Dalzell Street—a two-bedroom, new construction house, costing around $1,000.00.

Early in Nancy's second marriage, she occasionally worked as a domestic, but primarily, Nancy was a homemaker. Nancy cooked and sewed for her children and ensured the children attended a local Methodist Church.

Nancy was a diabetic, heavyhearted, and heavyset. During 1927, Nancy became sick and coincidentally died just one month after her father. Near age 50 Nancy reached the end of her fate and passed away. The family laid Nancy to rest at Lewis Chapel Cemetery.

Who can say for sure what happened to Nancy's children after her death in Shreveport. By 1930, the youngest offspring had settled in Louisiana with an older sibling; some siblings were enumerated in Caddo Parish, Louisiana under the assumed surname of Brown. Nancy named her children:

- Mattie Sims (Crawford) Jordan Heard Taylor
- Joseph "Joe" Sims, Rev.
- Ada Sharp Calhoun
- Ruby Lee Sharp Thompson
- Charley "Jim Bo" Henry Sharp
- S. B. Bryant (a boy)
- Rebecca Bryant Ball Lawson Eaton
- Mary Lou Bryant White

NANCY SIMS SHARP BRYANT FAMILY

Mattie Sims (Crawford) Jordan Heard Taylor

Like mother, like daughter—much of Mattie's life paralleled Nancy's life. Mattie was born during 1895 in Jefferson. As a child, Mattie attended the early Lewis Chapel MC and the school on the same grounds. In fact, Mattie's aunt Hattie helped Mattie learn her first poem that she recited for school: "I am the pet—not six yet. My name is Mattie, and don't you forget it."

By age 17, Mattie had met a man named Ennis Love; they conceived a child during 1912. Only one month of age, Mattie entrusted her first and only son Johnny Wesley to the care of her grandparents Berry and Becky (the same grandparents who raised Mattie).

Later, Mattie married Andrew Jordan in Lodi, Marion County, Texas and moved from Jefferson to Rustler, Louisiana. Next, Mattie moved to De Ridder, Beauregard Parish, Louisiana, living there for a stint. Mattie and Andrew returned to Jefferson and resided next door to her uncle Charley Sims and her grandfather Berry throughout 1920.

Mattie divorced Andrew and moved to Shreveport, Caddo Parish, Louisiana, where she married a second and third time. Next, Mattie married James "Jim" Heard during 1926 in Shreveport. Concerned for perseverance, Mattie divorced Jim.

Mattie was an attractive woman of medium height, slender build, narrow face, and brown skin. Though occasionally a bit impatient, Mattie was predominantly practical.

Her third marriage lasted until death. After consideration, Mattie married Rev. Theodore "Ted" R. Taylor during the Depression era and decided to settle in Shreveport.

In Shreveport, Mattie joined the Johnson Chapel UMC during June of 1937. Besides being tenacious about her third marriage and her Christian works, Mattie persistently paid her portion of the real property taxes on the Berry Sims Estate, and she received any applicable proceeds. Though Mattie made her home in Shreveport, she and her husband number three had no qualms about returning to Jefferson for the annual family reunion.

Around age 78 Mattie reached the end of her fate and passed away at the Fairfield Hospital in Shreveport. The family laid Mattie to rest at Lewis Chapel Cemetery.

Johnny Wesley (Love) Sims

Mattie's son Johnny Wesley (Love) Sims began farming with his great-grandfather Berry as early as age nine. Johnny attended the Lewis Chapel School and the Lewis Chapel MC, where he sang in the choir. When Berry died, Johnny was around age 15; from that point, Johnny helped Becky manage the farm. Later in life as a young man, Johnny also drove a truck for a sawmill, hauling logs and lumber. While Johnny stayed with Becky, she continually equipped Johnny with vehicles, to aid in farming and general transportation.

Johnny fathered children with four women, three of whom he married. According to Johnny, "I've been married three times; it took me the third time to get it right." Johnny was around age 23 or 24 when Rev. Amos Mayes performed the nuptials for he and Annie Mae Ruffin in Lodi. This second marriage lasted five or six years. Johnny also fathered several children with Lee Willow Zackery Williams. Between relationships, Johnny moved to California and worked in a shipyard. Upon returning to Shreveport during 1946, Johnny married Lula Harris, and their marriage lasted forty-seven years. According to Johnny, his children loved Lula—she raised them. Habitually, the children telephoned and spoke to Johnny for ten or fifteen minutes and spoke to Lula for thirty minutes. Johnny and Lula made their home in Shreveport on Alcorn Street. Through the years, Johnny occasionally traveled to Jefferson for the annual Sims Family Reunion.

In Shreveport, Johnny united with his mother's church, Johnson Chapel UMC, where he was a member of the choir until his health failed him. Being baptized was important to Johnny as was studying the Bible. He characterized himself as a Bible scholar, reading it through many times. As an adult, Johnny was baptized by immersion at a Baptist church in Bossier Parish, Louisiana. According to Johnny, "The Methodist just sprinkled you; you can not get to heaven by being sprinkled."

Regarding employment in Shreveport, Johnny maintained lawns for a number of years and worked with Kroger for thirty-six years. As a senior citizen, Johnny leisurely filled his day with joy rides to the store and as a lawn care overseer of only one yard with a bit of help. "I would sit up in the truck until he got done; he was real handy; he was a lawyer!"

At age 84, Johnny took pride in never being sick. During one of Johnny's last physical examinations, his health was good, x-rays were clear, and his heartbeat was steady. Johnny boasted of being five feet eleven inches (prior years he measured six feet) and 224 pounds with one bad, artificial knee. Complaining about the procedural side effects and painful physical therapy, Johnny waited a few years later to have the second knee replacement surgery. He was also a diabetic.

Johnny was born and died during the cold of January, but endured long enough to see his great, great grandchildren. At age 91 Johnny reached the end of his fate and passed away. The family laid Johnny to rest at Lincoln Park Cemetery, Shreveport.

Rev. Joseph "Joe" Sims

Nancy's first son the Rev. Joseph "Joe" Sims was born during 1897 in Lodi. At age 12, he confessed a sincere hope in Christ and joined the Lewis Chapel MC in 1909. Joe married Willie B. Crawford, making her a dazzling June bride in 1920. Joe and Willie B. began their life as husband and wife at the Berry Sims Estate, where they farmed a portion of the land and started a family. While Joe was young and spry, he fathered seven children; all of whom are now deceased, including his son Lorenzo born of Ruby Belcher in 1929 and died in 1930. Also during the early 1930s, Joe and Willie B. recommitted themselves to living in Lodi and raising their children in the church (Lewis Chapel).

As a maturing man, Joseph was apparently artistic and sensitive to the spirit. At Lewis Chapel, he gained his reputation as the *singingest* and *preachingest* person with much about to sob, sigh, and sing. Joseph sang in the church choir with "Doc" Hodge and sang in a gospel quartet with Warren "Muck" Taylor and Johnny Williams. Later, Warren "Muck" Taylor joined the national gospel group named the Pilgrim Travelers, and Joseph became a pastor.

Lewis Chapel, embodying other Black churches, produced a few homegrown pastors. Rev. Joseph Sims was one of those who grew out of the Lewis Chapel experience. He joined the ministry and began preaching during the Depression era. No one could recall whether the topic of Rev. Joseph Sims' opening trial sermon at Lewis Chapel was about sin, death, eternal life, or love. He first became pastor of a church in Sulphur Springs, Hopkins County, Texas and secondly a church in Ore City, Upshur County Texas. Although, preaching took Joseph and his family all over Northeast Texas, his 1937 completed Social Security number application indicated that he was unemployed, at the time. However during 1937, Rev. Joseph Sims was appreciably performing nuptials. Throughout the late 1940s, Joseph was a pastor in Daingerfield, Morris County, Texas. Joseph continued in the ministry until retiring during 1967.

Joe's personality was very outgoing, and he was always debonair. If it were winter, Joe completed his style with a coordinating hat, scarf, gloves, and coat. Any season, Joe was a very dignified dresser.

Other than having a polished and sophisticated appearance, Joe wanted his children to be of good character and succeed in life. Joe wanted everyone to graduate from college, and he wanted at least one to become a musician. Joe's wishes came true in his youngest daughter who attended college and developed into a musician. Joe known for his frankness was very strict and honest with his children:

- Valerie Sims Richardson
- Nathaniel L. Sims
- Willy Taylor Sims, Sr.
- Nancy Mae Sims Black
- Mattie D. Sims Armstrong
- Eva E. Sims

When Joe married Nellie Martin Brown, he was around age 70. Under a year into the marriage, as the 1968 Christmas season advanced, the Rev. Joseph "Joe" Sims reached the end of his fate and passed away from heart failure and hypertension at the Stevens Park Hospital in Dallas. The family held his funeral at Lewis Chapel MC and laid Rev. Sims to rest at Lewis Chapel Cemetery.

Ada Sharp Calhoun

Nancy's third child Ada was born during 1900 in Lodi. When Ada married Oscar Calhoun at age 18, she too became a housewife. As the title implies, Ada cooked, cleaned, and cared for her children. Ada and Oscar lived in Louisiana at their Shreveport residence for twenty-one years and conceived nine children (five boys and four girls). Ada and the children attended a local Methodist Church, and the family described Ada as very pretty and petite with a sweet personality, brown skin, and a head full of hair. Throughout the early 1930s, Ada feasibly took in laundry for extra family income.

Around age 40 Ada reached the end of her fate and passed away from a puerperal hemorrhage while giving birth to twin girls in a Caddo Parish hospital, who soon passed away. The family held Ada's funeral in Shreveport and laid her to rest at Lewis Chapel Cemetery.

Ada's children who survived to adulthood included:

- Genevieve "Jennie V." Calhoun Beard
- Charley Berry Calhoun
- Oscar Calhoun, Jr.
- Melvin Calhoun
- Allan Calhoun
- Raymond Calhoun

During October of 1986, Ada's offspring and Nancy's daughter Rebecca sold their undivided interest in the Berry Sims properties to Brooks Farms of Atlanta, Cass County, Texas. As a result, the Brooks Farms, a family partnership fell heir to the land for which Berry Sims and others had toiled—land for which they shed blood, sweat, and tears. Until this point, notwithstanding land leases, Berry's property had remained solely in family hands for over ninety years.

Ruby Lee Sharp Thompson

Nancy's fourth child Ruby Lee was born circa 1901 in Lodi. As Ruby matured, she also worked as a cook and in other domestic capacities as a means to survive.

During 1929, Ruby married her knight W. B. Thompson in Caddo Parish. Together, they resided on East Dalzell, as baron and baroness, calling each other darling. Though a loving and affectionate couple, Ruby and W. B. did not have any children together, as W. B. was significantly older than Ruby. W. B. treated Ruby as nobility, shepherding her sidesaddle atop their mule, in the early days. For gallivanting in later years, Ruby and her husband drove a Model T Ford relic.

Family described Ruby as pretty, dark-skinned, forgiving, friendly, and very helpful. Around age 50 Ruby reached the end of her fate and passed away in Shreveport at the family's main residence on Dalzell during 1951. Ruby's funeral was held in Shreveport.

Charley "Jim Bo" Henry Sharp

Nancy's fifth child Charley "Jim Bo" Henry Sharp was born circa 1902 in Lodi. For a brief stint as a little boy, "Jim Bo" stayed with Berry, Becky, and Johnny Sims. "Jim Bo" was fun-loving, short in height, and noticeably dark-skinned. Throughout the early 1920s, "Jim Bo" lived in Shreveport, Caddo Parish, where he married Lillie B. Freeman. After divorce or death of his first wife, "Jim Bo" supposedly married someone named Lou Ella. "Jim Bo" conceivably fathered one son who also died. Eventually, "Jim Bo" met and married Annie Salter Hanson in Grand Cane, De Soto Parish, Louisiana.

"Jim Bo" and Annie came to live in Jefferson, where "Jim Bo" was ambitious and a stable provider. He independently owned and operated a gristmill (grinding corn for others). Additionally, he ran a taxicab service, driving people to their appointments around town. Being a shade tree mechanic, he managed to own a truck and a car.

Unlicensed and unregulated, "Jim Bo's" Social Security number application indicated he was unemployed during 1944. However, "Jim Bo" made sufficient money working on cars. For leisure, "Jim Bo" loved to fish and watch the picture shows during his leisure time. In Jefferson, there was the Strands Theater and another movie theater. "Jim Bo" fished on Caddo Lake or any river branch, which did not require a license, unlike the Stafford or Black Cypress.

"Jim Bo" and Annie moved to Los Angeles, Los Angeles County, California after 1946, contending for a better life as suggested by his siblings and cousins. For a stint, "Jim Bo" continued with his avocation and vocation, repairing cars. During 1968, "Jim Bo" returned to Jefferson for maybe the last time, attending the 1968 Sims Family Reunion. He registered his address as 1473 East 58th Los Angeles, California. Unfortunately, much of "Jim Bo's" twenty-five year California stay was unpleasant.

As the 1971 Ides of March approached, "Jim Bo" reached the end of his fate and passed away at age 69 or 70, in Los Angeles at the Temple Villa Convalescent Hospital. The cause of death reportedly pertained to his cerebrum or brain. His body was cremated.

S. B. Bryant

Nancy's sixth child was her second son S. B. Bryant who was born during 1907 or 1908 in Jefferson. S. B. supposedly married three times while he lived in Shreveport. When S. B. was age 15 or 16, he may have married someone by the name of Hattie Mae. During 1923, S. B. married Ethel Proctor. Perhaps, his third wife was Clara Bevins. However, S. B. was widowed at his death and had not father any children.

While in Shreveport, S. B. resided at the family home. Though S. B. was unemployed for a period during 1942, he picked up odd jobs wherever he found work. S. B. believed in making his own way, and around 1944 without vacillating, S. B. moved to California for a better life. In California, S. B. stayed with his sister Rebecca until he found his own place. In San Diego, S. B. worked for the city during the day and at the navy base by night. His last known occupation was a janitor for the Lafayette Hotel.

On occasion, S. B. visited Lodi and Shreveport, such as the instance he drove back to Louisiana from California for his sister Ruby's funeral during the early 1950s. By his 1976 death, S. B. had struggled in San Diego County, California for thirty-two years.

S. B. had smoked cigarettes and been on oxygen at the University Hospital, UCSD Medical Center. S. B.'s death certificate described his cause of death as respiratory failure; chronic obstructive; pulmonary disease; and organic brain syndrome. Coincidentally, S. B. was born and died during April, and like his brother, S. B.'s body was cremated.

Rebecca Bryant Ball Lawson Eaton

Rebecca was one ballsy lady. During the WWII period, Rebecca moved mid-West and again due west in pursuit of Rosie the Riveter type jobs. This phase found Rebecca working at the North Island Naval Air Station. Loved ones remembered this same courage and commitment on display, as Rebecca witnessed for her Jehovah to all who would listen on downtown San Diego streets and in her home.

Rebecca's flare for fashion was evident in her stylish appearance, attire, and in her home décor. Into her 90s, she still arranged for manicures—she was always dressed and ready to serve others unto her God with courage and determination.

Born during March of 1909 at home, Mother Nancy named her seventh child Rebecca after her mother Becky. And Rebecca named her one daughter Eddie Mae. All of her life Rebecca oozed that same sturdy strength as her grandmother Becky. At age 97 Rebecca reached the end of her fate and passed away.

Mary Lou Bryant White

Nancy's eighth child Mary Lou was born during 1911 in Lodi. Mary like her other siblings attended school in Shreveport. During 1954, Mary became a dazzling June bride, marrying Leslie White in Shreveport.

Around 1961 or 1962, Mary and her family moved to San Diego. Mary loved to read, sew, and quilt. At the time of her marriage to Leslie, Mary possibly and temporarily worked outside of the home as a cook; but mostly, Mary was a housewife who took care of her home and family. Although she grew up in the Methodist Church, later in life, Mary joined the Jehovah's Witnesses.

Unfortunately, Mary was sickly—a long-term epileptic with seizures. At her death, she experienced acute cardio respiratory failure at Paradise Valley Hospital, National City, San Diego County, California. At age 73 Mary reached the end of her fate and passed away during 1974. The family laid Mary to rest at Greenwood Memorial Park.

Mary gave birth to seven children, five girls and two boys—her deceased children included:

- Mary Lou Wilson Kado
- Frank Faulkner, Jr., Rev.
- Louella Beasley Ray
- Alma Marie Sharp Merriweather
- Charles Edward Tibbs

***

Charley Edward Sims, Sr.

Berry and Becky named their only son Charley Edward Sims, Sr. He was born between 1881 and 1882 in Lodi. Some census records described Charley as being able to read and write; other records did not. He was recorded as at least receiving a third grade education at Lewis Chapel School. Every document checked and every person interviewed agreed that Charley was a farmer his entire life, and he had enough education to adequately manage and control more than 100 acres of farmland.

Charley married Carrie Jane Weaver at 7:30 in the evening on Halloween at the home of the bride's parents Mr. and Mrs. G. W. Weaver of Jefferson. Rev. D. C. Hailey their pastor performed the nuptials. Together Charley and Carrie conceived ten children (six boys and four girls). All of their offspring are now deceased. Charley and Carrie were married for approximately forty-eight years, and their address remained constant, Route 2, Lodi, Marion County, Texas.

As the quintessential farmer, Charley primarily earned a living from the land, cultivating and selling crops. Though he sought alternated streams of income, he never pursued a steady weekly or monthly paycheck from an employer. Charley shrewdly supplemented the family's income by periodically selling timber and leasing a portion of the land to those interested in minerals. Occasionally, Charley worked for hire by hauling logs with oxen or bulls and selling timer or lumber to the local sawmills. Additionally for temporary work and income, Charley helped construct Highway 49 between Jefferson and Louisiana during the early 1930s. Whether farming or logging, Charley usually left home during the mornings—so dark no one could see, not even him. He returned home the same way, in the dark.

For extra income, Carrie and Charley rented rooms in their home to teachers, such as Ms. Izora Wilkinson during the 1920s and Ms. Norman during the 1930s and Ms. Annie Jackson. Later in life and with some difficulty, Carrie persuaded Charley to arrange to receive the old folks' pension, i.e., the precursor to Social Security benefits. Eventually, Charley received $65.00 a month. As Charley aged and crop revenue decreased, this income helped supplement necessities. However during the physically demanding farming years, the family was never on public welfare. The land always yielded plenty to sustain and share.

There was always work to be done on the family farm. If Charley was not farming, there was work to do around the home or errands into town. For example during the autumn, Charley and Carrie used crop revenue to venture into town and purchase shoes and clothes for the children. During Charley's spare time, he made shoe last for the children's shoes using leather. Practically, Charley made chair bottoms by cutting a specific type of plant of a particular reed blade. Then, he plaited the woody stem or stalk, forming the chair seat. Once the chairs were constructed or repaired, Charley placed the chairs in the house or on the front porch.

Charley could be found on the front porch, leaning backward on his homemade cane-bottom chair during his limited leisure time; he relaxed in his special spot with either a toothpick or tobacco in his mouth. He would dip snuff and chew tobacco. To entertain the children and grandchildren, he would spit the snuff through two fingers, aiming for a target in the near yard or a distance away from the front porch. The young at heart gushed in delight at the pastime while dodging the projectile and running to the landing spot.

Charley's toothpicks were specially made from a tree twig or short switch.

Charley also savored coffee. Whenever the grandchildren asked him to share his coffee, he answered them with his nonsensical stock saying: "Coffee will make you black." However, Charley eagerly shared his shotgun by showing it to the grandchildren and shared his horses by permitting the grandchildren to ride. The grandchildren especially cherished the wagon ride into town whenever they visited.

Charley was a short Black man who always smiled. His smile was a real slow smile that made his face radiant. Partly because of his smile, he seemed a very humble, peaceable, and likeable person. Charley was famous for his original barbeque and his frequently repeated self-evident truth: "What's for you in this life, you'll get it; that's that not, you'll never reach it."

Family lore claimed, Charley hid money that the family never found—this missing money may have been the same money that Charley replevied from a failed Jefferson bank. Charley persistently journeyed to town every other day, demanding the return of his money until he finally obtained it. Evidently, Charley had opened a bank account with Rogers National Bank of Jefferson. Among the surviving papers of Carrie Weaver Sims, there was a 28 December 1934 bank draft receipt, payee Charley Simms of Lodi, Texas. While Charley was still physically able to farm the land, he doubtlessly established a lending relationship with a local bank, where he borrowed money from the bank to help produce and market his cotton crop.

Each of Charley and Carrie's children farmed a section of the land. The planted everything edible, except wheat and sugar cane. For example, they harvested cabbage, cantaloupes, cucumbers, greens, okra, onion, peanuts, peas, pepper, potatoes, purple peas, squash, sweet potatoes, tomatoes, watermelon, and all-purpose corn. After harvesting the corn, he transported the corn to a mill in town and paid to have the corn ground into meal. Apple, peach, and pear orchards as well as pecan trees were grown on the property. They built a water well, a chicken coup, and a smokehouse, on their property. Charley owned a white horse called Bullet; a brown mule; a black mule called Hattie—he owned pigs and cattle. He kept the horses and mules in a pasture and plowed the land using the same. Charley also hunted wild game.

As the children matured and married, some continued to work the land. Upon Ernest's 1933 autumn marriage, he and his new bride walked from the wedding ceremony to the cotton field, where they picked cotton in the back of Charley and Carrie's house. In all likelihood, once they picked the cotton, they stored it. Later Charley or his sons hauled the cotton and/or seed to the gin at Lodi or Smithland, Marion County to sell, ideally for a profit.

Cotton was Charley's chief cash crop. His two 1934 cotton producer certificates showed a total of seventy-five pounds of cotton produced and packaged. During May of 1935, the Cooperative Extension Work in Agriculture and Home Economics office sent Charley a letter, stating his ginning certificates were turned into Washington, D.C. for the replacement certificates, which permitted him to gin cotton during 1934/1935. On 22 August 1939, Charley received his 1939-1940 Marketing Year—White Cotton Marketing Card, permitting him to produce and/or market his cotton.

Evidentially, Charley participated in the War Food Program between 1944 and 1945, using 66 ¼ acres of his 98 ½ acres for growing and harvesting crops. During this growing season, Charley raised nine hundred pounds of cotton; sixty bushels of sweet potatoes; five bushels of Irish potatoes; twenty-five bushels of all-purpose corn; livestock and poultry: six cattle and calves; six cows and heifers; seventy hens and pullets; hogs; pigs; sows farrowed; and 100 chickens. With such an endowment at stake, Charley typically walked his property early during the morning hours, armed for inspecting the fence and enclosure.

During August of 1937, Rebecca Sims and heirs (her children and their spouses) accepted payment and conveyed to the American or Southern Liberty Pipe Line Company a right-of-way and easement. This right-of-way and easement allowed construction, maintenance, and operation of pipelines and telegraph and telephone lines through a portion of the 98 ½ acres of land described in the Charles Grayson Survey. The right-of-way and easement covered a strip of land twenty-five feet in width. Crop damaged would be determined upon completion of the line, and the agreed upon payment was $62.50 to Charley for the right-of-way and easement. This same company of Dallas paid Charley Sims $100.00 to release and quitclaim the company for all causes of action for damages on 17 September 1937.

The socially and politically conscientious Charley bravely registered to vote on 31 January 1938; Charley's poll tax receipt showed he was a fifty-eight-year-old farmer who had been a resident of the Lodi, Marion County, Texas his entire life. It labeled him as Colored. By the 1940s, Rev. Joseph Sims had moved to Daingerfield, Texas, and Johnny Sims had moved to Shreveport and onto San Diego. Therefore, the bulk of farming land fell to Charley. Charley Sims paid $12.53 in state and county taxes on the Berry Sims Estate, comprising 98 ½ acres and 34 acres on 19 January 1949. Additionally, Charley Sims paid $1.15 in state and county taxes, same date. Totaling the tax receipts, for years 1950-1954 alone, Charley paid approximately $108.00. Charley property paid taxes until his death.

Frequently, Charley rubbed and complained about his stomach; every blue moon he visited the doctor but never the hospital. Maybe ulcers or colon cancer were the source of his stomach problems. As well, his rheumatism arthritis was undocumented.

At age 72 or 73 Charley reached the end of his fate and passed away from a coronary thrombosis (heart attack) around two o'clock in the morning, while at home. The family laid Charley to rest at Lewis Chapel Cemetery.

Carrie Jane Weaver Sims

Carrie Jane Weaver Sims was the first born and eldest daughter born to Grandison W. and Malinda Norris Weaver. Carrie's arrival in Jefferson and the 1887 Christmas season were synchronized. Growing up, Carrie attended school at Union Chapel, from the first to eighth or ninth grade. There, Carrie received a sound foundation—she learned to master reading, writing, and arithmetic and to express herself. As the eldest, Carrie had chores and responsibilities, so she squeezed in her school lessons by lamp light. At age 19, Carrie married Charley Edward Sims, Sr., during 1906. Their home off Lodi Road was the birthplace of their ten children.

Rarely was Carrie only a wife and mother. After all, she had mouths to feed. Certainly, Carrie worked the farmland, but she made the land work for her. She was an entrepreneur, selling candy, gum, and farm products such as milk and butter. She tended truck patches, selling farm produce to the community; she harvested and sold crops such as cabbage, peas, corn, peanuts, and sweet potatoes. She raised Rhode Island Red chickens, white, and various other chickens, selling eggs and chickens to community folks.

With ten children to raise, Carrie worked in and out of the home. Carrie's 1938 poll tax receipt described her as a homemaker. Carrie earned a license to write and sell insurance, and from 1942 to 1963, she worked with Peoples Funeral Home and Burial Association of Marshall. Her 1947 Social Security number application labeled her as unemployed. However, she was at least selling burial insurance during this period.

By the late 1940s, all the children were adults, making their own way, and Carrie took comfort in continuing her church and community activities. Only later in life, such as when Carrie registered to vote during 1969, did she claim to be retired.

Carrie ensured the church was home and home was church. Once the children were in bed and the house was quiet, Carrie sang God's praises and church songs while they slept. Early in her marriage, she joined the Lewis Chapel MC. At church and in the community, Carrie rendered conscientious Christian service with every breath and deed until her last, and she raised all of her children in the Lewis Chapel experience. Five years before her death, on 22 August 1965, Carrie alongside one of her grandchildren were baptized by immersion in a branch at the foot of the graveyard, as it extended down the hill into the woods. Lafayette Jefferson, Sr. helped Rev. William F. Locket, pastor of Lewis Chapel conducted the baptism. This was the last known baptism by immersion at the Lewis Chapel MC.

Unforgettably, the Lewis Chapel MC burned on Communion Sunday, 06 May 1956. After the fire, the congregation held worship services at the old Lewis Chapel School building on the spot where the current church building is now located.

The 1956 – 1957 church leadership purchased the school building from the Jefferson Independent School

District along with an additional 2 ½ acres of land on 17 January 1957 under the direction of the District Superintendent Rev. Dr. Curtis S. Weaver, Carrie's brother. Other Lewis Chapel trustees and stewards involved were Lafayette Jefferson, Sr., James Bennett, and Oscar Perry, Sr. Besides Carrie, other church women who were helpful during this transition included: Bessie Darty, Pearl Criss, Ima Viola Sims Jefferson, and Hattie Mae Sims Tyson. Carrie's son Rev. Ernest Sims was pastor when the church burned.

Carrie understood the value of education and ensured all ten children began their education at Lewis Chapel School, during the 1920s and 1930s. Getting to school often involved hardships or extremes and likely a boyhood tussle or spat between the Sims and the Browns. On cold school mornings, the boys carried pine straw in their pockets and used it to start a fire for warmth while waiting on a school bus. If the Browns and the Sims bickered, they knew not to as they passed the home of grandparents Berry and Rebecca Sims, on their walk to and from school.

The best game in Lodi for venting frustrations and having pure fun was baseball. The Sims' boys played baseball during the 1930s. The baseball diamond was located below the Lewis Chapel School on the Oscar Perry place. They had just enough players to make a team—Milton Sims, catcher; Howard Sims, pitcher; Ernest Sims, outfielder; Clinton Sims, third baseman; Loyd Sims, second baseman; Charley Sims, Jr., shortstop; and Johnny Sims, first baseman. Often, their friend Ollen Morrow and Cousin Milton Weaver joined the Lodi baseball team. Besides the Lewis Chapel/Lodi team, the community had two additional teams: Union and Logan. After the baseball game, three things were certain: home-brewed beer, barbeque, and a fight. For the barbeque pit, they dug a hole in the ground; burned wood all-night to crack the coal; then they killed a hog. After throwing the hog over the coals, they cooked all-night. They saved roasting trimmings for last. Someone made the home brewed beer. Maybe the Sims boys occasionally fought on their way to school or after the baseball games but not among themselves.

The ten Sims children were healthy. No one was under a doctor's care except Charley, Jr. who supposedly contracted Typhoid fever. Carrie practiced preventive medicine. She gave the children popular, cure-all medicines, such as Black-Draw or Cal-O-Tabs to ward off colds every autumn and winter. If the children did develop a cold, Carrie always returned to the dependable yet dreadful castor oil.

Carrie was full of ingenuity, decorating her Christmas trees with Christmas cards. She was certainly charitable, granting right-of-way access across her property to the neighboring Calhouns and Coopers. Socially, she was a member of the Charity club (a community outreach organization). Politically, Carrie registered to vote and voted. On particular concerns, Carrie would not hesitate to pen a letter to her state legislator.

When her sons were called to serve in the U.S. Army during WWII, Carrie charted their comings and goings in her journal. Showing her business acumen, she tried to keep track of their military benefits. Carrie wrote the Veterans Administration (VA) on 08 May 1937, referencing Milton's military insurance policy. The reply letter of 18 May 1937 from the VA provided Milton's widow as the principal heir and the balance due on the estate as $532.00. On 25 April 1938, Carrie again wrote to the VA that her father was growing feeble and that she was seeking an appointment as guardian. The VA dated their reply on 10 May 1938 and instructed Carrie to let them know when the appointment occurs. After such an appointment, they would reconsider her claim. Maybe, Grandison Weaver, Milton's maternal grandfather, was named as a co-beneficiary or second beneficiary on Milton's insurance policy, considering Carrie's persistence. During October or November 1942, Carrie wrote to the military again. This time, she evidently wrote Milton's squadron, stating she was dependent on Milton for support and explaining an insurance error. The squadron commander written reply requested an affidavit as to the truthfulness of Carrie's dependency on Milton and explained that the insurance error was corrected. This issue was not resolved to Carrie's favor.

The 1910 census indicated Carrie and Charley were renting their home, and the 1930 census showed that they owned their home. However throughout the latter 1930s and early 1940s, they were paying a mortgage note to W. H. Thomas, as evidenced by handwritten receipts. During 1936, they paid $20.00 toward mortgage and note, and during September 1941, they paid $5.00 toward mortgage and note. Again during November of 1941, they paid $10.00 with a balance of $85.00 on mortgage and note.

Between 1939 and 1942, Carrie's house needed repairing. Struggling, yet purposeful, family and friends began demolishing a portion of the house in hopes of salvaging the remainder and rebuilding on the identical spot. A worker must have unintentionally removed structural support beams; because, the house fell to the ground like timber. Neighbors, workers, and all around shook in their boots at the sensation and sound of the tremor.

Charley and Carrie lived in a farmhouse with a front porch that stretched the width of the house and a purple wisteria, which screened the sunlight for those sitting on the porch. They entertained countless and frequent guests from their front porch swing and chairs with abundant food, fellowship, and an open door. Some guests stayed for weeks at a time. Carrie cooked as though she was cooking for a hotel, and she always kept a gift wrapped to give as a parting present for the expected and unexpected company.

Huge oak trees blanketed both sides of the house. A wisteria vine and a rose bush greeted everyone as they walked through the picket fence, stepping onto the pristine white sand-dirt front yard. A dirt and rock pathway led to either of the two glass and wooden front doors. Helping to shape their wood-frame house were two front windows and a two-tier roof. Upon entering their home, three bedrooms were located to the left, and the living room, dining room, and kitchen were located on the right. The edges of the back porch, led to more gardens, pastures, the cotton, and other crops. Gardens were spaced around the perimeter of the house. On the left side were the white water well and the used wash pots. On the right rear were outdoor privy facilities, a smokehouse, and a chicken coup.

It is from this home that the Sims Family Reunion continued with the same traditions of Rebecca (Becky). The reunion was always the highlight of Carrie's life, as were the family reunion preparations. Carrie kept it going, notifying everyone far and near. Old and young eagerly anticipated the wonderful annual celebration of family and the best food. The only dreaded reunion moment for the children was when the older relatives attempted to kiss the children on their cheeks, especially the relatives who had snuff in their mouths.

By the time the Sherman, Grayson County, Texas family arrived for the reunion, the sun was usually still asleep but not Carrie nor Charley. Charley handled the barbequing, which lasted all-night. After digging a pit in the ground, he then built a fire using hickory wood at another spot. As the hickory wood turned into ember chips, he maneuvered the embers under the barbeque and in the pit. If Charley dozed off during the night, he would perk up and keep replacing the smoking embers until daybreak.

Before daybreak, Carrie was awake and cooking breakfast, in the kitchen. For the morning homecoming meal, Carrie cooked ample food, making the best buttered biscuits, fruit preserves, rice, and fried chicken, served with a glass of cold buttermilk.

She would choose either a chicken from her own yard or coup or another meat from the smokehouse, where hams, slabs of bacon, smoked sausage, beef, and other selective meats hung. They made a twine from a plant and used it to hang the meat in the smokehouse; otherwise, the meat hung from hooks. One grandchild recalled, "One time my grandmother told Chester to catch a chicken and to chop off the chicken's head using the axe. Chester held the chicken and told me to chop it off, and I cut his finger—not off but I cut it. We laughed." For frying, Carrie battered the chicken with meal, milk, and eggs.

For milking the cows, Carrie always used water buckets. Once Carrie poured the milk from the water bucket to the churn, she occasionally permitted the grandchildren to churn the milk. Churning of the milk involved using crock jars of the number ten or twenty variety and a round stick. The churn stick resembled a broom handle with a flat board on the bottom of it. Carrie used an up-and-down motion, bringing the butter to the top of the milk. She then took a spoon and dipped all the butter from the top. At this point, the butter was neither necessarily smooth nor curdy. Next, Carrie reduced the butter further by patting the milk out of it before placing it into a butter mold for chilling in the icebox along with the milk. Blocks of ice purchased in town refrigerated the icebox.

Carrie gathered the rice, which was encased in small wooden barrels, and the flour and meal were packed in bags/cloth sacks. Often, folks transformed those sacks into dresses and skirts or quilts and curtains

After Carrie completed breakfast, she started preparing the evening homecoming meal. She made every meal one could cook from beef or pork on her big, beautiful black cook stove with a place for the wood and multiple eyes or burners. Positioned atop the cook stove was a white overhead warmer, and the warmer had an extremely large oven on the side. The large side oven is where Carrie placed the wood and boiled the water.

Carrie filled her sideboard with cakes and pies and spread other desserts on top, for everyone to eat and enjoy. The sideboard stood in the dining room and was similar to a dining room buffet. She made a variety of fruit preserves and placed them in jars. Even Carrie's safe, which resembled a china cabinet, held desserts instead of her dishes or dinnerware.

Carrie's cooktop stove was used to heat the bathwater for their large tin tubs. All their water was drawn from water well, outside. A grandchild recalled once having the privilege of drawing water from the well. Undisputedly, Carrie's well water was some of the best cold water anyone could ever drink. There was no need to chill one's beverage made from the well water because the water was always ice cold.

Outside, Carrie boiled the well water for washing clothes by building a fire pit beneath large black, cast-iron pots. She used a rub-board for some of the clothes, but items such as sheets and solid white clothes, she boiled these things in the black cast-iron pots. Once the water heated, she added the lye soap to the pot and began punching the clothes using an up-and-down motion. As the clothes and household linens were cleaned, she hung everything to dry on the outside clothesline. Wife, mother, homemaker, all three characterizations denote work, and Carrie definitely worked her entire life.

Carrie's smile was mainly in her eyes; it was as though her eyes just twinkled. Carrie's eyes certainly dimmed and

185

clouded at the passing of her life partner Charley. Alone, Carrie welcomed in a stray dog and started writing a diary or journal of sorts. A loving and generous soul, Carrie wrote funeral remarks or resolutions to be read at the funerals of untold friends and family. With the one exception found below, all funeral remarks have been lost, destroyed, or simply missing.

Though Carrie sprained her hand during 1960, by all accounts, she mostly maintained good health with few exceptions. Cousin Bessie Martin kept Carrie once when she was released from the hospital, after receiving treatments for a severe cold. Again, Carrie was hospitalized after an automobile accident on 26 November 1969, staying in the Marion County Hospital for seven days.

Lastly, she was hospitalized at her stroke and death. According to Carrie's youngest Ester Weaver Sims Cole Hawkins: "[Her] blood pressure went up; she became helpless; she couldn't walk. One leg was drawn back. She was in intense pain. She didn't want anyone to touch her. She got sick in the night. Dr. Douglas said to bring her up the next morning. He finally came in—gave her a shot—she rolled her eyes—looked at him—rolled over, and she never said another word."

Around age 82 Carrie reached the end of her fate and passed away Wednesday the eighth of April, eight o'clock in the evening at Douglas Memorial Hospital from a dissecting aneurysm; arteriosclerosis; and aortitis. Signaling Carrie's impact on the community, a death notice appeared in the local newspaper. The family laid Carrie to rest at Lewis Chapel Cemetery.

Note: Glimpses into Carrie's remaining years are captured in the below excerpts, a recasting of her inexplicably fragmented journal or diary, correspondences, and

186

receipts. Verbiage remains intact from original except editing for corrections in spellings, punctuation, and grammar; adding abstracts of business letters; and adding explanatory details (side bars). All additions, corrections, and sequencing were made for grammar compliance or clarification, enhancement, and review purposes.

***

Remnants of Carrie's Journal Entries

1955

07 January 1955, paid $2.42 in taxes on the G. W. Weaver Estate, comprising 80 acres, 1/9th interest; abstract 12, William K. Allen Survey (grantee).

08 September 1955, butane system put in, a [new] cooktop stove—two heaters, by Oney Butane Company, Jefferson, Texas; Edgar Willis, agent.

SIDE BAR: The Oney Butane Company's building was located on Polk Street in Jefferson during 1967, telephone number, 665-2551.

1956

14 January 1956, paid $19.79 in taxes on the Berry Sims Estate, comprising 98 ½ acres and 34 acres.

20 March 1956, well curbs put in C. J. Sims well.

SIDE BAR: Well curbs were retaining walls, a concrete barrier inside well perimeter.

03 August 1956, Friday, Dear Daughter, I went to Lodi this afternoon and saw Lillie who was locating a pig, so she says it is o.k., ready, and waiting. So, I will have a pen built, and as soon as you send the $5.00, I will go and get it. She says it is really a nice pig. I saw hers, and it is fine. So, I am doing pretty good—still able to be up and about. I went to the doctor Wednesday night, so I have a prescription to be filled, and maybe I will get along better. Maybe, when I can get it filled. So, I will look to hear from you real soon. All send love. From Mother.

SIDE BAR: Carrie sent this letter to her daughter Malinda in Sherman. Grammar and word usage remained intact from original.

25 October 1956, [Rev.] A. L. Gabriel, [passed].

SIDE BAR: The Reverend Albert Louis Gabriel was born in Freestone County, Texas to James "Jim" Gabriel and Jane Shelton Gabriel and became a Methodist Church minister, serving Texas for over fifty years.

U.S. Postage Stamps were three cents each.

1957

Paid 1957 tax on Berry Sims Estate, 139 acres, Charles Grayson Survey.

Received a refund check of $8.14 from Upshur-Rural Electric Cooperative Corporation, serving East Texans.

1958

17 January 1958, a State Department of Public Welfare field
worker, Gaines D. Freeman, wrote Carrie a letter,
indicating he was scheduling an appointment for 21
January 1958 at one o'clock in the afternoon at his
office. Freeman instructed her to bring tax receipts
and explained he would address her concerns about
glasses.

19 January 1958, purchased my glasses in Marshall, price
$21.95 from Texas State Optical, Marshall, Texas;
received ? 14 January 1958.

May 1958, Henry Weaver [took] $3.00 out of all the Weaver
heirs mineral check. [He] forged his sister, Carrie's
name [in order to] take out the $3.00 of her money
and will not give it up. May this be remembered for
Henry Weaver.

04 June 1958, the Iran Drilling Corporation of Longview,
Gregg County, Texas wrote Carrie asking her to sign a
lease, permitting the company to drill on property for
minerals. Their letter indicated that Carrie owned an
undivided interest in the minerals, covering the Becky
Sims 98 ½ acres, under re-survey, 107.14 acres. The
letter states further that approximately 56 mineral
owners existed in said tract, including Arkansas
Louisiana Gas Company. Evidently, Arkansas
Louisiana Gas Company had farmed out their lease to
Iran Drilling Corporation. Company letter was signed
by A. Z. Skeetes and W. C. Curry. The letter granted
the regular one-eighth landowner's royalty.

June 1958, Leola [White Sims] left the children.

12 June 1958, House insurance paid up from 12 June 1958 to
12 June 1959; $2,000.00 insurance on house and
household goods; $1,000.00 on each. Insurance with
Ned Ford, Jefferson.

22 June 1958, Fourth Sunday, Dedication Service in new
Lewis Chapel Church. Cornerstone to be laid fourth
Sunday in July or September.

SIDE BAR: After Lewis Chapel MC burned on Sunday
morning, 06 May 1956, church services were held at
the old elementary school building, in the spot where
the church is now located.

14 July 1958, lease papers returned and signed. Leased
to A. Z. Skeetes and W. C. Curry for Charley Sims
heirs. Charley Sims passed on 21 September 1954;
Carrie J. Sims, widow—ten children.

15 July 1958, Curtis Weaver paid Ernest Sims' funeral bill,
cash; partly paid, balance $71.00 due.

SIDE BAR: Ernest's siblings later reimbursed their uncle
Curtis. Rev. Curtis S. Weaver was a brother of
Carrie's, and Rev. Ernest Sims was Carrie's son who
died during 1957, at Brooks Clinic.

July 1958, paid to Sister Hattie Hodge $20.00 out of the
money for the road leading to Holland Well.

16 September 1958, This one spot has been my home for fifty
years, and anything I can sell off this spot where I live

will go to help me along while I live alone and no one to help me. Charley Sims died on 21 September 1954. I have lived here alone with exception of one child and another here at times with me. No one has lived with me since he passed.

SIDE BAR: Charles Sims (Loyd's son) and Clifton Earl (Clinton's son) lived with Carrie at various points for an extended stay, as did other grandchildren. Albeit, no one lived with Carrie for the total fifteen years between Charley's death and Carrie's death.

28 September 1958, Lewis Chapel cornerstone laid, fourth Sunday.

September 1958, Glover Butler passed, one o'clock in the afternoon at his home, Lodi, Texas.

19 October 1958, Layman Day held at Lewis Chapel, [on] third Sunday; a wonderful program, rendered. Sunday school taught by Professor Eddy Coleman; also addressee for the day's program; topic: Seek Ye First. Solo performed by Mrs. Mattie Jones. C. L. Lewis, charge lay leader, in charge for the day.

November 1958, hope to pay tax during December 1958 for this year.

09 November 1958, went to Plainview for a WSCS group Meeting, from Lewis Chapel; chair with president of WSCS.

SIDE BAR: WSCS was the former women's group in the Methodist Church; more recently aka the United

Methodist Women; now United Women in Faith.

13 November 1958, Anna McIntosh passed; funeral set for 18
November 1958, Plainview church, [Rev. Fred] F. D.
Mays officiating.

17 November 1958, W. S. Ford well on homestead; drilling
started and continues each day up to present-time, 01
December.

17 November 1958, bought overhead ceiling from Mr. Ford;
amount due Mr. Ford $5.00 for same; to be paid on or
before 01 December 1958.

SIDE BAR: The 1900 and the 1920 population census data
showed the Ford families as neighbors to the Sims
families.

November 1958, overhead ceiling put up by Bennie Martin.

23 November 1958, Mr. Eddy Coleman and C. W.
Westbrook went with Lewis Chapel group to Mount
Carmel on Sunday evening; $11.00 [collected] in
meeting; wonderful short saying by Mr. Coleman.

SIDE BAR: Mount Carmel, Lewis Chapel, and Union
Chapel were apart of the same Methodist Church
circuit.

December 1958, Mattie Taylor sent $3.00 [toward] 1958 tax—
kept with tax notice for this year.

December 1958, Hattie Hodge $3.00 [toward] tax for 1958.

December 1958, Skeetes and Curry threw up ? for well on
location in the spring of 1958; 98 ½ acre tract; lease
started June 1958; erosion still unchecked in
December 1958. Request for damage of
peanut crop, labor, fertilizer, and time.

02 December 1958, order sent to Lane Bryant for coat and
gloves; coat $29.98 and gloves $1.98. [Order] returned
from Lane Bryant, 12 December. Also asked for
return of money, 12 December.

SIDE BAR: Lane Bryant was a mail order catalog for mature,
full-figure women.

03 December 1958, order sent to ? for touch-up pencil.

08 December 1958, paid [Warren P.] W. P. McGuffin,
groceries.

SIDE BAR: W. P. McGuffin was a grocer in Lodi who sold
groceries, clothing, fabric, and hardware in his general
merchandise store. He also operated a gas filling
station and a post office from the same Lodi
establishment.

08 and 09 December 1958, second work on Sims well
location.

13 December 1958, first snow, Friday night and Saturday
morning.

13 December 1958, paid Southern Ind Ins $2.10—three
months.

16 December 1958, received $1.00 each from Malinda and
Loyd [toward] 1958 tax.

16 December, baked a fruitcake.

25 December 1958, Christmas gifts [given] to C. J. Sims: Ben
Atkins $5.00; Malinda $5.00; Howard $1.00;
Corrie $1.00; Charley [Jr.] $2.00; [another
party gave] $5.00; [another party gave] $2.00; and
seven pairs of stockings; two towels and pillowcases
given by Corrie and Howard.

29 December 1958, a minister preached, four and twenty
black birds.

29 December 1958, $1.00 for a four-year subscription to *Farm
Ranch*.

SIDE BAR: Colonel Frank P. Holland launched *Farm and
Ranch* using a list of subscribers to another Texas
periodical. With the aid of W. A. L. Knox, *Farm and
Ranch* (based out of Dallas) served the interest of Texas
agriculturist for more than fifty-five years.

31 December, $1.00 sent for pen desk set.

1959

01 January 1959, new well went in production; will be ninety
days (31 March 1959) before one can consult
authorities concerning offset or proceeds.

06 January 1959, a thousand friends, not a friend to spare; he
who has an enemy, will meet him everywhere.

06 January 1959, sweet potato crop sold: one bushel to Hun Livingston $2.00; 1½ bushel to Mr. M. McDonald $3.00; 1 bushel to Sallie Stevenson $2.00; ½ bushel to Mrs. Chism $1.00; ½ bushel to postman $1.00; ½ bushel to Mr. McDonald's mother $1.00.

08 January 1959, order sent to National Bellas Hess for two slips, tea rose [color].

SIDE BAR: National Bellas Hess was a mail order company (catalog store) for women, operating from North Kansas City, Missouri.

09 January 1959, insurance sent to United Insurance Company, Atlanta, Texas $3.20.

19 January 1959, mailed Family Life premium; sent for book [about] funeral occasions, notice to fire, forest man.

20 January 1959, paid $18.43 in state and county taxes on the Berry Sims Estate, comprising 98 ½ acres and 34 acres.

20 January 1959, lawyer consulted about the new Ford well must call back to see the lawyer in three weeks.

26 January 1959, paid Mr. Ford $5.00 for the material bought [during] November 1957.

27 January 1959, 1 Timothy; Galatian 2; Revelations 17; Daniel 7.

20 February 1959, Lewis Chapel, C. J. Sims program with Rev. Amos Terrell; total proceeds $100.00; flower basket

bought for the church from this effort by C. J. Sims.

08 March 1959, appreciation service for the pastor at two o'clock in the afternoon; Rev. B. H. Rosebough, pastor. Pastor Edward of Jackson Temple, Marshall, brought the message for this occasion.

October 1959, house insurance paid with Ned Ford, Jefferson, Texas.

25 October 1959, [John Henry] J. H. Belcher passed, ten o'clock in the evening. Buried, 01 November, three o'clock.

29 October 1959, went to Atlanta to shop with my brother Rich and his wife; bought my coat.

30 October 1959, [money] sent to *Texarkana Gazette* for payment, first month.

02 November 1959, $10.00 due Mr. Jim Bennett; $3.00 due Mrs. Anna Turner; $2.00 due Bill McGuffin; hope to pay all during November 1959; my legal accounts for October 1959.

SIDE BAR: Bill McGuffin was son of Warren P. McGuffin.

02 November 1959, received the cake from Ester.

03 November 1959, received first issue of *Texarkana Gazette*. Went to Linden with Mrs. Belcher.

04 November 1959, $1.00 order sent for picture, Christmas cards $1.00.

05 November 1959, order sent to National for hat and gloves.

07 November 1959, A. Z. Skeetes came by; says he will drill Sims well number two in the near future and will help with porch repair.

22 November 1959, $6.00 to Sister Hattie Hodge; $6.00 to Mattie Taylor; $6.00 for herself for wood sold above tax for 1959. The same to be held by them, to be used for 1960 tax or to use, and they will be responsible for the tax for 1960 to the amount of $18.00—the amount of wood sold and divided in three parts as taxes are divided. Let this be remembered that said amount is in these hands, which will be required for next year's tax 1960: Hattie Hodge; Carrie J. Sims; Mattie Taylor.

24 November 1959, paid Miss Anna Turner.

07 December 1959, Christ was never in Christmas. Galatians 4:9-11.

10 December 1959, made fruitcake.

18 December 1959, sent a letter to Will Norris; to I. G. Weaver; to A. Z. Skeetes; Velma Grisson. Fant insurance paid. Ninety-four-year lady, full of fun, not dead yet. Not to old to learn. Keep alive while you live.

25 December 1959, [some children and spouses and grandchildren] came home for a short visit for Christmas; leaving for home on 27 December 1959 and [some] leaving on Saturday 26 December 1959.

December 1959, Vaughria Livingston passed at her home in

Jefferson from suffocation in storm pit [Vaughria] and three others; one woman, two children, seven years of age, twins.

SIDE BAR: Kerosene lanterns in the storm cellar (pit) were the culprit. Storm cellars and fallout shelters were prevalent during this era.

Christian Crusade PO Box 977, Tulsa, Oklahoma. Please send me your calendar free.

December 1959, Christmas gifts to mother, C. J. Sims: Malinda $10.00; [daughter and spouse] $10.00; [son and spouse] $3.00; [friend] $2.50; [son and spouse] scarf, stockings; [son] a small Bible.

1960

Trust in the Lord. Wait on him. He may not come when you want, but he is always on time. Don't worry about tomorrow, just be real good today. The Lord is right beside you, he will guide you all the way. Have faith, hope, and charity—that is the way to live. How do I know, the Bible tells me so.

15 / 16 January 1960, sent $1.20 to Robert Nichelson for garden seed.

16 January 1960, Read Jeremiah, tenth chapter through. Find out about the Christmas tree; beginning at the second chapter—unequal comparison of God and idols. The prophet warns the people. Hear ye the word, which the Lord speaketh unto you.

24 January 1960, general freeze, rain, and ice. Rain on twenty-third and twenty-fourth, then freeze on twenty-fourth—white ice everywhere.

27 January 1960, bought gas $10.80.

19 February 1960, sent license application with $1.00 enclosed; sent to Mrs. [Mamie L.] Fant in Linden. Balance due on license $4.00 to be paid to Mrs. Fant at an early date.

25 February, gas bought, ten o'clock in the morning, during snow $12.00.

03 March 1960, Subject: What the Singing Convention Means to the Local Church, by C. J. Sims. Sunday at Lewis Chapel Church.

March 1960, Bills pending for March: Mrs. [Mamie L.] Fant $4.00 on license; Curtis Weaver $5.00; Grubbs $4.60; Haggard $5.00.

SIDE BAR: Grubbs was a furniture and appliance store located on Polk Street in Jefferson. Haggard was a two-story furniture store located on Austin Street. Some people paid insurance premiums at the furniture store in Jefferson.

15 March 1960, put radio in shop.

18 March 1960, borrowed from Ned Ford $15.00 for repair of glasses, 10 percent interest, due $16.50 within forty-five or sixty days. Paid. Hair dressed; radio brought home from shop for repair.

SIDE BAR: There was a hair salon in Jefferson with four or
five beauticians who washed, dried, pressed, curled,
and waved the Black women's hair. Appointments
were not necessary; hair service was available on a first
come, first serve basis.

20-26 March 1960, Ninth PTA Congress at Smithland
Elementary School, Smithland, Texas.

22 March 1960, eyes examined; glasses left in shop for repair
same day; paid $10.00; balance due $4.35 when glasses
returned; .50 cents extra fee. Paid.

28 March 1960, glasses received from Texas State Optical,
Marshall, Texas. Paid.

01 April 1960, gas bought—past due $2.00; plow due $1.25;
fish due $2.15; Hattie M. paid $2.00; Rawleigh man
paid.

SIDE BAR: The Rawleigh man was a door-to-door salesman,
selling liniments, ointments, and spices such as the
vanilla bean spice from Madagascar. William T.
Rawleigh of Illinois The W. T. Rawleigh Company
was started during the late 1800s.

11 April 1960, hand sprang; doctor treated, 12 April; cast
removed, 19 April; Dr. DeWare treated. $5.00 due on
doctor bill.

21 April 1960, sent order off to National Bellas Hess.

26 April 1960, third trip to doctor for sprain left wrist; doctor
bill due; medicine $1.00.

27 April 1960, $10.00 due Haggard Furniture Company, old account. Paid.

07 May 1960, put lay-a-way with J. B. White; paid $1.00; balance $5.35. Paid.

SIDE BAR: J. B. White was the name of a regional department store founded by James Bryce who immigrated to U.S. during the 1860s. He set up business in Augusta, Richmond County, Georgia during the 1870s. Through various periodic mergers with Chaflin Company of New York and Mercantile Stores of Ohio, J. B. White eventually joined Dilliards during the late 1990s.

14 May 1960, paid on stove repair to Oney Butane Company, Jefferson, Texas; balance $8.00.

14 May 1960, deep freeze bought and delivered; first payment due, 25 June; $12.00 per month; thirty-six months to pay.

09 June 1960, paid Ned Ford in full for money borrowed $16.50. Paid on freezer bill for convenience; first payment due on 25 June 1960.

June 1960, balance on accounts for June: to T. R. Grubbs, Tire and Appliance on bags $4.98; to Benefield $5.15. Paid to Beatrice on pig $2.00. Paid on lay-a-way $6.98. To Dr. DeWare $9.00.

SIDE BAR: T. R. Grubbs was Thomas Rayford "Ray" Grubbs.

August 1960, Family Life $2.00; Fant $1.25; Fish $4.75; Watkins $3.00; H. Pruitt $2.00; United $2.00; on bags $2.00.

10 August 1960, borrowed $2.00 from H. A. Pruitt; to be paid soon.

08 September 1960, payment of $5.00 to Terry DeWare Clinic and Hospital, Jefferson, Texas.

05 November 1960, paid $17.40 in state and county taxes on the Berry Sims Estate, comprising 98 ½ acres and 34 acres.

01 December 1960, Southern Fidelity Life Insurance Company, Marshall, Texas issued an assumption certificate for a policy with Southern Industrial Life.

1961

January 1961, Ben Atkins passed at home.

08 June 1961, Jennie Gilham.

17 November 1961, paid $17.40 in state and county taxes on the Berry Sims Estate, comprising 98 ½ acres and 34 acres.

1962

February 1962, John Glenn, first man flight.

08 April 1962, George Hill.

05 May 1962, TV went out.

07 May 1962, TV picked up.

24 May 1962, Scott Carpenter, second man flight. TV returned.

August 1962, Chanie McIntosh passed.

29 October 1962, [TV] turned back to T. R. Grubbs Company; picked up by worker, Kerst.

30 October 1962, house insurance taken out with D. C. Daniels, Marshall, Texas of the Old American County Mutual Fire Insurance Company, Dallas, Texas; $5.00 per month; paid $10.00 for two months.

11 November 1962, House insurance policy with Old American County Mutual Fire Insurance Company, Dallas, Texas, $5.00 per month.

13 November 1962, Odessa Calhoun.

15 December 1962, Oza Martin died.

20 December 1962, telephone put in.

25 December 1962, gas bought.

1963

February 1963, [On the death of] Mrs. Anna Turner. There is an open gate at the end of the road, through which each must go alone, and there is a light we cannot see, our Father claims his own. Beyond the gate our loved ones find happiness and rest. And there is comfort in the thought that a loving God knows best. On Sunday evening, 24 February 1963, God called from our midst, Sister, Anna Turner—one who has served and shared in the many problems of life, giving in deeds, words and comfort to those whom she was able to reach and [she] was always ready to share whenever she was called. It was a pleasure to have a part in whatever was needed for her church and community. Until her health failed, she was always ready to go to the house of the Lord and play her part in whatever way she could. Sometimes mid scenes of deepest gloom, sometimes where Eden's flowers bloom, by still waters or troubled sea, still tis his hand that leadeth me. To the family, I commend you to him, who will lead you at last to that blessed abode, to the city of God, at the end of the road. Humbly submitted Lewis Chapel Church. W. F. Lockett, Pastor.

SIDE BAR: Odessa Calhoun, Jennie V. Gilham, Anna Turner were friends of Carrie as opposed to known relatives.

28 April 1963, Henry Jackson.

18 December 1963, paid $7.23 in state and county taxes on the Berry Sims Estate, comprising 98 ½ acres and 34 acres.

1964

28 January 1964, paid $26.46 in school taxes for Marion County, associated with the Berry Sims Estate,

comprising 98 ½ acres and 34 acres.

February 1964, Fant Security Association of Linden, Texas—insurance policy premium changed to $2.81; [premium] had been $1.25 since I first joined; it went up without notice.

U.S. Postage Stamps were five cents each.

04 December 1964, paid $7.30 in state and county taxes on the Berry Sims Estate, comprising 98 ½ acres and 34 acres.

29 December 1964, paid $26.46 in school taxes for Marion County, associated with the Berry Sims Estate, comprising 98 ½ acres and 34 acres.

1965

20 May 1965, made an application for a hospital room expense policy with Southern Fidelity Life Insurance Company, Marshall, Texas. Monthly premium $3.15; daily hospital room benefit $8.00.

22 August 1965, C. J. Sims baptized by immersion by Pastor W. F. Locket.

23 November 1965, paid $7.22 in state and county taxes on the Berry Sims Estate, comprising 98 ½ acres and 34 acres.

12 December 1965, paid $26.04 in school taxes for Marion County, associated with the Berry Sims Estate, comprising 98 ½ acres and 34 acres.

1966   No findings in journal, diary, letters, or receipts.

1967

25 April 1967, filed a claim under Old American County
        Mutual Fire Insurance policy, and the company sent
        her Proof of Loss forms.

03 May 1967, land insurance added by agent from Dallas,
        Texas who made inspection and payment of damage
        cooktop stove; $1,000.00 added to the house building,
        making $2,000.00 on house; the sum of $3,500.00 on
        house and household goods. Policy to be sent soon.
        Agent from Dallas, Texas.

26 October 1967, paid $7.48 in state and county taxes on the
        Berry Sims Estate, comprising 98 ½ acres and 34 acres.

26 October 1967, paid $26.04 in school taxes for Marion
        County, associated with the Berry Sims Estate,
        comprising 98 ½ acres and 34 acres.

26 October 1967, paid $2.03 in taxes on the G. W. Weaver
        Estate [Carrie Weaver Sims Estate], comprising 8.88
        acres, William K. Allen Survey (grantee).

1968

19 November 1968, paid $10.64 in state and county taxes on
        the Berry Sims Estate, comprising 98 ½ acres and 34
        acres.

19 November 1968, paid $26.04 in school taxes for Marion
        County, associated with the Berry Sims Estate,

comprising 98 ½ acres and 34 acres.

19 November 1968, paid $2.03 in taxes on the G. W. Weaver Estate [Carrie Weaver Sims Estate], comprising 8.88 acres, William K. Allen Survey (grantee).

1969

28 January 1969, voter registration certificate, issued for year beginning 01 March 1969 and ending 28 February 1970; age 76; retired.

18 August 1969, How wonderful to meet at the home coming each year with family, folks, and friends. This group present at the home of Mrs. Carrie J. Sims, Jefferson, Texas Route 2, Box 252. Our Father we dedicate our lives to thee. May we dedicate our lives and our homes to thee. May we find within the walls of our home the love, faith and peace, which comes from thee. Through Jesus Christ our Lord, Amen. Oh, give thanks to the Lord, for his mercy endureth forever. The Lord is my shepherd, I shall not want! [Words written by Carrie J. Sims on the occasion of 1969 Sims Family Reunion].

04 September 1969, bought on charge account, [Harvey] H. A. Pruitt General Merchandise, $18.57 in groceries, and an $8.88 balance brought forward.

02 October 1969, paid by cash $2.50 to [Harvey] H. A. Pruitt General Merchandise, bought on charge account in groceries $25.53.

SIDE BAR: The Pruitt store was located near the First

National Bank, downtown Jefferson located on
Walnut Street; there the Black population of Jefferson
gathered and greeted one another, whenever they
ventured to town, especially on weekends. On the
side of the store was a place to park. In later years,
customers could reach the H. A. Pruitt Grocery, Feed,
and Hardware Company store by dialing 665-2352.

27 October 1969, paid $14.18 in state and county taxes on the
Berry Sims Estate, comprising 98 ½ acres and 34 acres.

27 October 1969, paid $26.04 in school taxes for Marion
County, associated with the Berry Sims Estate,
comprising 98 ½ acres and 34 acres.

27 October 1969, paid $2.03 in taxes on the G. W. Weaver
Estate [Carrie Weaver Sims Estate], comprising 8.88
acres, William K. Allen Survey (grantee).

01 November 1969, bought on charge account [Harvey] H. A.
Pruitt General Merchandise $28.68 in groceries.
Grocery list included: bread, chicken, ice cream,
margarine (two packages), pocket knife, tang, one-half
gallon buttermilk, pet milk (four cans), and fish.

04 November 1969, paid by cash $2.50 to [Harvey] H. A.
Pruitt General Merchandise.

26 November 1969, [in automobile accident], Thanksgiving,
on the way home from Thanksgiving dinner; stayed in
hospital one week, seven days.

29 November 1969, bought on charge account, [Harvey] H. A.
Pruitt General Merchandise, $1.10 in dog food.

SIDE BAR: After Charley's death, Carrie came to have a dash-a-hound (dog), and she tagged it by the name of Beaver.

04 December 1969, paid by cash $2.00 to [Harvey] H. A. Pruitt General Merchandise, bought on charge account in groceries, $16.25.

U.S. Postage Stamps were six cents each.

27 October 1969, voter registration certificate, issued for year beginning 01 March 1970 and ending 28 February 1971; age 79.

1970

January 1970, journal /diary included local address for welfare office.

02 January 1970, C. J. Sims entered the Marion County Hospital on Thanksgiving evening, after having been in a [automobile accident on 26 November 1969; stayed] there for seven days; returned home. Had a hospitalization policy with Southern Fidelity. The policy was held in the office until the day I left for home. Having to this date, 2 January 1970 no word as to the results of this policy. Was under the care of Dr. R. D. Douglas. Hoping to hear from the hospital or Dr. Douglas soon, as next payment will soon be due for January 1970. Hoping for reply.

03 January 1970, bought on charge account in groceries $25.21 from [Harvey] H. A. Pruitt General Merchandise.

05 January 1970, paid by cash $2.50 to [Harvey] H. A. Pruitt General Merchandise.

06 January 1970, opened a bank account with the First National Bank in Jefferson using a check for $200.00.

13 January 1970, paid bills—Old American House Ins, light bill paid; gas bought $6.50 due; sent for insurance policy.

15 or 16 January 1970, sent in $1.00 for hospital policy; policy to be sent soon; hospital policy [with] Southern Fidelity, Marshall, Texas; claim still held at hospital, Jefferson, Marion County; Dr. Douglas in charge.

24 January 1970, received insurance policy paperwork from Direct Extra Cash Plan of Omaha, Nebraska; policy offered hospital confinement coverage at monthly premium of $6.50.

26 January 1970, opened a bank checking account with First National Bank, Jefferson using a check in the amount of $200.00

February 1970, from [automobile accident] Thanksgiving November [1969] Southern Fidelity, Marshall, Texas; $340.00 paid in cash.

05 February 1970, paid by cash $2.50 to [Harvey] H. A. Pruitt General Merchandise, bought on charge account in groceries, $37.48.

11 February 1970, wrote a $75.00 check, payable to herself and cashed it at First National Bank of Jefferson.

20 February 1970, paid by cash $1.20 to [Harvey] H. A. Pruitt General Merchandise.

20 February 1970, Texas State Optical or Dr. Payton's letter indicated that one or the other examined Carrie's eyes. Eyeglasses were not prescribed, and a return visit was not warranted.

Bills for March 1970, to be paid in April, light bill $5.52; gas bill $0.00; house insurance $8.00; family life $3.00; Fant Security $2.81.

05 March 1970, paid by cash $2.50 to [Harvey] H. A. Pruitt General Merchandise, bought on charge account in groceries, $20.43.

25 March 1970, Fant Security paid and Family Life paid.

April 1970, telephone bill was .33 cents, and her telephone number was 214-665-3540. A telephone call placed to Atlanta, Texas #214-796-4684 appeared on Carrie's bill. Bill stamped, Paid.

04 April 1970, paid by cash $2.00 to [Harvey] H. A. Pruitt General Merchandise.

SIDE BAR: The heirs of Carrie Jane Weaver Sims settled all outstanding accounts, such as those with Lewis and Walker Funeral Home, Harvey A. Pruitt General Merchandise, etc.

***

CHARLEY and CARRIE WEAVER SIMS FAMILY

Charley and Carrie named their children:

- Ima Viola Sims Jefferson, Centenarian
- Howard Cleveland Sims
- Ernest Sims, Rev.
- Malinda Elizabeth Sims—named after Carrie's mother
- Charley Edward Sims, Jr.
- Loyd Edward Sims
- Hattie Mae Tyson—named after Charley's sister
- Clinton Sims
- Milton Sims—named after Carrie's brother
- Ester Weaver Sims Cole Hawkins—named after Carrie's birth family

Centenarian Ima Viola Sims Jefferson

During the autumn of 1907, Charley and Carrie welcomed their first child Ima Viola who became the family's standard bearer of care. Growing up, Ima explained her caretaker role: "We never did fight too much. I always took care of the children. Mama and Papa could go where they wanted, day or night. I loved my brothers and sisters. I whipped them at times. Mama and Papa knew they were safe. They were not worried, wherever they were going. I did not let any of them get hurt. When Mama and Papa would leave, I made a cake; if it turned out really good, I saved it for them. Me and my oldest brother Howard—whatever I was doing, he was right in with me; he was going to help."

Around age 20, Ima married her seventy-year life partner Lafayette Jefferson, Sr. Together they gave life to thirteen children and attributed their matrimonial longevity to their strong faith in God; belief in family; and devotion to their church and charity.

While a member of Lewis Chapel, Ima served as treasurer for the Women Society of Christian Service and is recorded as a member of the Eastern Star and the Charity Sisters Club. Within the family Ima was a pillar of strength. When her life partner became ill, Ima remained his helpmate and caregiver.

At age 95 Ima expressed she had really lived—she had made it through all of the stumbles and milestones—she had done all that was required of her as a good steward and faithful caregiver—plus, she had even traveled across the U.S. Her only wish was to go west, maybe see the dessert, to see the mountains, the ancient red wood trees, to see Hollywood.

At age 100 Ima reached the end of her fate and passed away. The family laid Ima to rest at Lewis Chapel Cemetery.

Howard Cleveland Sims

Charley and Carrie named their second child Howard Cleveland Sims—he was born in Lodi approximately three years into his parents' marriage. As a little boy, Howard and his big sister followed their grandfather Berry around as he cultivated the farmland. Howard was always affixed to his eldest sibling whenever tasked, in trouble, or when taking care of their younger sisters and brothers. Howard gained early education at the early Lewis Chapel School and continued his education at Central High School.

During the autumn of 1931, the Methodist Episcopal minister Albert E. Liles wed Howard to Corrie Lee Moss Sims Manuel in Marion County. Though the bride and groom initially resided at the home of the bride's parents, Howard farmed the land belonging to his parents, raising food for consumption and crops for income. Howard not only continued to farm in Jefferson; but also, he obtained work, cutting crossties. The thick rectangle wood blocks that shored up the railroad metal tracks were called crossties. He and his wife began living at the sawmill quarters in shotgun-shaped houses in Bivins, Cass County, Texas, near Atlanta, where Howard cut logs for the Grogan Sawmill.

During 1945, the couple moved to Sherman, Grayson County, Texas, staying with his sister Malinda and her family, for a length of time. Howard accepted any work he found. He worked at Grayson Hotel and Joe's Café—a café in the city for whites only. There, he cooked, cleaned, or completed assigned task, out of the customers' sight, as required. Reminiscence of his childhood growing up on the family farm, Howard also maintained lawns, finding yard work in town.

As Corrie bore no natural children, she and Howard raised several adopted sons who are deceased. Howard and his family settled on Broughton Street in Sherman.

Howard smoked Camel cigarettes, practically a pack-a-day. Every time the church doors opened, Howard was in attendance and active. He joined the Saint James UMC, in Sherman. There, he was president of the usher board, served on the steward and trustee boards, and was the caretaker of the grounds. Howard was a member of the citywide usher board and served as president. Howard approached life as though he was part of a cooperative partnership and believed in decency and order.

As the 1969 Christmas season advanced, at age 60 Howard reached the end of his fate and passed away in his Sherman home. Howard possibly developed lung cancer considering his heavy cigarette smoking lasted thirty years of adulthood. The family held Howard's funeral at Saint James UMC, Sherman and laid Howard to rest at Lewis Chapel Cemetery.

Rev. Ernest Sims

Charley and Carrie named their third child Ernest Sims—he was born during 1911 in Lodi. He too attended early Lewis Chapel School and Central High in Jefferson.

When Ernest married Ollie Mae Bennett Perry during 1933, it was cotton-picking time. After Rev. Amos Mayes performed the wedding ceremony, the couple picked cotton in the rear of Carrie's house. Initially the couple stayed with Carrie, for a time.

Ernest became a farmer and later a minister. Rev. Ernest Sims and his family eventually moved into their family house near Lewis Chapel MC, as he was the pastor of the Lewis Chapel Methodist Church when the church burned during 1956.

Ernest and Ollie Mae conceived twelve children. Several of their children died at infancy or during early childhood. Ollie Mae died during 1954. To help raise the children, Rev. Ernest Sims married Leola White as the 1956 Christmas season approached. In less than three months later the Reverend Ernest Sims died. As circumstances developed, Ernest's children did not need raising. The siblings met and decided to ask their stepmother to leave. Leola left the children June 1958.

At age 48 Rev. Ernest Sims reached the end of his fate and passed away at six o'clock in the morning from heart disease and hypertension at Brooks Clinic in Atlanta, Cass County, Texas. He spent nine days in hospital, suffering two years from a heart condition. The family held Ernest's funeral at the Lewis Chapel old school building.

Malinda Elizabeth Sims

Charley and Carrie's fourth child Malinda Elizabeth
was born the fourth of July in Lodi during 1913—but Malinda
was their first to finish high school. However, she had to
attend three schools, in three towns, and live with three
families to complete high school. Malinda began her
education at old Lewis Chapel School in Lodi. Moving to
Marshall, she resided at Annie Emory's home and attended
Pimpton High School. At last in Sherman, she stayed with
Cousin Sallie (Sarah) Weaver White Vaughn, and graduated
from Fred Douglas High School. The Fred Douglas High
School was across the street from Cousin Sallie's home.

If Malinda's high school autograph book is any
indication, she enjoyed high school. Malinda had a group of
girlfriends named: Oneta, Bernice, Lottie, and Minnie;
Malinda's friends shortened her name to Linda. Excerpts
from Malinda's high school autograph book included the
following preferences, prose, and poetry. Jefferson is my
home, Sherman is my station; I just came here to get an
education. Malinda's favorite things included: fried chicken;
cooking; the song, *Just a Little While to Stay Here*; the dance, the
one-step; music on the radio; baseball; poppies (flowers).
Though Malinda loved Mrs. A. E. Lamplin—her English
teacher, Malinda's favorite subject was cooking (home
economics) and favorite hobby was talking to her girlfriends in
the senior and junior classes. Malinda's boyfriend was A. J.
Lewis, in the senior class. For a sweetheart she wrote, You will
always be wondering. For the favorite or popular high school
slang, Malinda wrote, Git stuff.

After high school, Malinda married her beau on a
rainy day in Durant, Bryan County, Oklahoma. At the start of
their marriage, they stayed with Cousin Sallie (Sarah) Weaver
White Vaughn throughout 1930. From there, Malinda

moved to and from three different Sherman addresses before settling at Sycamore. Malinda and her spouse conceived four children—three of whom are deceased.

Malinda was active in OES, number 28, Golden Link, and president of Fred Douglas PTA; Malinda was equally devoted and dedicated to Saint James UMC, Sherman, Grayson County, Texas. From age 16, Malinda's life of commitment and service to the Saint James UMC included manifold activities: Sunday school adult class teacher, Sunday school superintendent, church secretary, usher, chairperson of six committees, Communion stewardess, member of WSCS, president of United Methodist Women, mission coordinator Christian social involvement in the Sherman-McKinney district, United Methodist Women, and lay delegate to the annual jurisdictional church conferences.

To help nurture and sustain the family, Malinda worked at Clark Cleaners, 310 North Maxey, Sherman, throughout 1952, and occasionally, Malinda did light cleaning as a domestic. Her primary job outside of the home was one where she cooked for the Bells and the Hopkins families of Sherman.

Malinda was a magnificent cook. Family members continued to praise and crave Malinda's cooking, especially her not too sweet, not too tart apple pies with the cinnamon layer underneath the crust. A few of Malinda's adages in latter years included sayings such as: "If that don't beat a hen-a-pecking;" "How nice;" and "Prayers go where you can not." As well, a few of those favorite things from her youth remained with her or developed as she matured such as listening to the baseball game over the radio, reading, cooking, and gardening, growing flowers and vegetables.

Malinda's children remembered a loving mother very involved in her children's lives and education—whether walking the children to and from school or helping with their homework or serving on the parent, teacher board. Every summer, Malinda and her brothers in Sherman took their children to the Sims Family Reunion. They securely rode the 200-mile ride to Lodi in a quilted and tarp-covered flatbed pickup truck.

At Malinda's funeral, a lifelong friend described Malinda as straightforward, reserved, and articulate. Malinda's minister portrayed the image of Malinda praying and crying and crying and praying when her health failed but never losing her faith. A former student of the days when Malinda was PTA president, for eight years, recalled Malinda leading the way for school integration and imaged her leading the way heaven-wide. A Jefferson childhood friend told the story of the annual community homecoming. The friend and Malinda were admiring those who had returned for the occasion. Seeing all the beautiful people finely dressed inspired Malinda to remark, "One day, I am coming back wearing a wide hat."

As the 1996 Thanksgiving holiday advanced, at age 83 Malinda reached the end of her fate and passed away at Wilson N. Jones Hospital in Sherman from heart and kidney failure with diabetes and hypertension as contributing factors. By the hundreds, everyone who knew Malinda attended her funeral, offering condolences to one another. An odd and unpredicted sleeting rain fell the day of Malinda's funeral. Though Malinda did not intend to make Sherman her home, she suffered her station for over sixty-five years, and now Sherman is her resting place at the Westhill Memorial Park.

Interestingly or oddly, it rained at Malinda's death, rained at her marriage, and could have rained at her birth. Malinda's mother Carrie named her daughter Malinda in honor of her mother Malinda Norris Weaver, and Daughter Malinda continued the naming tradition. Likewise, Malinda carried her tradition of generosity, giving goodbye gifts to all visiting family and friends.

Charley Edward Sims, Jr.

Charley and Carrie named their fifth child Charley Edward. He was born during 1915 in Lodi, and attended the old Lewis Chapel School, as a young boy. Maturing physically and spiritually, Charley confessed a hope in Jesus Christ at Lewis Chapel MC. Charley was the second sibling to graduate from high school, graduating from Central High School in Marion County.

After graduation in 1937, either that July or November, Charley married at the parents' home his sweetheart for life, with Charley's cousin Rev. Joseph Sims performing the nuptials.

With difficulty finding work, Charley and his bride moved from Jefferson to Sherman and dwelled with his sister Malinda for nearly five months, until they found a home of their own. Throughout 1938 Charley and his new bride resided at 317 North East Street (sister Malinda's address), And when Charley applied for a Social Security number, he was working at Lee's on 103 South Travis Street.

Once settled, Charley and family immediately joined the Saint James UMC. There, Charley became a certified lay speaker, trustee board member, official board treasurer, stewards board member, church school superintendent, choir president, and Methodist youth fellowship co-sponsor.

As extra income, Charley hauled wood; that is, he drove his pickup truck to Oklahoma to buy the wood and returned to Sherman to sell it. The family also used the flatbed truck to travel to East Texas in the summer for the annual family reunions or during the winter holidays. For the Christmas season travel, they placed a charcoal iron bin in the truck to keep the children warm. The coal remained secure, as did the tarp covering the truck-bed. Later, Charley secured employment as a maintenance worker and as a library aide at

Austin College in Sherman. Charley also worked as an engraving apprentice. Throughout the 1960s, the family resided at 520 East College in Sherman.

During the early 1970s, Charley and his family relocated to Fort Worth, Tarrant County, Texas. After relocating to Fort Worth, Charley and his family were among the charter members of the Campus Drive UMC. At Campus Drive, Charley served as trustee, Sunday school teacher and superintendent, finance committee chairperson and member, and choir member. Charley was active in his community, as a Master Mason in the Grand Temple Lodge, number 75, Free and Accepted Mason of the Prince Hall Affiliation of the Grand Lodge of Texas.

Charley had a successful professional career as a master engraver and owner of Eloquent Trophy and Engraving Shop located in the Sims Professional Building, Fort Worth.

Charley considered military service and began basic training. Carrie's writings charted Charley's entrance and stations. Charley reported to the army, arriving at Fort Riley, Kansas, subsequently deploying for Fort Sam Houston. However, military records personnel did not locate a service record for Charley, basing their search upon Charley's social security number. Health reasons prevented Charley from serving on active duty. Of Carrie's ten children, only two actually served on active duty, Clinton and Milton.

Charley wanted to attend the August 1992 Sims Family Reunion; because, he felt it would be his last. By September, Charley was hospitalized and supposedly suffered a stroke during surgery. Afterward, he never regained consciousness.

At age 77 Charley reached the end of his fate and passed away. Innumerable people attended the funeral, in Fort Worth, paying their last respects. The family laid Charley to rest at Cedar Hill Memorial Park, Arlington, Tarrant County, Texas.

Loyd Edward Sims

Charley and Carrie named their sixth child Loyd Edward Sims; he was born circa 1917 in Lodi. Loyd attended early Lewis Chapel School and Central High School in Jefferson. Getting to school was no walk in the park. Loyd, Charley, and other siblings walked through the woods, over Sand Road, to catch the school bus. Their walking distance from their home to the bus stop seemingly equaled their bus ride distance. More indicative of the times was this scenario. The boys carried pine straw in their pockets, so when they reached the bus stop, they could light the pine straw to stay warm, on frigid mornings while waiting for the school bus.

Loyd started out farming in tandem with his siblings, but he soon started driving a truck, hauling lumber and started dating. As a young man, Loyd dated while working for Charley Morgan Sawmill in Jefferson/Lodi. During this interval, he and the young lady conceived a child. During 1941, Loyd decided to marry LeVelma, and Rev. James Jones performed the nuptials. LeVelma's father was Henry Weaver's brother-in-law. Initially, Loyd and his new bride resided at Carrie's home, but they soon moved onto Tom Cooper's place. Tom Cooper had a few piddling rental houses on his property, which were near Carrie's home and land.

Next, Loyd secured a job at the Grogan Sawmill in Bivins. There, Loyd and LeVelma tolerated the dilapidated and degrading sawmill quarters in Bivins and conceived their second child. Making their pallet more palatable was Howard and his wife who lived and worked there around the same stretch.

In a moment of epiphany, Loyd decided to move to Sherman, where he stayed with his younger sister Ester Weaver Sims Cole Hawkins for a break before eventually finding and moving into his home on North East Street. Loyd married Cloria Goodman McKinney, and together they raised their family.

Finding familiar employment, Loyd worked as a truck driver; instead of hauling lumber, he delivered furniture. Loyd drove a furniture truck for twenty-seven years, working for Knights Furniture of Sherman and driving all over the country. Loyd's most dangerous furniture delivery was on the occasion when he innocently stumbled into an imminent cross fire between escaped convicts and police. Loyd hid by lying down behind the sofa, the third house away from where the shoot-out occurred. The May 1978 shoot-out in Caddo, Bryan County, Oklahoma made local headlines and the highway patrol's yearbook. Among the dead were three escaped convicts, two deputies, and one constable. Loyd, undaunted by the danger, continued truck driving and delivering furniture after the incident.

At Saint James UMC, Loyd served as steward, trustee board chairperson, and official board chairperson, for decades.

Growing up, Loyd was never sick. He recalled his mother Carrie keeping them healthy with Cal-O-Tabs (an over-the-counter medication) at night and castor oil the next morning. Much later in life, Loyd experienced sinus problems and underwent prostrate surgery. He loathed the winter season, passionately expressing his preferences for 100 degrees and the comforts of a shade tree or shadow to ease the stinging sun rays. Regarding health remedies, Loyd felt equally passionate concerning the pointlessness of prolonged use of prescription medicine: "You can take anything so long until you cannot do without it, and it is not doing you any good."

At age 85 or 86 Loyd reached the end of his fate and passed away during March of 2004. The family laid Loyd to rest at Bethel Bells Cemetery, Bells, Grayson County, Texas.

Hattie Mae Tyson

Charley and Carrie named their seventh child Hattie Mae who is remembered for sewing quilts, her green thumb, and making lye soap. Her quilts were vibrant as her garden of all things green, yellow, and red and as comforting as her food. Like her sisters, Hattie's cooking especially her baking was something sweet, and her Lewis Chapel church work was without question.

Affectionally called Aunt Lady, she described herself as the "Jill" of all trades. She expressed a keen wit, sharp tongue, and fiscal savvy who kept the Sims Estate property taxes paid and all land lessors in check.

With no natural children, she raised her grandniece as her daughter and embraced all children, especially bonding with school age children from the junior high school, where she worked as an office aide. Some of these favorite youths called her Aunt Tag.

Born 1919, Hattie Mae married Ed Tyson during September of 1937. At age 89 Hattie Mae reached the end of her fate and passed the last day of December 2008. The family laid Hattie Mae to rest at Lewis Chapel Cemetery.

Milton Sims

As though permanently parched, Milton would yell at bedtime, "Papa, I want a drink of water—drink Papa drink." Charley and Carrie was named their eighth child Milton Sims in honor of Carrie's sick and dying brother Milton Weaver. During 1921 in Lodi, Milton came to tug at everyone's heart;

those who knew him called him "Bit" or "Bitty-B." Milton satisfactorily finished the grammar grades at Lewis Chapel School, during 1940; afterward, he attended Judea High School in Jefferson.

Supposedly, Milton married very young to an even younger bride. Their union lasted only a few months; the bride returned home to her parents in Corinth, as though their union was an aberration. Afterward, Milton had a relationship with another lady. This relationship also soon ended.

Milton decided to join the Civilian Conservation Corps (CC Camps) workforce, signing up in Jefferson or in Waco, McLennan County, Texas. After working with the CC Corps, Milton joined the U.S. Army.

Carrie tracked Milton's movement as she had for Clinton and Charley, Jr. Milton went overseas, October 1944 and returned from overseas, 28 August 1945. Milton came home for a visit. He departed from overseas, 19 August; arrived in Boston, Massachusetts, 28 August and remained there three days. He started for home and arrived at home, 06 September for a thirty-day furlough. At the end of the thirty days, he extended fifteen more days; he returned to camp, 20 October 1944.

According to Milton's military service record received from the U.S. Army, Milton achieved the rank of private first class. He entered military service on 11 September 1942 and exited on 24 February 1946. His assignments or geographical locations included: Detachment Number Two Headquarters and Jackson Barracks. Milton took the military induction in Jefferson and accepted military separation at Camp Fannin, Smith County, Texas. Milton used Route 2, Box 29 Lodi, Marion County, Texas as his home of record and applied for the National Service Life Insurance. This $5,000.00 insurance policy became effective on 01 August 1943 and was payable upon his death.

After Milton returned to his Jefferson home from overseas, he met a vacation Bible schoolteacher from Houston. By August of 1946, he and his fiancée were married in Marion County. Almost abruptly, the couple (a veteran and schoolteacher) moved to Houston—the bride's hometown and resided at 2919 Jenson Drive. Coincidentally, Moscoe Dixon and his wife Bessie Riser of the Union community had also resided on Jensen Drive the previous year.

At Milton's 1946 Social Security number application, he was unemployed but soon secured employment as a longshoreman, in the shipping industry. Milton retired from Armco Steel during 1983.

In Houston, Milton married again; he and the third wife did not have any children. Throughout 1958 Milton's address was 2612 Chenevert Street Apartment Six, Houston.

Milton lost his wives through divorce or death. By 1985, Milton was residing in his two-story duplex at 2612 Truxillo Street, Houston. Throughout 1991, his home was worth $14,400.00 in land and $34,300.00 in improvements, totaling $48,700.00 assessed value.

The young Milton was fun-loving and outgoing. He, his brothers, and cousins played baseball, and Milton also sang in a music quartet. As an adult, Milton was sad and a loner. Alone in his home, Milton drank light brew (as opposed to ardent miltons), seemingly trying to drown abject sorrows or quench a thirst from early childhood. Adhering to a self-imposed solitary confinement, Milton did not attend his mother nor father's funeral.

At age 67 Milton reached the end of his fate and passed away alone in his Truxillo Street duplex during 1989. Someone discovered his body and death. The family laid Milton to rest at Houston National Cemetery.

Clinton Sims

According to Clinton—the storyteller, "You know I never went to a doctor or sick call until I was in '*service*.' In '*service*,' they kept putting me on sick call. They told me to have my teeth fixed—I wouldn't let them pull them. So, they decided that they would make me have them filled. I had them all filled, and when I got out of '*service*,' those fillings dropped out piece by piece. I could take my tongue and shoot a piece of it out. Later, I had them all pulled. Now, I got a set of teeth I wear once a week—every Sunday—I wear them to church."

Whoever sat down to talk with Clinton Sims was in for nonstop laughter. Clinton Sims may have been the ninth child born to Charley and Carrie, but his life was by far the most colorful and comical.

Clinton was born during 1923 in Lodi. He too attended the Lewis Chapel School and Judea High School. Growing up he worked hard and played hard. Clinton said the only major accident he ever had was riding on the handlebars of a bicycle, belonging to the only boy who had a bike in Lodi. They were riding down a red hill, seemingly going 40 or 50 miles an hour. Years ago, according to Clinton, many of the Lodi roads were dirt-packed and red hills. The boy's bike hit a tree root in the road and threw Clinton sliding on his face into the dirt and ditch. The boy landed on top of Clinton, and Clinton woke up with bumps and bruises.

Young Clinton had a relationship and fathered a child. Still a young man and unemployed at his 1942 Social Security number application, Clinton meddled and meandered a bit in towns such as Baytown, Sherman, and Jefferson, finding odd jobs here and there.

During 1942, Clinton and others who were employed at a worksite were playing dominoes and card games when they were caught in a Baytown 48-hour hurricane. According to Clinton, "When I looked around everybody out there was gone. I left my paycheck; I left everything; I left clothes, down there; I just brought what I had on. I didn't even go back to the camp, but the hurricane took all of that. The old man running a café there—his car was floating in water, way down the street. That man prayed—that's how I got out of there. Everybody got still. He prayed, and by the time, he stopped praying, a truck came along. We all loaded in the truck, and they carried us downtown. I got rid of them cards. I was not going to pray with cards in my hand. We played cards out there every time we got a chance. Since then, I never went back to Baytown."

Afterward, Clinton straggled to Sherman and stayed a stint with his brother Charley. While there, the military called Clinton to report to the U.S. Army. Mimicking Baytown, Clinton abruptly left and left a paycheck in Sherman, from another of his odd jobs. According to Clinton, "I was up for the examination, and they didn't even let me come back home; I had to catch a bus." Clinton was drafted into the U.S. Army during 1944 and discharged during 1947.

When asked for his wedding date, he stalled, but Clinton clearly remembered his length of military duty, saying, "I was in the 'service' two years, six months, and twenty-two days." Clinton appeared for basic training in New Orleans, Louisiana in preparation for his assignment to the South Pacific in the Philippines. Clinton arrived home on his first furlough, 03 June 1945 and left for California, on 11 June 1945. According to Clinton, "The morning they told me, I was up to go home, they said 'we got a charter plane back to the States.' I told them, you let that plane go ahead; I will catch the boat. I came home on a ship in 1947." Clinton never flew in an airplane; he obviously preferred ground transportation.

After Clinton returned home from the army, one winter was so cold that the car froze and would not start. Clinton's remedy was to set a fire under the car, explaining, "When ice gets under an automobile, you make a fire for it and warm it—that joker will crank."

After the army, Clinton visited places such as Sherman and Houston but eventually settled back home in Jefferson. During 1947, Clinton married his sweetheart for life at Rev. James "J. P." Patrick's home.

Through the years, Clinton worked as a self-employed farmer, a rubber plant laborer, and a Jefferson Independent School District employee. Clinton also kept the grounds and handled necessary maintenance at the Lewis Chapel Cemetery.

Upon seeing and talking with Clinton, seldom would he complain about any ailment, although high blood pressure, sinus/allergy problems, and emphysema greatly affected him. Instead at almost every meeting, Clinton brought much laughter, by telling stories such as the one about not having much money to buy gasoline. "I would save gas down hill; cut the key off and coast down hill; see way back when (well they cut out the hills now) way back we had red clay and steep hills."

Almost age 80 Clinton reached the end of his fate and passed away during 2003 at his home in Jefferson. The family held his funeral and laid Clinton to rest at Lewis Chapel Church and Cemetery, Jefferson.

Ester Weaver Sims Cole Hawkins

Charley and Carrie's youngest daughter came along when Charley was about age 45 and Carrie about age 40—no one dared call Ester a change of life baby. Oddly, just after Ester's early September birth, her paternal grandfather Berry died late that same September; and her aunt Nancy died that October, same year. Ester remembered never having a bicycle and never learning how to ride a bicycle, but that was about the only thing she did not have. Ester recalled being wealthy in all of the ways that mattered—church, family, friends, and God's love.

According to Ester growing up on the family farm is where she learned her first lessons about survival, sacrifice, and service. Her formal education began at Lewis Chapel Elementary through the ninth grade and Jefferson Central High through the tenth grade. Following her older sister Malinda, Ester took the train to Sherman, stayed with Malinda and completed high school at Fred Douglas, in Sherman. She was the first of her siblings to attend undergraduate college; at Wiley College in Marshall, Texas, she studied accounting and bookkeeping.

After Wiley, Ester returned to Sherman, continued staying with Sister Malinda and secured a job with the chain store called Three Sisters. The dress shop name, the income, and the work appealed to her. Ester dressed windows, sold merchandise, and handled receiving and shipping, which was in line with her accounting studies. Ester recalled from this experience to her last days, she could size a person at a distance.

The 1940s and 1950s found Ester married, divorced, re-married, and moved back and forth between Sherman and Fort Worth. This period solidified her pattern of dropping whatever she was doing and going to the aid of her siblings, when and where needed.

In Fort Worth for a season, Ester stayed with her Weaver uncles: Morris Wellington and Isaac "Ike" Gilham and their respective wives. Living together and helping each other, they all had the best of time spoiling one another with care, generosity, and food. Ester and her uncles loved fishing and the movie theaters. Her Weaver uncles taught her to drive an automobile, and her husband James Arthur Hawkins purchased Ester's first car. While in Fort Worth, Ester also helped her brother Charley, Jr. in operating his Mainline Office Supply business and helped in chartering their church—the Campus Drive UMC.

Ester and her lifelong partner James Arthur returned to Jefferson, building their home in the Union Community on approximately one acre of land as part of Weaver Estate, belonging to her mother, Carrie Jane Weaver Sims. Here, Ester perfected her cooking and award-winning baking skills in the vein of her mother Carrie, her sister Malinda, and her uncle Morris. Here, Ester greatly contributed to her church and community.

Ester survived her parents, each of her nine siblings, and both of her husbands. Years before her death, Ester signed a warranty deed, giving this book's author her interest in the Weaver Estate as well as bequeathing the author of this book her Jefferson home and land. However, another Sims relative disputed this author's ownership of the bequeathed house and one acre of land. Likewise, Ester transferred her interest in the Sims Estate to another niece who like this author helped care for their beloved aunt Ester doing her latter years.

At age 89 Ester reached the end of her fate and passed away, leaving a legacy of Christianity, pragmatism, strong work ethic, and a belief in the value of returning to the land and living off the land. The family laid Ester to rest at Lewis Chapel Cemetery.

***

Centenarian Hattie Mae Sims Hodge

Remarkably, Berry and Becky's youngest child lived until age 103, twenty days short of her 104th birthday. Her name was Hattie Mae—she was born just two days prior to the 1883 Ides of March in Lodi, fated to live and tell the family stories. Predictably, Hattie attended Lewis Chapel MC and the early Lewis Chapel School. Hattie grew to reach five feet four inches or so with very long and very dark colored hair, which did not seem to gray until she turned at least 100. Uncommonly for the times, Hattie did not marry until age 25. A Hodge relative, named Gussie Young, introduced Hattie of Lodi to Isom Hodge, Jr. of Linden after he had lost his first wife. Hattie married Isom during 1908 in Cass County, Texas, making their home and raising their children in Linden.

After Hattie and Isom married, they raised Isom's two sons from his previous marriage and eight children of their own. The growing Hodge household was always alive with activity—from farm life, Christian service, school lessons, sports, to homegrown entertainment, where everyone played a role. Their youngest child captured the early years in the Hodge household, located just beyond the Linden and Jefferson Highway.

"Our parents were Christians, hardworking people, caring, and always helping people. We grew up on the farm. It was never a dull day at our house. We all were active in church and school activity. Most of us were in sports during the winter months. We would sit around the fireplace at night eating peanuts and playing games. We made up plays, sang, and performed before our parents. We would put chairs in the living room for our other audience. We played with our dolls and cut out pictures from the catalogs. During summer months in the evening, we played games with our friends outside and ate watermelon.

Christmas time was big at our house. One Christmas just before Santa Clause was supposed to arrive, we sneaked a peek at what we had. We ate some of the candy; normally, we were supposed to eat the candy on Christmas day. After eating it beforehand, we did not have much candy left. Dad said to Mama, 'I bought more candy than that'. We just stood there looking sad. We never did that again.

We were never hungry. Some children ate three meals a day. We ate four. As soon as our parents' backs were turned, we would go out to the smokehouse and get some ham and to the henhouse, getting eggs to cook. Mama would tell us to leave one egg in the nest, so that the chick would know to lay more.

I remember the storms. Seems like they would come every night; we would have to get up and get dressed and head for the storm cellar. I hated that. We would put our clothes and shoes in a place so we could get them quickly if we had to get up and go."

Springtime was planting time on the family farm, and all of the children learned the value of tilling the soil—the land yielded the best comfort food with the highest nutrient value and the sweetest, mouth-watering fruit. Farm life was not all theatrics and Oscars and savory meals or sweet food, though—life on the farm had its rewards. The family worked hard, but the loving Hodge household made physically demanding work tolerable and expeditious.

Although Hattie made an abundant life in Linden with her husband, family, and on the family farm, Hattie periodically worked outside her home in a domestic capacity. However, Hattie's 1965 Social Security number application was stamped with the word, welfare.

Enriching her life, Hattie often attended the Sims Family Reunion as evidenced by oral history and the 1969 reunion sign-in sheet. Through the years, she maintained ties with her Lodi family—the Sims. Hattie helped pay property taxes on the Sims land and received applicable proceeds, per Carrie's journal entries. Further, Hattie named one of her brother's children in honor of herself—Hattie Mae. Her memories of her father, mother, and maternal grandmother remained strong, and many of these memories she shared with her youngest grandson.

Hattie united with the Linden Church of Christ during 1951. However, when her death occurred, she was affiliated with the Salem Missionary Baptist Church of Linden.

At age 103 Hattie reached the end of her fate and passed away at 8:30 in the morning at the Linden Municipal Hospital from profound dehydration; azotemia; and severe arteriolosclerosis. The family laid Hattie to rest at the Salem Cemetery, Linden, Cass County, Texas.

Clearly, Hattie and Isom conceived eight children. However, the birth order of the children remains guesswork, with contradictory public records and oral history. All eight of the children were born in Cass County, all attended Cass County public schools, and all received a strong Christian foundation. Hattie's deceased issue included:

- Zettie Mae Hodge
- Clarence Hodge
- Gertie Mae Hodge Singleton
- Ivory Pearl Hodge Sims Whaley
- Oscar Douglas Hodge
- Novelle Hodge Richardson Jackson
- Odelle Hodge Allen

CENTENARIAN HATTIE MAE SIMS HODGE FAMILY

Zettie Mae Hodge

Hattie's daughter Zettie Mae did not marry nor have any children of her own. Feasibly, Zettie worked occasionally and lightly as a domestic, and practiced her Christian faith, religiously being a friend to all.

At age 32 or 33 Zettie reached the end of her fate and passed away while at home from a debilitating paralysis, which confined her for about two years.

Clarence Hodge

Hattie's son Clarence married three times and fathered five children. Like his older sister Zettie, Clarence received his early education in the Linden schools and his Christian training at the Linden Sunrise Missionary Baptist Church. He lived in Dallas majority of adulthood and lived with a hearing deficiency. Clarence was a typical fun-loving Texan; he loved playing dominoes and watching baseball.

At age 92 Clarence reached the end of his fate and passed away. The family laid Clarence to rest at Salem Cemetery, Linden.

Gertie Mae Hodge Singleton

Hattie's daughter Gertie Mae—like her siblings Zettie and Clarence, she grew up in the Linden public school and the Sunrise Missionary Baptist Church. Gertie met her husband at a school dance, and during 1936, Gertie married Lester B. Singleton at the county courthouse. Through the years, they conceived seven children; of whom, six survived to adulthood.

As wife and mother and with very active roles in her church and community, Gertie did not work outside the home for income. She volunteered weekly for the Red Cross at the local Baptist hospital and participated in the pastor's aid club, mission board, Sunday school, and the deaconess board at Mount Olive Baptist Church. In Orange, Orange County, Texas, where they lived, Gertie created a scholarship fund for Mount Olive college-bound students. Gertie's constant encouragement to the youth involved the themes of praying, completing their education, and remaining in the Lord.

At age 77 Gertie reached the end of her fate and passed away. The family laid Gertie to rest at Magnolia Memorial Garden Cemetery.

Ivory Pearl Hodge Sims Whaley

Hattie's daughter—Ivory Pearl stood out in distinction. Taking the height of her father, she seemed to soar at five feet nine inches tall. Though Ivory inherited her mother's hair length, Ivory's hair was seemingly pure red and her skin, a light-tone. Those prone to musing would wonder whether her red hair somehow empowered Ivory.

Harebrained rabbits and even the snakes scurried for shelter upon encountering Ivory in the field. She was able to pick cotton and pull it in a 150 or 200-pound sack. While growing up and early in her marriage, Ivory worked on the family farm and in the home.

There, Ivory raised her ten children to be law-abiding, hardworking, self-sufficient, and to fear God. Ivory married twice. As a homemaker, Ivory made pillowcases, sheets, quilts, and clothes for the children. During the early years, the only items she bought from the store were flour, meal, and baking soda; the family planted everything else on the farm harvesting for consumption or for sale. At breakfast, food galore lined a twelve-foot table; typically Ivory prepared bacon, sausage, ham, grits, rice, eggs, and biscuits.

Eventually, the family moved to Greenville, Hunt County, Texas. From there, they moved onto Fontana, San Bernardino County, California. Occasionally, Ivory worked as a domestic in Greenville. After moving to California, Ivory scheduled an appointment for a physical examination with her physician, for insurance purposes.

Hearing the words, cervical cancer from her physician was even too much for Ivory's strong frame and will to bear. The anguish of cancer and all it involves prevented Ivory from having a peaceful death. At age 72 Ivory Pearl reached the end of her fate and passed away from cancer. The family laid Ivory to rest at Salem Cemetery, Linden, Cass County, Texas.

Oscar Douglas Hodge

Hattie's son Oscar Douglas, like his siblings received his foundation in the Linden public school and Sunrise Missionary Baptist Church. Oscar Douglas never married and fathered three children. Oscar lived and worked in Linden and Texarkana, Texas, the majority of adulthood.

At age 75 Oscar Douglas reached the end of his fate and passed away.

Novelle Hodge Richardson Jackson

Hattie's daughter Novelle married twice and conceived two children. Novelle lived in Linden, Dallas, and Denton, Denton County, Texas.

At age 71 Novelle reached the end of her fate and passed away.

Odelle Hodge Allen

Loved ones remembered Odelle best as loving her family, church, and community. Her life story is being told by her grandson and other family researchers.

Interestingly, Mother Hattie's youngest daughter, Odelle lived longer than each of her siblings. If science has identified a longevity gene, Odelle may have had it, as she too approached centenarian status. Amazingly, two of her first Sims cousins either approached or reached centenarian status: Rebecca (age 97) from Aunt Nancy's branch and Ima (age 100) from Uncle Charley's branch.

Made by love, Odelle was born during January of 1923. In love, Odelle married her beloved George Edward Allen during May of 1943. Consumed by love, Odelle gave birth to eight children. Surrounded by love, Odelle Hodge at age 95 reached the end of her fate and passed away during December of 2018. The family laid Odelle to rest at Salem Cemetery, Linden, Cass County, Texas.

***

Milus Sims

After Emancipation, some of the newly freed fled
bondage in search of lost loved ones. Others stayed in place,
forming families out of necessity rather than blood relations.

Possibly owing to the enumerator's error, Peter, Will
Ann, Berry, and Milus were found grouped together at 1870
census; presumably, they had resided in the Peter Perry
household for at least five years. They may have been
grouped because of blood relations or simply banded
together to survive. Berry and Milus could have been Peter's
nephews, given Peter behaved as their uncle or surrogate
father. Will Ann may have been their biological mother,
surrogate mother, or aunt. Peter Perry may have raised and
kept Berry and Milus relatively safe, as children; however, as
adults, they made a life for themselves.

At the start of adulthood, Milus and Berry trustingly
lived near each other and married around the same time.
Milus married Angeline (Angelina) Love during 1874.
Throughout 1880, Milus and Berry were neighbors, and
their proximity probably paved the way for their young
children to play together. Coincidentally, both Milus and
Berry had a child to die during the same year, perhaps
simultaneously. Berry's daughter Jane, and Milus' son,
Avenger died between 1879 and 1880.

Among the first acts of adulthood, Berry and Milus
dropped the Perry surname (as transcribed at the 1870
census), and they begin transacting business using the Sims
surname. The year, Berry fell behind on paying property
taxes; the tax collector wrote a note in the property tax
ledger that Berry's brother would pay the taxes due.

Beyond 1880, Milus and his descendants appeared in
the Cass County, Texas census records and land records.
However, Milus may have eventually moved back to the

Shreveport, Caddo Parish, Louisiana area, at least for a pace. Berry's eldest granddaughter Mattie supposedly contacted her uncle Milus upon moving to Louisiana.

Milus passed away around 1915, and the family laid Milus to rest in Cass County.

Milus' deceased children included:

- William "Willy" Sims
- Avenger Sims
- Maggie I. Eugenia Sims Chatman
- Silvestor / Silvestine Sims
- Alberta Sims Williams Collins
- Minnie C. Sims Gardner
- Goldie Sims Heath
- Ethel Sims Williams Hancock

End note: Oscar Perry's Affidavit of Heirship during April of 1920 presented Peter Perry and Will Ann as being married during or thereafter slavery without children. Berry Sims' eldest grandchild Ima could no longer remember Berry's mother nor reconcile his brother Milus Sims. However, the eldest Ima still had a memory of a half brother Phil Ross; whereas, family elders interviewed such as Johnny, Lafayette, Sr., and others remembered brother Milus and not the half brother Phil. Hopefully another family historian will explore the whereabouts of the Milus Sims descendants, finding a DNA connection.

THIS IS AN ACCOUNT OF THE SIMS FAMILY.
MAY THEIR STORIES BE REMEMBERED AND
SPIRITS HONORED.

And they assembled all the congregation together on the first day of the second month, and they declared their pedigrees after their families, by the house of their fathers, according to the number of the names, from twenty years old and upward, by their polls.

Numbers 1:18 KJV

BRANCH SIX

......

THE WALTON FAMILY TREE

Squire and Sarah Walton

WHEN SQUIRE AND SARAH WALTON APPEARED IN 1870 Marion County, Texas, Squire was age 60, born circa 1810 in Alabama, and working as a laborer. Sarah was age 45, born circa 1825 in Alabama, and keeping house. Squire and Sarah (Sallie) were not located at subsequent census records, beyond 1870. Whether Squire and Sarah came to Texas as free persons or as enslaved persons remains an open question, as do many, many aspects of their past. There is limited oral history to supplement the census accounting of Squire and Sarah Walton other than confirmations of their daughters:

- Rebecca
- Mary

At the 1870 census, Rebecca (age twelve) and her sister Mary (age four) were living at home with their parents Squire and Sarah. Rebecca Walton became Rebecca Walton Sims, and Mary Walton became Mary Walton Martin Lucky. See their entries at the Sims Family and the Martin Family, respectively.

Probably Squire had already died by the time Hattie Mae Sims Hodge was born 1883; because, Hattie left no oral history regarding Squire.

However, Hattie passed along one story pertaining to Sarah (Sallie) though. When Hattie was a little girl, between the ages of five and seven, she walked to her grandmother's home to collect a bundle of coal for a neighbor, so the neighbor could use the bundle as fireplace kindling. Hattie commented to her grandmother that she did not have anything in which to carry the coal, and she did not want the coal to burn her. Grandmother Sarah (Sallie) told Hattie not to worry that she would show her how to scoop the coal into her arms without it burning her. Hattie also recalled that Grandmother Sarah (Sallie) wondered aloud about their old homestead and people in Georgia or Alabama.

Squire and Sarah (Salllie) Walton reached the end of their fate and passed away.

Theoretically, Squire and Sarah Walton, Rebecca and Mary's parents, came to Texas as slaves with either of their immediate 1870 neighbors. Hopefully another intrigued descendant will explore and develop their history.

In may be interesting to note that Squire and Sarah's immediate neighbors at the 1870 Marion County, Texas census were Ann Virginia Allen Ward Bynum and James D. Todd. Ann Virginia was also from Alabama and the daughter of William K. Allen, a Texas land mogul from Tennessee. By 1860, Ann Virginia had married Robert H. Ward, a farmer and attorney from Alabama. At Robert's death, Ann Virginia inherited real and personal property, from Robert. By 1870, Ann Virginia had married Alfred (Alford) L. Bynum, another farmer. Also, a Black domestic servant was plainly working in the 1870 Bynum household. The Ward lineage and the Todd lineage were both slaveholding families in Marion County, Texas. Whereas, the Ward family came to Texas circa 1847, James D. Todd was an earlier Texas settler, merchant, and railroad financier from Georgia.

THIS IS AN ACCOUNT OF THE WALTON FAMILY.
MAY THEIR STORIES BE REMEMBERED AND
SPIRITS HONORED.

His seed shall be mighty up earth: the generation of the upright shall be blessed.

Psalm 112:2 KJV

BRANCH SEVEN

. . . .

THE WEAVER FAMILY TREE

Robert "Bob" and Ann Weaver

REGARDING ROBERT "BOB" WEAVER'S BEGINNINGS, ROBERT WAS plausibly related to a Lee family from Tennessee. A woman by the name of Lettie Lee was enumerated with Ann and Robert at the 1880 Marion County, Texas census. Lettie was labeled as being Robert's mother and age 90. Through connection or coincidence, Charles Lee and his family were living next door to Robert and his wife Ann at the 1870 census. Robert's neighbors at the 1870 census such as Charles Lee and Peggy Weaver were also listed as being from Tennessee.

Public record documentation bears out that Ann and Robert "Bob" Weaver became a family unit who lived in Marion County, Texas. Ann and Robert conceived thirteen children. Although, by 1900, only seven children had survived. The given names of Ann and Robert's children included:

- Thomas
- Ducas

- Jake
- William
- Robert
- Grandison W.
- Richard
- Sallie (Sarah)
- Mary
- Caroline
- Adaline M.

The matriarch Ann Weaver was possibly born during the 1820s or the 1840s in Tennessee or Missouri. Robert Weaver was born during either 1812 or 1823 in Tennessee. Judging their reported ages, both Ann and Robert were slaves; whether Ann and Robert migrated to Texas as enslaved or as free persons is unknown.

As newly freed persons, Ann and Robert initially lived between the scions of the Locketts and Nance families; in view of their proximity to these two former slaveholding families, Ann and Robert probably entered sharecropping or tenant farming agreements with either of these two families, post-Emancipation

Throughout 1880, Ann and Robert feasibly worked for landowner Ann Virginia Allen Ward Bynum who lived nearby. Though Robert and Ann worked the land as laborers, no evidence surfaced indicating that they purchased land. Perhaps vestiges of the slave system prevented Ann and Robert from actually owning Texas land. Instead, post-1880 Ann paid property taxes on a few cattle and a mule.

Robert probably died prior to the 1900 census. By this time, Ann was a widow, living side by side to her sister Minerva Lewis in a narrow, wooden shotgun house behind Grandison and Malinda Norris Weaver's home. Ann had moved into her son Grandison's home by 1910.

244

However at least three months before Ann's death, she was perhaps living with or visiting another son in McLennan County, Texas; because, that is where she died on 04 March 1913. Within a few days, a train to Jefferson transported Ann's body, and the family held her funeral at Union Chapel with Rev. C. S. Williams offering the eulogy. An anonymous friend generated the death notice that appeared in the *Jimplecute*; the local newspaper tribute described Ann as a Christian who believed in God's love and proclaimed that the Union community loved Ann in return.

Somewhere between ages 73 and 93 Ann reached the end of her fate and passed away from pneumonia during 1913. The family laid Ann to rest at Union Chapel Cemetery.

Thomas, Ducas, Jake, William, and Robert, Jr.

The Marion County, Texas early census records only provided names for eleven of Ann and Robert's thirteen children, and far too scant oral history survived regarding the lives of five of their sons:

- Son Thomas could have been born in Texas either 1843 or 1860 and was a laborer.

- Son Ducas was born circa 1858 in Texas.

- Son Jake was born during 1878 in Marion County. His name appeared on several land transactions during the late 1800s. A photograph of Jake also survived, and he stayed with his mother during 1900.

- Son William was born circa 1878 in Texas.

- Son Robert, Jr. was born circa 1880 in Texas.

Sons Thomas, Ducas, William, and Robert, Jr.—all hypothetically died either tilling the soil, hanging by a rope, or from illness. Beyond the early census, there was nil accounting of their lives.

Mary and Caroline

Likewise, little is known about Ann and Robert's daughters Mary and Caroline.

- Mary was born either 1867 or 1868 in Texas. Possibly Mary married James Green, as provided by a county marriage record. Gravesites for a Mary Green and a James L. Green are located at the Lewis Chapel Cemetery.

- Daughter Caroline could have been born during 1873 in Texas and could have been the Weaver daughter that married Robert Ford and moved to Lamar County, Texas. The 1920 and 1930 Lamar County, Texas census records do provide for a Carrie Ford as wife to a Robert Ford.

Grandison W., Richard, Sallie (Sarah), Adaline M.

However, regarding Ann and Robert's remaining four children—two sons and two daughters, much oral history and many public records sources survived the journey between then and now. See below the section headings and sketches, illuminating the lives of their children: Grandison W., Richard, Sallie (Sarah), and Adaline M. Weaver.

Grandison W. Weaver and Malinda Norris Weaver

Ann and Robert's son Grandison W. Weaver was born between 1860 and 1866 in Texas. Early in life, he worked as a laborer who later became a farmer. Grandison exchanged wedding vows with Malinda Norris Weaver during 1887 in Jefferson, and John Jackson pronounced them husband and wife. Immediately, Grandison and Malinda started their family; conceived twelve children; and lived in Jefferson their entire lives. Malinda was wife, mother, and homemaker. Grandison and Malinda named their children:

- Carrie Jane Weaver Sims
- Henry Lee Weaver—named in honor of the Lee relatives.
- Richard McCallihan Weaver, Rev.
- Grandison "Grant" W. Weaver, Jr.
- Milton Weaver
- Eula V. Weaver Rice
- June Weaver
- Curtis Shedwell Weaver, Rev.
- Isaac "Ike" Gilham Weaver
- Spencer Weaver
- Otis Weaver
- Morris Wellington Weaver

A story that survived the generations involved Grandison's land acquisition. Reportedly, Grandison woke early one morning, heeding the early bird catches the worm adage, hitched the mule to the wagon, and rode to town. Before anyone else was the wiser or could stop him, Grandison had bravely purchased enough land for a family farm and home.

One might wonder whether Grandison experienced a
vicarious triumph from his land purchase, considering he was
likely purchasing land his father had previously worked as a
laborer. During October of 1899, Grandison purchased
approximately 61 acres of land, a portion of the William K.
Allen Head Right Survey from the heirs of Ann Virginia Allen
Ward Bynum with Sylvanus Grady Echols as agent. The
patch of land cost $40.00 cash with $82.00 due on 01
November 1900, at 10 percent interest. Amazingly,
Grandison paid this note on 24 November 1900, according to
his bankers, T. J. Rogers and Sons. Grandison and Malinda
owned their farm at the 1910 Marion County census. The
family farmed the land, growing produce for profit and
consumption; they had horses, mules, cows, pigs, chickens,
and various trees including pear, peach, mulberry, and fig.

Although Malinda lived a distance away in the Union
community, her Norris family who primarily lived in the
Valley Plain and Kellyville communities, did not abandon
Malinda, as her father Richard had. Occasionally on Sundays,
Sam (her nephew) and his wife Maggie would visit Malinda,
bringing food and the children. Often, Daughter Carrie Jane
Weaver Sims and a few of her children accompanied the
Norrises for Sunday family gatherings at Malinda's home.
Some of Joseph Smith's nieces (Joe married Patsey Norris) also
visited Malinda, often staying for weeks at a time. The Smith
nieces affectionately nicknamed Malinda, Aunt Babe.
Invariably, the nieces climbed the mulberry trees in Malinda's
yard, and the mulberries stained their clothes. Without
exception, Malinda would chastise the playful nieces. Malinda
would call the grandchildren, nieces, and nephews endearing
terms such as, baby and sugar, until they misbehaved. At the
point of disobedience, she would straighten out the willful.

Malinda spent countless hours on her feet in her
kitchen cooking and baking for her family without a thought

about herself. Undisputedly, Malinda made the best biscuits. Anyone approaching her home would smell the fresh baked biscuits even from a distance, as the fresh-baked scent permeated the air. Malinda's biscuits were light, fluffy, easy to pull apart, and best served with a glass of buttermilk and pear preserves. Every crumb of Malinda's T-cakes were delicious, even to the finicky.

Sampling her own kitchen creations, Malinda came to be on the heavy side as an adult. She inherited smooth, soft brown skin, and she stood approximately five feet ten inches, rising nearly two inches taller than Grandison.

Weaver family sentiment described the Weavers, in general, as ungenerous. Considering the difficulty in their initial land acquisitions and Malinda's abandonment as a child, perhaps a tight rein philosophy and practices were understandable.

Grandison was generous where it mattered. He worked from sunup to sundown for his family—farming to feed the family, but he refused to share his favorite snack of nuts and fruit even with the grandchildren who would sit and watch him enjoy every morsel. If any of the little ones dared to ask Grandison to share his snack, he would affectionally and guiltily reply, "Get out of here." Providing food for the table was a different matter—one in which Grandison and Malinda worked in tandem. Grandison provided the sustenance from the land, and Malinda prepared ample to spread along the table.

Though Grandison always wore overalls when farming, he came to the table immaculately clean and neatly dressed. Grandison smoked a corncob pipe, using his homegrown tobacco that he labeled, daddy bush. Sometimes, Grandison spat his tobacco into a spittoon; otherwise, he impressed the young grandchildren by jetting the tobacco across the yard, indelibly hitting a mark.

As Malinda and Grandison aged and could no longer farm, they periodically received income from gas and oil leases such as in 1925 and 1930.

At age 67 Malinda she reached the end of her fate and passed away during February of 1937, in Jefferson from influenza and endocarditis. Son Morris and Daughter Eula helped care for their father Grandison after Mother Malinda's death. About a year or so later around age 75 Grandison reached the end of his fate and passed away at home. At their deaths, the family certainly wept and mourned.

Carrie Jane Weaver Sims

Carrie Jane Weaver was the eldest child of Malinda and Grandison; she was born during their first year of marriage. Carrie favored her mother Malinda in appearance and grew to become a five feet five inches—shorter than her mother and 135-pound—smaller frame than her mother. Carrie was full of intelligence, love, and twinkling eyes. Around age 19 Carrie married Charley Edward Sims, Sr. See Carrie Jane Weaver Sims' entry at the Sims Family.

Henry Lee Weaver

From the stories shared regarding Henry Lee Weaver, Malinda and Grandison's first son, one could conclude that Henry Lee had a mean spirit. His sister Carrie wrote these words in her journal: "Henry Weaver took $3.00 out of all the Weaver heirs' mineral check, May 1958. He forged his sister Carrie's name in order to take out the $3.00 of her money, and he will not give it up. May this be remembered for Henry Weaver." None of Henry's nicknames: Buddy, smart Negro, or Jack (because of his one peg leg), were said in an affectionate manner. Henry owned a car when others did not. Reportedly, he would drive pass someone walking and not offer that person a ride even though he was going to that person's house. Henry was intentionally mean to his sister Eula and her children (Verna and Edgar) when they returned to Jefferson, from Arkansas and moved into the home of their ailing father Grandison. On another memorable occasion, Henry became furious with his brother Spencer and purposefully cut down the pear tree, preventing Spencer from picking the pears from the tree.

Others described Henry Weaver, saying his name was his currency. Others described his appearance as a dark, Black man with gold crowns on his teeth, smooth skin who always dressed neatly. Henry was an industrious man who worked a variety of jobs, often two at a time. He wrote and sold insurance. Years earlier, Henry fell from his horse and broke his leg. Despite this trauma, he believably accomplished more work with one poorly functioning leg than the average person did with two properly functioning legs. Henry finagled land leases, both writing and buying them; dealt in timber; and hewed crossties with an axe. Working from sunup to sundown, he made approximately twenty to thirty crossties a day. Later, he sold the crossties in town. Additionally, Henry farmed the land and worked on the railroad. He was dependable and a responsible man who served as the informant at his mother's death certificate and signed the birth certificate of his younger brother Isaac "Ike".

Though Henry was most industrious as evident by community sentiment and mean spirited according to a few family members, he had his pride. Throughout the 1950s, Henry worked for McDonald Lumber Company, Batson, Hardin County, Texas. A particular payday after work, Henry stood tall and proud, talking on the sidewalk in town while a co-worker went inside to obtain their pay. The co-worker returned and grew impatient to tell Henry that he had received the pay and was ready to leave. Henry became irritated at the interruption, as he had been trying to carry an impressive conversation with another member of the upper crust. In response, Henry replied, "it is yours, you keep it," meaning the pay.

He lived comfortably and owned a beautiful home. Henry positioned his home between his father's home and his uncle, Richard Weaver's home, just off Thompson Camp Road.

Henry Lee Weaver was born during October of 1889 in Jefferson. During the 1916 Christmas season, Henry married Edith Smith in Jefferson; they conceived one daughter who passed very young during September of 1917. During January of 1920, Edith passed in Jefferson from pneumonia. Four years and six months later, Henry married Edith's sister Betty Smith in Jefferson. Henry and Betty did not have any children.

At age 79 Henry reached the end of his fate and passed away during February of 1969. The family laid Henry to rest at Union Chapel Cemetery.

Rev. Richard McCallihan Weaver

Malinda and Grandison's second son became a Methodist minister. Rev. Richard McCallihan Weaver was born during 1892 at the Weaver home in Jefferson. Family friend Jennie V. Gilham later certified as to Richard's birth. In tandem with Henry Lee, Richard worked on the home farm. Between farming and marriage, Richard was drafted into the U.S. Army during WWI.

After returning home from wartime military service, Richard married Verna Burns. Richard and Verna married on 01 January 1920, the day Henry's first wife died and the month of Richard's birth. At the start of Richard and Verna's marriage, they lived a year or two in Jefferson before moving onto El Paso, Texas, staying there for five years. Then, they returned to Jefferson before relocating to Fort Worth. There, they stayed until 1938. During the 1930s, Richard worked on the Texas and Pacific Railroad as a laborer, which took him among places such as Marshall, El Paso, and Fort Worth, Texas.

Also after Richard's Europe infantry days in France, he worked for the railroad and continued to buy French bread every two weeks on payday. Richard and Verna's four children looked forward to their payday meal of fried catfish, with a complete compliment of side dishes, plus treats of orange slice candy and fresh bananas. After their meals, the family spent enjoyable evenings storytelling.

Richard was one of the first in their Fort Worth community to buy a car, a Model T Ford. Though Richard always purchased the best of everything, he valued his family above all else.

Richard was called to the Christian ministry during 1937, which he faithfully served in the West Texas Conference for twelve years. Throughout 1942, the family resided at 5627 Fletcher, Fort Worth. During 1949, Richard was transferred to the Texas Conference, where he served until his death. As a Texas Methodist Church minister, Rev. Richard Weaver was also a pastor of the Saint James UMC in Sherman.

The U.S. Army took a medium height, medium build, twenty-five years of age, dark brown eyed, and black haired farmer, exposed him to the horrors of war, and sent him home eighteen months later with an honorable discharge and his life. Fortunately, for all whom Richard touched and lead to Christ, he made the world a better place with dignity and mercy.

At age 61 the Reverend and Private Richard McCallihan Weaver reached the end of his fate and passed away during 1961 from a heart attack while at his home. The family laid Rev. Weaver to rest at Union Chapel Cemetery.

Richard and Verna were proud parents of:

- Aaron Weaver
- Willie Mae Weaver Walton
- Ethel Raye Weaver Davis
- Walter Weaver

Grandison "Grant" W. Weaver, Jr.

Grandison, Jr. or Grant W. was born during 1894 in Jefferson. Conforming to the norm, Grant worked on the home farm, as a young person and married during the month of his birth, January. Perhaps family, not finding the right person, or financial obligations tied Grant to the land longer than his siblings, as he did not marry until around age 30.

After Grant married Olivia (Doll) Ross, they stayed with family friend Jennie V. Gilham for a stint in Jefferson. Courageously refusing to accept the life handed down to him, Grant and Olivia relocated to Chicago, Cook County, Illinois, to start anew in an industrial city.

By 1937, the family was residing at 3809 South Wabash Avenue in Chicago, and Grant was working at 600 West Forty-first Street, Chicago for American Smelting and Refining Company. Throughout the 1950s, Grant resided at 4215 Langley Avenue, Second Floor, Chicago, where he likely resided until death.

As a free-willed adult, Grant converted from Methodism to the Church of God in Christ denomination and faithfully served as deacon, trustee, and Sunday school teacher.

For unknown reasons, Grant only returned once to Jefferson, for a visit. However, Grant maintained communications with at least his brother Isaac, as Isaac attended Grant's funeral.

The first week of November 1968, at age 74 Grant reached the end of his fate and passed away in Chicago. The family laid Grant to rest at Lincoln Cemetery.

Milton Weaver

Grandison and Malinda's third son was also born during January, keeping pace with the previous two. Milton Weaver was born during 1896 in Texas. Milton labored on the family farm but not for long. Baseball was his passion. He loved to play baseball and played at every opportunity on any of the three community teams.

Milton served in the military during WWI as a private in the 368th Infantry Division. During 1919, Milton married Bessie Dixon. Bessie owned a big rooming house, where she raised her sisters after her mother's death and accepted boarders, in their home. The income from the boarders helped them earn means to survive. The boardinghouse stood across the street from a sewer pipe company located on Phennie Avenue in Texarkana. Bessie cooked for the household and sold dinners to the men who worked for the company. Milton and Bessie resided at the boardinghouse.

After Milton contracted tuberculosis, he returned to Jefferson. At age 25 Milton reached the end of his fate and passed away during 1921 from T.B. as pronounced by Dr. J. W. Peebles. The family laid Milton to rest at Union Chapel Cemetery.

Eula V. Weaver Rice

Grandison and Malinda's second daughter Eula V. was born on Valentine's Day in Jefferson. She too worked on the family farm. At some point, Eula married Edgar Lorenzo "Love" Rice, Jr. in Jefferson. Eula was a pretty woman and Edgar, a handsome man. They began married life in the Union community and conceived two children, one a beauty queen Verna Mae Rice Sedberry Warren and the other a fine-looking son Edgar Lorenzo Rice, III.

The decision was made to move to Little Rock, Pulaski County, Arkansas, for a better way of life. Edgar ventured to Little Rock alone. After finding a suitable home and employment, he then returned for the family. Edgar drove a wagon from Jefferson to Little Rock, and the ferry took the wagon, mules, and family across the Red River.

Around 1939, Edgar remained in Little Rock while the family returned to Jefferson. Eula worked as a maid at the Excelsior Hotel in Jefferson, during the 1940s. Upon the return of Eula and the children from Arkansas, older brother Henry was very cruel to his younger sister. Eula and the children stayed with Eula's father Grandison throughout his illness and until his death.

Later, Eula and her family lived in Rice Bottom, aka the boon docks or the river bottom, before moving to Thompson Camp Road in Jefferson. Eula made the Richard Weaver Estate her last home, from where she served her church, community, and family.

At age 73 Eula reached the end of her fate and passed away during 1971. The family laid Eula to rest at Union Chapel Cemetery.

Verna Mae Rice Sedberry Warren

Eula's beautiful daughter Verna Mae was born 01
September 1922 in Little Rock. Verna, like her mother Eula,
was surrounded by men the majority of her life. She married
twice; conceived two sons; and had at least ten uncles. Verna
inherited her big, beautiful eyes and long eyelashes from her
father; she even won a beauty pageant while attending college.
Verna received her high school diploma from Central High in
Jefferson; a B.S. in Home Economics from Prairie View A and
M University, Waller County, Texas during May of 1943; and
a Masters in Social Work from University of Southern
California. Before pursuing her graduate degree, Verna
worked several years as an educator in Texas.

During the 1940s, Verna and her second husband
moved to Los Angeles County, California, where she faithfully
worked for thirty years as a social worker. Upon retirement,
Verna surrounded herself with beautiful flowers; she opened,
owned, and operated Flower Things, a flower shop, which
became Verna's garden of heaven on earth.

With deep religious convictions, Verna remained
faithful to the Methodist Church and ministries in Texas and
California. Verna participated in other civic organizations
such as the National Association of University Women and
Prairie View Alumni Association. Often, she traveled back to
Prairie View for the class reunions.

A few months before her 73rd birthday Verna reached
the end of her fate and passed away the Fourth of July 1995.
The family laid Verna to rest at Inglewood Park Cemetery,
Inglewood, Los Angeles County, California.

June Weaver

Grandison and Malinda's son, June was born circa 1901 in Texas. He attended school throughout 1919 and mostly worked on the home farm during his early years. For a stint, June worked in Marshall for Cousins George and Mattie Lewis; they paid him 12 ½ cents by the row of cotton. Later, June drifted to Sherman and stayed with Cousin Sallie (Sarah) Weaver White Vaughn. June was in Fort Worth during the 1950s, working at the Army Depot and staying with his brother Isaac "Ike" Gilham Weaver.

All of sudden, June Weaver disappeared. Carrie placed an ad in a newspaper in an effort to find her brother June. Except for one story, he was never heard of again. According to Isaac, June Weaver settled in Oklahoma, changed his name, and owned or worked on a horse ranch. Could June have worked on the famous Ranch 101? Supposedly, June made sufficient income from the horse ranch, enough to cover expenses for a return trip to Texas. But June never returned. As often as June's ministering brothers traveled the Texas Methodist Church circuits, seemingly, someone ought to have heard something else. No one is truly certain as to why June left Texas or when or which direction the wind took June or what was his fate.

Rev. Curtis Shedwell Weaver

Rev. Dr. Curtis Shedwell Weaver was born during 1902 in Jefferson to Grandison and Malinda. Curtis attended school during 1919 and worked on the home farm with his brother June. Curtis graduated from Central High School with a diploma during 1924 and later graduated from Wiley College of Marshall, Harrison County, Texas. Curtis furthered his theological training and higher education at

Clark University, Gammon Theological Seminary, and Clark Interdenominational Theological Center, Atlanta, Fulton County, Georgia. After a six-year period, he received his A.B. and B.D. degrees during 1949.

The Texas Methodist Church Conference granted Curtis his local ministerial license, and he began serving as a supply pastor in the Texas Annual Conference of the MEC (later to become the Texas Conference of the Central Jurisdiction of the Methodist Church). The conference admitted him for a trial basis on 25 October 1936 and admitted him with full connections in the Texas Conference during 1940. The conference ordained him an elder during 1942. Throughout his thirty-six-year ministry, the Reverend Doctor Curtis Weaver served numerous circuits and churches in both pastoral and superintendent appointed positions. Coincidentally, he was the district superintendent of Lewis Chapel MC when it burned Sunday morning of 06 May 1956. After thirty-eight years, he was granted the retired relation status on 28 May 1975. Though retired, he continued religiously serving as pastor for another ten years. Rev. Weaver's orotund voice and genuine benevolence led countless souls to Christ.

Rev. Dr. Curtis Weaver was also trustee-emeritus of Wiley College, serving on many boards and conference committees. Similarly, he was a member of Greenleaf Masonic Lodge, number 147.

Curtis married Patsey Charleston Jones, and they conceived one son Curtis Martin who developed into a commercial artist. Though the family traveled throughout Texas, Houston remained their home.

Around age 90 Rev. Weaver reached the end of his fate and passed away. The family trio was laid to rest at Paradise North Cemetery, Houston, Harris County, Texas.

Curtis Martin Weaver, Jr.

Curtis their artistic son was born during June, married during June, and died in the January cold. Curtis received his early education at a one-room school in the Union community. Following his parents, Curtis continued primary and secondary school education in Angleton, Brazoria County, Texas and Huntsville, Walker County, Texas. For a stint during 1943, young Curtis worked for Ivan Hudspeth in Huntsville, Texas. Curtis followed his parents to Georgia and concentrated on higher education at Clark College in Atlanta, Georgia and later Howard University in Washington, D.C.

Curtis' college years were interrupted, as he was drafted into the U.S. Army. After serving his country a few years, Curtis received an honorable discharged and returned to the U.S. During the mid-1940s, Curtis drove a taxicab in Atlanta, Georgia, but commercial art was his passion, pride, and primary income. Later he found employment as a commercial artist with a Texas gas company. Besides painting, Curtis sang and wrote poems.

Curtis' battle with adult onset lupus prevented him from consistently pursuing his passion and leading a full life. Though Curtis was very intelligent and gifted, he became despondent with the disease, drifting between Connecticut and Texas, between sickness and health. Lupus shortened the life of a six-foot one inch tall, skinny, dark brown man known as the artist.

Around age 50 Curtis reached the end of his fate and passed away. The family laid Curtis to rest at Paradise North Cemetery, Houston, Harris County, Texas.

Isaac "Ike" Gilham Weaver

Grandison and Malinda's son Isaac Gilham Weaver was affectionately called "Ike" or "I. G." and named in honor of Jennie V. Gilham's husband I. G. Isaac too was born during a January in Jefferson. Though he worked on the farm, his parents ensured Isaac attended elementary and high school. Growing up, Isaac naturally dated, and around the age of consent, Isaac and girlfriend Izora Luster conceived a daughter they named Earline. Early in life, Isaac left Jefferson. He too stayed with Cousin Sallie in Sherman, staying until he was ready to venture out on his own, making his own way.

Isaac became a maintenance man. For years, he worked repairing or rebuilding appliances and automobiles in Fort Worth. If Isaac was not working, he was hunting with his two hound dogs. If he was not working or hunting, Isaac was chauffeuring his extended houseguests to church or the drive-in movie theater in his 1950s Buick. The three bedrooms of Isaac's 1950s house were huge, accommodating several beds, pallets, and plenty of guests. Throughout the 1950s and 1960s, Isaac resided on Terrell Street, and he became the Cousin Sallie of Fort Worth for the multitude of Norris, Sims, and Weaver family members. Throughout the early to mid-1970s, Isaac's home and business were at the same location on Marion.

Isaac married twice—first to Hattie Ella Corsey in Sherman, Grayson County, Texas. The second marriage occurred when Isaac was age 70; Isaac married Etta Mae McKie Yeldell in Fort Worth. After his second marriage, Isaac made his home and business at the Dunlap address.

Surviving his only daughter and grandson, at age 91 Isaac reached the end of his fate and passed away during 1995 from stomach cancer. The family laid Isaac to rest at Cedar

Hill Memorial Park Cemetery, Arlington, Tarrant County, Texas.

Earline Weaver Donelson

Earline was Isaac Gilham Weaver's only child. At an early age, Earline moved to Louisiana. There, she studied beauty culture at Alexander Beauty School; earned a beautician's license; and worked for Montgomery Ward for fifteen years.

During the 1950s, Earline moved to Chicago. Imitating her father, Earline went into business for herself, establishing a beauty and hair business in Chicago. During 1957, she opened her own shop located at 1240 South Christiana on the West Side of Chicago. Later, she moved her business to the South Side at 6319 South Racine.

Earline married a Donelson and conceived one son who preceded her in death. During 1968, when Grant passed in Chicago, Isaac attended his brother's funeral and surely visited with his daughter Earline.

At age 64 Earline Weaver Donelson reached the end of her fate and passed away during 1987 at Saint Bernard Hospital, Chicago. Coincidentally, like her uncle Grant Weaver, Earline was laid to rest at Lincoln Cemetery.

Spencer Weaver and Otis Weaver

Grandison and Malinda finally conceived children (a set of twins) who were born during a month other than January. They named their twins Otis and Spencer. Unfortunately, Otis did not survive. Otis' death led Malinda to be over protective of Spencer. Malinda initially thought and behaved as though Spencer was weak. As a result, everyone petted and doted on Spencer. Possibly Spencer was

262

puny and petite for a young boy, but he clearly developed a loud mouth with a strong propensity for foul language. With his treasure chest of memory, he could tell an enthralling story.

Spencer was not too frail to work on the family farm nor too sickly to attend school as an adolescent. He grew up modeling the boys of his day, interested in appearing sharp. He kept his hair edged high in the back. At night, he placed a stocking cap on his head, greasing the way for the appearance of slick hair on the next day.

Mirroring his uncle Henry Weaver, Spencer too had his share of false pride. Years ago, a person hired Spencer to repair the fence along the highway. Spence did not want anyone to know he was working, so whenever anyone passed, Spencer foolhardily placed his hand in his pocket as though he was not working. Through the years, Spencer took odd jobs, yet always adequately providing provisions for his family.

Emulating his brothers, Spencer married during his birth month. Spencer married Murrie Greenwood during the 1930s with Rev. James A. Johnson officiating. The couple conceived one son Clarence Edward Weaver. Spencer was born, married, and died in Marion County.

After all was said and done, Spencer was proven strong—around age 80 Spencer reached the end of his fate and passed away. The family laid Spencer to rest at Union Chapel Cemetery.

Morris Wellington Weaver

At some point, Grandison and Malinda's youngest child Morris Wellington Weaver learned to cook and especially bake. Maybe Morris learned a thing or two about cooking maybe from his mother—someone had to cook for his father after the 1937 death of his mother Malinda. Morris attended the Marion County, Texas public schools and Prairie View A and M University, Texas.

After college and after the death of Morris' father during 1938 or 1939, Morris moved to Fort Worth and probably initially stayed with his brother Isaac. Ike's Fort Worth home became a safe haven for boarders, until they were able to live independently, just like Sallie's home had been in Sherman. In Fort Worth, Morris met and married Willie Mae Gaines.

During WWII, Morris was inducted into the military from Fort Worth and later honorably discharged as a private first class. He probably perfected his cooking craft during his military days if culinary arts and science was his military occupational specialty (MOS).

Reasonably, Morris could have been assigned to one of the army bases in Colorado. After Morris' honorable discharge from the military, he worked at Star Baking Company in Colorado Springs, El Paso County, Colorado. Or, Morris possibly relocated to Colorado, heeding the example set by Cousin Inez Weaver Reeves. Inez had attended the University of Denver in Denver, Colorado.

After Colorado, Morris returned to Fort Worth and became an instructor at the Lone Star Cooking and Baking School. Fort Worth was his home away from home, whether residing on Humbolt or East Mulkey Street.

While Morris was among his family, he felt truly at home and was happiest. Morris often visited his sister Carrie, staying the weekend whenever there was a family gathering. He contributed jubilance to the family gatherings by baking and entertaining the family with his dancing. Morris had a fishing boat and a 1939 small Ford car, both of which he kept shiny, clean, and in working order. When Morris turned the corner, driving his car, it appeared as though he was riding on two wheels.

Around age 66 Morris reached the end of his fate and passed away in Fort Worth during the January cold of 1978. The family laid Morris to rest at Cedar Hill Memorial Park, Cemetery, space one, Arlington, Tarrant County, Texas.

Richard Weaver, Sr.

Ann and Robert's son Richard Weaver, Sr. was born between 1869 and 1874 in Texas with 1870 being the most frequently supplied birth year. Richard married Mary Lee Etta Williams during the 1895 Christmas season with A. J. Singleton officiating. The couple conceived seven children but only five survived to maturity:

- Inez Weaver Reeves
- Asa "Acie" Weaver
- Jesse Weaver
- Richard Weaver, Jr.
- Sallie Gray Weaver Green Hill

Richard's home was located just above his brother Grandison's home; in fact, they shared the same 40 acres of land until 1917 when they peacefully partitioned the property, both taking 20 acres each. Initially, they purchased the 40 acres from Walter P. Schluter during 1913.

Around age 83 Richard who was born and bred a Marion County farmer reached the end of his fate and passed away. Dr. R. D. Douglas labeled apoplexy as the primary cause of Richard's death. The family held Richard's funeral on 15 September 1944 at Union Chapel with Rev. Albert Louis Gabriel officiating and laid Richard to rest at Union Chapel Cemetery.

Inez Weaver Reeves

Richard and Mary named their first born Inez. She surely stood up to the responsibility of being the eldest child! Jefferson may have been her birthplace; in other respects, the classroom and the roadways were her homes. She graduated from Central High School in Jefferson; earned her B.S. from Prairie View A and M University, Texas; and attended graduate school at Wiley College of Marshall, Texas; Tuskegee Institute (now University), Alabama; and the University of Denver, Colorado.

Inez traveled Texas, the mid-West, and the South, teaching and endorsing the importance of education. Inez taught school for thirty-seven years in the Marion, Bastrop, Cass, and Titus counties of Texas.

In Jefferson, Inez taught at a two-teacher school—one teacher for grades one through four and another teacher for grades five through eight. She did not teach because of the salary; the pay was not any more money than a man made from cutting crossties.

Additionally during the Depression, Inez was the can supervisor, for a governmental program providing communities with food. In a building between the church and school was a processing and distribution factory, of sorts. The factory staff or workers killed calves for canning; they also canned fruits; and pressure-cooked other foods. Inez was responsible for distributing equal food portions to families.

Inez was most concerned about lifting others as she climbed and truly valued her family and education. No matter where she traveled, promoting education, Inez tried to attend the Sims Family Reunion. Inez was an independent woman, ahead of her time, really. She married later in life and bore no natural children. However, Inez raised one nephew in Mount Pleasant, Titus County, Texas.

Inez was a member of the Urissia Christian District Club, Texas Colored Federation Club, and the National Federation of Colored Women. She sponsored the Phyllis Wheatley Girls Club and was a member of the OES, chapter number 236. Inez's warm smile portrayed her naturally caring character, though the (now démodé/passé) gold crowns on some of her teeth tarnished the image. Inez had equal portions of gracefulness, height, and a heavy voice. Her hair was cut short in the back and curly on the top or in the front.

Around age 89 Inez reached the end of her fate and passed away September 1985. Out of community statute and respectfulness, her death notice appeared in the local weekly newspaper. The family laid Inez to rest at Union Chapel Cemetery.

Asa "Acie", Jesse, Richard, Jr., and Sallie Gray Weaver

Biographical sketches for Richard and Mary Lee Etta's other four offspring have been omitted:

- Asa "Acie" Weaver
- Jesse Weaver
- Richard Weaver, Jr.
- Sallie Gray Weaver Green Hill

However, their birth, marriage, and death dates may be found at the Time and Events section heading.

Sallie (Sarah) Weaver White Vaughn

While no oral history survived regarding some, this is not the situation with Sallie (Sarah) Weaver White Vaughn, her two spouses and three children. Ann and Robert's daughter Sallie was widely known, respected, and loved.

Ann and Robert's Sallie grew up in Jefferson, and around age 20, Sallie married a local fellow—a Mulatto named Sydney J. White, in Jefferson. For some reason, the last day of the year appealed to Sallie and Sydney, so they began their life as husband and wife, on that day. Soon after their marriage, they conceived a son Sydney A. White, Jr. and moved to Sherman. Sallie and family possibly traveled on the Sherman, Shreveport, and Southern Railway or the Texas and Pacific, segregated train car. The line ran amid Jefferson, Fort Worth, and Paris, Lamar County, Texas.

In Sherman, Sallie joined the Saint James UMC, where she met Mack Vaughn, another church member. Around 1892, Sallie married Mack. Mack's origins are unclear—he could have been a Creek freedman or a descendant of the Melungeons from Kentucky. Locally, Mack worked at the brickyard and at the oil mill in Sherman.

For a brief period, Sallie and the children resided on North Branch Street, but their East College Street address became home for whoever knocked, seeking lodging or help starting out in life. Sallie's open arms philosophy had less to do with economics and more to do with empathy and experience, considering she too left her sister Adaline M. and brothers Grandison W. and Richard, Sr. in Jefferson, at the start of her first marriage.

Sallie was an early Saint James UMC pioneer. Sallie believed in God and Saint James UMC, working as a good and faithful servant her entire life. Even as a senior citizen, Sallie still walked from home to her neighborhood church, where she taught Sunday school. On the way, Sallie gathered a church crowd with her strident, Sunday morning street commands, directed to the little, rowdy tag-alongs: NOW, NOW, DICK and JANE! COME ALONG! DON'T DO THAT! Among Sallie's myriad service activities, she was a member of the Sunday school board, president of WSCS, and a church trustee.

Sallie worked like a drudge. Sallie did laundry for others, to earn a means to survive and support others. Monday mornings were for washing clothes and linens and hanging the wash loads outside on the clotheslines to dry. On Tuesdays, she ironed all-day; and on Wednesdays, she returned everything to the people with the help of a grandson James and his little red wagon. At summertime, especially after Daughter Lucille became of age, Sallie traveled many summers to Sulphur Springs, Murray County, Oklahoma, where she worked as a laundress in the bathhouses. Sallie was generous with her hard-earned money. For example, she saved fifty silver dollars and contributed the fifty silver dollars to Saint James during the 1940s.

Her heart and home in Sherman, were always open to family, friends, and strangers alike. Almost every Norris, Sims, and Weaver relative that came to Sherman stayed with Sallie for a spell; some stayed a week or two; some stayed the entire summer. Malinda Elizabeth Sims stayed the longest; because, she went to Sherman to finish high school. Sallie put everyone to work, no matter how long they stayed. Great-niece Ester recalled her stay with Sallie. "I spent an entire summer before I went off to college, with Aunt Sallie." Sallie did not believe in leisure time—she found work for all household boarders or visitors and relatives. Niece Ethel Raye recalled: "I worked as hard as I ever worked while staying with her. MONDAY MORNINGS, I KNEW WHAT WE WERE GOING TO DO—WASH CLOTHES AND HANG THEM ON THE LINE OUTSIDE, to dry. She worked the stew out of me. She allowed me to go to the movies once only because she knew the boy, and she chided me so on what to do and what not to do—how I was to behave!" Sallie believed in strict decorum. No smoking—no drinking—no carousing—no trifling behavior, and certainly no disrespectfulness were her clarion calls. Whoever stayed with Sallie, attended mandatory church with Sallie. Nonconformists did not stay too long.

Son Sydney, Jr. went off to war during WWI and died a hero. Regarding Sallie's offspring, besides Sydney, Jr., her other two children were:

- Lucille
- Annie

Plausibly, there was a third daughter named Carrie who appeared on the 1900 Grayson County, Texas census. There is no oral history of Carrie—she possibly died very young. Grandson James explained that his grandmother Sallie always opened her doors to boarders for temporary lodging.

Sallie outlived both her husbands and her only son. Around age 80 Sallie reached the end of her fate and passed away December 1948 in Sherman. Rev. J. E. Richardson offered the eulogy, and the funeral was held at Saint James UMC. Sallie likely left explicit instructions that her cherished OES diamond-studded pendant, from the organization be placed on her burial dress lapel.

Sydney A. White, Jr.

Sydney A. was born in Jefferson circa 1886 to parents Sallie and Sydney J. White. Son Sydney A. never married nor fathered children.

Between the ages of twenty and thirty, Sydney chose to enter military service, and he gave his life to his country during WWI. At one point, a plaque hung on the wall in the basement of the Grayson County courthouse in Sherman, honoring Sydney and other fallen WWI soldiers. Reportedly, Sydney was one of the first soldiers killed while allegedly attached to the 25th Infantry. Years ago, the Sherman retired veterans named their veterans' center and auxiliary in Sydney's honor.

Detailed documentation of Sydney's honored military service did not materialize other than two entries: an unexplainable claim supposedly filed by his mother Sallie, appearing by chance in the Civil War Pension Index and a head-stone application showing Sydney either died at a Honolulu, Hawaii military post hospital or his body was delivered to the Honolulu post. Without deeper discovery, whether Sydney served on active duty with one of the all Black regiments, serving across the Americas: 9th Cavalry, 10th Cavalry, 24th Infantry, 25th Infantry or with the overseas combat forces: 92nd Infantry Division or 93rd Infantry Division and their respective infantry regiments, 369, 370, 371, 372, remains to be determined.

Around age 30 Sydney reached the end of his fate and passed away. The family laid Sydney to rest at West Hill Cemetery, Sherman.

Lucille Ophelia Vaughn Jenkins Galbreath

Lucille was born circa 1896. Sallie sent both of her girls to college. Lucille and her younger sister Annie attended Samuel Huston College in Austin—now Huston Tillotson College. However of the two, only Annie graduated. With three years of college, Lucille began teaching. In all likelihood, she taught in a town near Little Rock, Arkansas and in Amarillo, Randall County, Texas.

When Mother Sallie could no longer care for herself, Daughter Lucille returned to Sherman, to help. Lucille did not have children, though she married twice—once to a Jenkins and next to Jesse Dea Etrice Galbreath.

Around age 56 Lucille reached the end of her fate and passed away December of 1952 in Sherman.

Annie Lee Weaver Rebecca Vaughn Gilham Allen Bell

Born in Sherman, Annie Lee Weaver Rebecca Vaughn was approximately five years younger than her sister Lucille. Annie had a plethora of names, which are not included here; probably her unattainable school or college records would provide the only documentation of her entire name. When Sallie was upset with Annie, she uttered Annie's entire name. Grandson James recalled, this tirade took more than a minute to verbally complete. As a memorial, Sallie named Annie in honor of every relative, including the Lee relatives believed to be from Tennessee.

With Annie's three marriages, her name became even longer. Annie married Frank Gilham (various spellings) in Sherman, around 1926. They conceived one child James. During the Depression era in Sherman, Annie married her second husband Edgar "Tige" Allen. Annie and Edgar owned and operated a neighborhood restaurant with chili as the restaurant's specialty. Throughout the 1940s, the restaurant stood directly in front of their Sherman home. Lucille disapproved of Annie's second husband, and eventually, they divorced. Annie married for the third time. At last, Annie married Theodore Bell around 1953, in Sherman.

Embracing her mother's example, Annie was a very active church member. Specifically, she was involved in planning the Saint James UMC anniversary program during February of 1967. Annie was also president or participant of the WSCS, and she served on the trustee board, historical committee, and the administrative board.

Annie's strong Christian service and spiritual mindedness as well as her practical and meticulous nature carried her throughout her long life. Annie, her mother Sallie, and her sister Lucille each died during December, and the family laid all to rest at West Hill Cemetery, Sherman.

James Vaughn Gilham

Inspired by his uncle Sydney, James served in the U.S. military. Dedicated not desperate, James served during both WWII and the Korean War and served in two branches—the U.S. Air Force and the U.S. Army. As a wounded and scarred paratrooper James physically suffered for the remainder of his life.

James began his life being inspired by his grandmother Sally's work ethic, aiming to fulfill her dream of a college education for her whole family. Like his mother Annie and aunt Lucille, James enrolled in Samuel Huston College in Austin—now Huston Tillotson College. By the time James enlisted in the military, he described himself as an electrician.

College educated—electrician—paratrooper—father— James Vaughn Gilham at age 82 reached the end of his fate and passed away.

Adaline (Ada, Addie) M. Weaver Norris

Ann and Robert's Adaline M. was born during 1875 in Texas. Around age 22, Adaline wed Sanford Norris, a distant relative by marriage, in Jefferson. She lived in Jefferson her entire life and worked as a midwife in the community. Adaline passed between 1907 and 1909. See Norris Family.

THIS IS AN ACCOUNT OF THE WEAVER FAMILY. MAY THEIR STORIES BE REMEMBERED AND SPIRITS HONORED.

Put me in remembrance: let us plead together: declare thou, that thou mayest be justified.

Isaiah 43:26 KJV

AFTERWORD—THREE UNRESOLVED RELATIONS: ROSS, ELLISON, and FORD

ROSS

Trudging from South Carolina, old man Phil Ross, Sr. came to Texas before Texas was a state, as the slave of Willis Whitaker, Sr. Belzora Cheatham, descendant and family historian of Chicago, Illinois, best tells Phil's story. Phil Ross is included here in this context because the eldest Sims descendant Ima Viola Sims Jefferson remembered Phil Ross and Berry Sims as being half brothers. According to Ima, later in life, Phil and Berry happened upon each other in Marion County, Texas and visited one another every blue moon. Upon interviewing the elder Ross matriarch Hattie Wallace Brown, she was unaware of Berry Sims and Phil Ross being half brothers; the only connection she described was the coincidence of both Phil and Berry being short and dark. Hopefully another researcher will unearth this truth.

ELLISON

Depending on with whom you speak, Jane (Janie) Ellison was either a cousin or an aunt. All remember her as having a sweet personality and having a nice appearance; although, one account described a low, dumpy woman. Some believed Jane was related on the Norris or Weaver side of the family.

Jane reportedly moved to El Paso, Texas with an Anglo family for whom she had initially worked as a domestic. Likewise, Jane possibly traveled with the same or a different Anglo family to various places such as Seattle, King County, Washington.

Everyone remembered Jane as being an ambitious and wealthy woman who eventually owned a ranch, which bred and raised cattle and quarter horses in El Paso.

At some point, Jane supposedly married; maybe, she met and married someone in El Paso. No one seemed to remember the husband; perhaps the husband died before memories took shape. Jane bore no natural children of her own. Instead, she persistently tried to persuade her Sims family members to visit and live with her; amazingly, everyone always declined even in the face of paid roundtrip tickets—even in the face of a promise to pay for college tuition. In one example, a Sims relative actually returned the unused ticket to Cousin Jane.

Occasionally, Jane traveled home to Jefferson for visits with Cousin Carrie. Periodically, Jane gave Carrie presents and sent the Sims descendants care packages. No one seems to know with certainty how Jane acquired her money. However, all agree that she had plenty, enough to own a ranch. In fact, before Jane died, she gave some of the Sims descendants diamond rings, for use as emergency bargaining chips. Upon Jane's death, someone sent Carrie two hefty trunks filled with Jane's remaining personal belongings. The State of Texas supposedly became the eminent heir to Jane's real property. Carrie's diary recorded Jane's death as 16 June 1935, El Paso, Texas.

FORD

Regarding the Ford connection to the Sims family, this relationship does not seem to have been a familiar one, unlike the Ford connection to the Weaver family. The foremost mention of the Ford surname appears in a sharecropping agreement, where Berry Sims was working the land at the Ford Plantation during 1881, in Marion County, Texas. Sharecropping and tenant farming were prevalent after Emancipation and during Reconstruction. The newly freed were not necessarily sharecropping at their former owners; rather, they typically opted to sharecrop at locations where work contracts were most favorable.

Whether, this 1881 Ford Plantation was situated in the same spot as the land owned by John V. Ford, slaveholder of 1850 Cass County and 1860 Marion County, Texas, is unknown. However, John V. Ford is a promising candidate to have owned a place labeled as Ford Plantation, rationalizing he owned more than 2,600 acres of land and owned sixty-two slaves (thirty-four males and twenty-eight females) who existed in ten slave houses. During 1860, John V. Ford was age 35 and a farmer from Madison County, Alabama.

As Mr. Ford evidently entered into tenant or share agreements with the newly freed, at least one freedman complained that Mr. Ford was not honoring the labor agreement. The Freeman Bureau personnel ordered Mr. Ford to deliver the withheld crop and he complied. Later, John V. Ford became a stockholder of the Citizens Savings Bank of Jefferson. Although John V. Ford died during 1878, his land could have been sold and continually farmed by others under various arrangements.

The other business deal between the Sims and Fords seemed to lean toward codependence. Rebecca née Walton

Sims and Berry Sims lived near a William S. Ford family at the 1920 census as did Charley Sims and Carrie née Weaver Sims. Charley and Carrie permitted William S. Ford to set up oil well drilling on the Sims Estate during the 1950s. William S. Ford fathered a son called Ned.

Ned became an insurance salesperson and neighborhood banker, of sorts. Ned sold Carrie household insurance during the late 1950s and lent Carrie money during the late 1950s and early 1960s. Ned Ford's lineage traces back to his paternal grandfather Spencer Ford who operated a local sawmill and employed Black labor. Ned's great-grandfather was William Thompson Ford of Virginia. There is no known connection between John V. Ford and William Thompson Ford, a Confederate Civil War veteran.

There is one other Ford mention that may help substantiate a blood relation between the Fords and the Weavers. Reportedly, one of Ann and Robert Weaver's daughters married a Ford. This Weaver daughter supposedly lived in Paris, Texas, and named one of her children, Robert "Bob" Ford in honor of her father, Robert "Bob" Weaver. Hopefully someone will explore this connection and document the family folklore.

And now abideth faith, hope, charity, . . .

1 Corinthians 13:13 KJV

A NEW BEGINNING

CARRIE, A WEAVER BY BIRTH WROTE IN her journal that Ann Weaver and Minerva Lewis were sisters. Coincidently, both of the sisters, Ann and Minerva, reported to the 1880 census takers that their parents were from Virginia. Through the years, memories fade and stories twist, but excerpts from Carrie's fragmented and sporadic journal have held up with public record documentation or corroboration from other memories.

From memories and research to publication, the family has now a recorded genealogy of the seven interwoven families of Lewis, Martin, Norris, Perry, Sims, Walton, and Weaver. The genealogy presented here covers mainly four generational bloodlines from Ann and Minerva to Ester. A remaining question is whether the present generation will reap the full reward of their ancestors' legacy of:

- Christ Jesus,
- land ownership,
- duty, and responsibility

The complete history for the fifth, sixth, and seventh generations has yet to be written—it's up to the next group of genealogists and family historians to write the next chapter. The book author hopes that this recorded genealogy spurs more in-depth discovery, discussion, documentation, and preservation by publication.

Halleluiah, glory to God, and A-men, the second edition of *And It Came To Pass* is now recorded! However, the book author realizes as generations pass away, that genealogy will pass away. Even, the knowledge absorbed from this family history book—it too shall pass away. All things come to pass, even heaven and earth, in the face of the next thousand years of rain, wind, and sand. There will come a time when *they knew Joseph not.* There will come a time when all will carry a new name. Between then, now, and eternity, the book author hopes that our recorded genealogy strengthens and encourages all generations on their path to eternity.

He . . . and the thing that is hid bringeth he forth to light.

Job 28:11 KJV

SELECTED SOURCES WITH LOCATORS

FAMILY PAPERS

Hagerty Papers
Rebecca McIntosh Hawkins Hagerty Papers, 1823-1901, Marion and
Harrison Counties, Texas (University Publications of America, 1987);
microfilm part of the Records of Ante-Bellum Southern Plantations
From the Revolution Through the Civil War, Series G, Part 1, Reel 42.
Accessed Marietta Public Library, Cobb County, Georgia.

Berry Sims Papers
Jones, John G., W. T. Peyton, W. H. Gibson, Sr. *Ritual And Degree Book
of the United Brothers of Friendship.* Kentucky Standard, Louisville. [Ritual
book shows Berry Sims' handwriting (script) and fraternal membership].
Merrill, S. M., Bishop, LL. D., A *Digest of Methodist Law: Helps In The
Administration Of The Discipline of the Methodist Episcopal Church*, revised
1892, Cranston and Curts, Cincinnati and Hunt and Eaton, New York.
[Only the title page survived. Title page shows Berry Sims' handwriting
(script) and indicates a Methodist church affiliation].

Carrie Jane Weaver Sims Papers
Insurance Policy Papers, various years and companies.
Letters to and from governmental (federal and state) agencies, various.
Letter from Carrie Jane Weaver Sims, Jefferson, Marion County, Texas
to daughter Malinda Elizabeth Sims, Sherman, Grayson County, Texas,
1956.
Recordings of Births, Marriages, and Deaths as kept in Carrie's Bible.
Bible was in possession of Loyd Edward Sims, Sherman, Grayson
County, Texas, now deceased. Photocopy of family records pages
retained by book author.

Recordings of Births, Marriages, and Deaths as kept in Carrie's Bible. Bible in possession Ester W. Sims Cole Hawkins, Texas. Photocopy of family records pages retained by book author.
Tax Payments Receipts, various years.
Voter Registration Certificates 1968-1970.

Malinda Elizabeth Sims Papers
Diary and Journal of Carrie Jane Weaver Sims, 1950s through 1960s. Diary and journal given to book author by Malinda Elizabeth Sims. [Only fragments survived].
Fred Douglas High School Class of 1933 Commencement Exercise Program. Program given to book author by Malinda Elizabeth Sims.
Fred Douglas High School Memory Book. Memory book given to book author by Malinda Elizabeth Sims.
History of the Sims Family Reunion, written by Ester W. Sims Cole Hawkins, 1987. History given to book author by Malinda Elizabeth Sims.
Saint James Methodist Church, Sherman, Texas Souvenir Booklet, 1967. Booklet given to book author by Malinda Elizabeth Sims.

BIRTH CERTIFICATES

Hill, Sallie Gray Weaver. Local File Number unknown, page 300, Marion County Clerk's Office, Jefferson, Texas.
Tyson, Hattie Mae Sims. No identifying locators. Marion County Clerk's Office, Jefferson, Texas.
Weaver, Isaac "Ike" Gilham. Local File Number unknown, page 519, Marion County Clerk's Office, Jefferson, Texas.
Weaver, Richard McCallihan, Rev. Local File Number unknown, Marion County Clerk's Office, Jefferson, Texas.

BOOKS

Afro-American Encyclopedia, Volumes 8 and 9. North Miami, Florida: Educational Book Publishers, Inc., 1974, pages 2349, 2350, 2810.
Aptheker, Herbert. American Negro Slave Revolts. New York: International Publishers, 1970, pages 84-85, 93.
Ashe, Arthur R., Jr. A Hard Road to Glory A History of the African American Athlete 1619-1918. New York: Warner Books, Inc., 1988 pages

30, 46, 49, 67, 84, 99, 113-115, 126.

Bailey, Ouida. *Selections From Marion County Scrapbook.* Jefferson, Texas: *Jefferson Jimplecute*, page 111.

Barr, Alwyn. *Black Texans A History of African Americans in Texas, 1528-1995*, Second Edition. Norman, Oklahoma: University of Oklahoma Press, 1996, pages 37, 54, 67-68, 91, 96, 102, 108, 137, 167, 169, 175-176, 179, 181, 188, 196, 231, 245, 247.

Bennett, Lerone, Jr. *Before the Mayflower A History of Black America*, Sixth Edition. Chicago, Illinois: Johnson Publishing Company, 1987, pages 173, 464, 473-474, 476-477, 482, 493, 507, 512-513, 515, 517, 519, 521, 536, 538, 549, 551-552, 558, 570, 575, 579, 593, 597, 599, 601, 603, 605, 614, 636, 638.

Campbell, Randolph B. *An Empire for Slavery The Peculiar Institution in Texas 1821-1865*. Baton Rouge, Louisiana: Louisiana State University Press, 1989, pages 52, 54-56, 125, 156-157, 192, 226-227, 233, 252-253, 275.

----. *Grass-roots Reconstruction in Texas, 1865-1880*. Baton Rouge, Louisiana: Louisiana State University Press, 1997, pages 8-14, 98, 99, 101-103, 106, 111, 128-129, 131, 137.

Carroll, John M. *The Black Military Experience in the American West*. New York, New York: Liveright, 1971, page 216.

Cawthon, Juanita Davis. *Some Early Citizens of Marion County, Texas*. Privately printed, 1996, pages 15, 21, 26-29, 45, 46, 54, 68-71, 76, 80, 84, 93, 96, 100, 103.

Cheatham, Belzora. *The History of Whitaker Memorial Cemetery, Cass County, Texas*. Privately printed, publishing date unknown, pages 2-3.

Cross, Melba C. *Patillo, Pattillo, Pattullo and Pittillo Families*. Fort Worth, Texas: American Reference Publishing, 1972, pages 67, 69 153-154.

Crouch, Barry A. *The Freedmen's Bureau and Black Texans*. Austin, Texas: University of Texas Press, 1992, pages 2-3, 13-14, 94-97.

Department of Public Safety. *Oklahoma Highway Patrol's Yearbook*. May 1982, Volume 2.

Ericson, Joe E. *Banks and Bankers in Early Texas 1833-1875*. New Orleans, Louisiana: Polyanthos, Inc., 1976, pages 33-34, 38-39, 45, 50.

Fehrenbach, T. R. *Lone Star A History of Texas and the Texans*. New York: The MacMillian Company, 1968, pages 393-396.

Francis, Lee. *Native Time A Historical Time Line of Native America*. New York: Saint Martin's Press, 1996, page 210.

Hafner, Arthur W., Fred W. Hunter, and E. Michael Tarpey, editors.

Directory of Deceased American Physicians 1804-1929, Volume 2. Chicago, Illinois: American Medical Association, 1993.

Haley, Alex. *Roots*. Garden City, New York: Doubleday & Company, Inc., 1976.

Hornsby, Alton, Jr. *Chronology of African-American History Significant Events and People from 1619 to the Present*. Detroit, Michigan: Gale Research, Inc., 1991, pages 63, 67, 71, 76, 91.

Greene, Robert Ewell. *Who Were the Real Buffalo Soldiers?: Black Defenders of America*. Fort Washington, Maryland: Privately published, 1994, page 12.

Katz, William Loren. *The Black West*, Third Edition revised and expanded. Seattle, Washington: Open Hand Publishing, Inc., 1987, pages 46-47, 198, 329.

Levine, Michael L. *African Americans and Civil Rights from 1619 to the Present*. Phoenix, Arizona: The Oryx Press, 1996, pages 279-282.

Litwack, Leon F. *Been in the Storm so Long*. New York: Alfred A. Knopf, Inc., 1979, pages 545-546.

Massey, Sara R., editor. *Black Cowboys of Texas*. College Station, Texas: Texas A and M University Press, 2000, pages xv, xvi, 38-45, 206-214, 318.

McComb, David G. *Texas An Illustrated History*. New York: Oxford University Press, 1995, pages 27, 30, 32-33, 41-43, 48-49, 53, 60, 63, 65-67, 75, 77, 85, 130-131.

McKay, Arch, Mrs. and Mrs. H. A. Spellings. *A History of Jefferson Marion County Texas 1836 – 1936*, Second Edition. Privately printed, publishing date unknown, pages 15-20, 22-23, 28, 31-32, 37-38, 41-42.

McKelvey, Greta. *And It Came To Pass*, First Edition. Private Publishing, 2006.

McKenzie, Fred. *Avinger Texas, USA*. Naples, Texas: M and M Press, 1991, pages 178, 204-211.

———. *Hickory Hill*. Avinger, Texas: M-M Press, 1999, pages 207-211, 381, 395.

Meltzer, Milton. *In Their Own Words A History of the American Negro 1619-1865*. New York: Thomas Y. Crowell Company, 1964, pages 183, 186, 187, 188.

———. *In Their Own Words A History of the American Negro 1865-1916*. New York: Thomas Y. Crowell Company, 1965, pages 173-174.

Mills, Gary B. *Of Men and Rivers The Story of the Vicksburg District*.

Vicksburg, Mississippi: U.S. Army Engineer District, 1978, pages 54-59, 219, 221.

Morgan, Ted. *A Shovel of Stars The Making of the American West.* New York: Simon and Schuster, 1996, pages 252-254.

Mundie, James A., Dean E. Letzring, Bruce S. Allardice, and John H. Luckey. *Texas Burial Sites of Civil War Notables.* Hillsboro, Texas: Hill College Press, 2002, pages 11, 277.

Newton, Michael and Judy Ann Newton. *Racial and Religious Violence in America: A Chronology.* New York: Garland Publishing, Inc., 1991, pages 195, 247, 252, 254, 256, 270, 280, 286, 303, 308, 316, 317, 326-327, 337, 339, 347, 348, 351, 354, 356, 363, 370-371.

Poinsett, Alex. *Walking With Presidents Louis Martin and the Rise of Black Political Power.* Lanham, Maryland: Madison Books, 1997, pages 59-72, 142-143, 148, 153.

Ramsdell, Charles William. *Reconstruction in Texas.* Austin, Texas: University of Texas Press, 1970, pages 21, 26-27, 40, 48.

Rice, Lawrence D. *The Negro in Texas.* Baton Rouge, Louisiana: Louisiana State University Press, 1971, pages 18-22, 88-89, 93, 95, 103, 116-117, 154-157, 188, 204-205.

Richardson, Thomas Clarence. *East Texas its History and its Makers.* New York: Lewis Historical Publishing Company, 1940, pages 546, 602, 733, 735, 737, 773, 838, 1104-1105, 1107-1110, 1111.

Richter, William L. *The Army in Texas During Reconstruction, 1865-1870.* College Station, Texas: Texas A and M University Press, 1987, pages 17, 33-36, 177-179.

——. *Overreached On All Sides: The Freedmen's Bureau Administrators in Texas 1865-1868.* College Station, Texas: Texas A and M University Press, 1991, pages 45-47, 113, 202-207, 283-286.

Russell, Jan Jarboe. *Lady Bird A Biography of Mrs. Johnson.* New York: Scribner, 1999, pages 27, 30, 64-65, 67-69, 242-244.

Russell, Traylor. *Carpetbaggers, Scalawags and Others.* Jefferson, Texas: Marion County Historical Survey Committee, 1973, pages 5-11, 14, 33, 42-44, 62-70, 74, 80-89, 92-94, 96, 104-105.

Smallwood, James M. *Time of Hope, Time of Despair.* Port Washington, New York: Kennikat Press Corp., 1981, pages 26, 31, 38, 43, 49, 54, 65, 68, 74, 80, 83, 86, 103, 135, 141, 143, 157.

Stewart, Jeffrey C. *1001 Things Everyone Should Know About African American History.* New York: Doubleday, 1996, pages 51, 52, 223.

Tarpley, Fred. *Jefferson Riverport to the Southwest.* Austin, Texas: Eakin

Press, 1983, pages 21, 47-48, 57-58, 67-69, 81-84, 92-95, 98, 103, 107-112, 116, 125-135, 192-193, 217, 238, 253, 257, 265-267, 290.

Texas Almanac 1996-1997. Dallas, Texas: The Dallas Morning News, 1996, pages 39, 40-45, 64.

University of Chicago Press. *The Chicago Manual of Style*, Fifteenth Edition. Chicago, Illinois: University of Chicago Press, 2003. [Style manual consulted].

U.S. Army Corps of Engineers. *Red River Waterway Project, Shreveport, LA, To Daingerfield, Texas, Reach Reevaluation Study In-Progress Review*. Vicksburg, Mississippi: U.S. Army Corps of Engineers, Vicksburg District, 1994, pages 37-38, 42, 50-55, 59, 63, 66, 71-72. Also available online at http://www.clidata.org/Reports/DaingerfieldReach/ Watercraft (accessed January 2003).

Varhola, Michael J. *Everyday Life During the Civil War*. Cincinnati, Ohio: Writer's Digest Books, 1999, pages 26, 232.

Waldman, Carl. *The Encyclopedia of Native American Tribes*. New York: Facts On File, 1988, page 34.

Williams, Juan. *Eyes on the Prize America's Civil Rights Years, 1954-1965*. New York: Viking Penguin, Inc., 1987, pages 143, 285.

Williams, Willy Alvin. *Lewis Chapel United Methodist Church*, Lodi, Marion County, Texas. Privately printed, 1999, page 5.

Winegarten, Ruthe, Janet G. Humphrey, and Frieda Werden. *Black Texas Women 150 Years of Trial and Triumph*. Austin, Texas: University of Texas Press, 1995, pages 43, 47-48, 50.

World Book Encyclopedia. Chicago, Illinois: World Book, Inc., 1990, Volume 19, Letter T, pages 187, 205-208.

DEATH CERTIFICATES

Bryant, S. B. File Number 76-052123. California Department of Health Services, Sacramento, Sacramento County, California.

Calhoun, Ada Sharp. File Number 6056. Louisiana Bureau of Vital Statistics, New Orleans, Orleans Parish, Louisiana.

Dixon, Moscoe. File Number 35231. Texas Bureau of Vital Statistics, Austin, Travis County, Texas.

Hodge, Hattie Mae Sims. File Number 09911. Texas Bureau of Vital Statistics, Austin, Travis County, Texas.

Hodge, Zettie Mae. File Number 40941. Texas Bureau of Vital Statistics,

Austin, Travis County, Texas.

Lewis, Charles Monroe Lewis, Sr., Dr. File Number 493. Arkansas Bureau of Vital Statistics, Little Rock, Pulaski County, Arkansas.

Lewis, Felix, Jr. File Number 34539. Texas Bureau of Vital Statistics, Austin, Travis County, Texas.

Lewis, Isaac. File Number 53517. Texas Bureau of Vital Statistics, Austin, Travis County, Texas.

Norris, Alex "Alec". File Number 56650. Texas Bureau of Vital Statistics, Austin, Travis County, Texas.

Norris, Edmund. File Number 37909. Texas Bureau of Vital Statistics, Austin, Travis County, Texas.

Norris, Sanford. File Number 71349. Texas Bureau of Vital Statistics, Austin, Travis County, Texas.

Schuford, Annie Myrtle Norris Glover. File Number 38073. Texas Bureau of Vital Statistics, Austin, Travis County, Texas.

Sharp, Charley "Jim Bo" Henry. File Number 71-036612. California Department of Health Services, Sacramento, Sacramento County, California.

Sims, Berry. File Number 31248. Texas Bureau of Vital Statistics, Austin, Travis County, Texas.

Sims, Carrie Jane Weaver. File Number 36592. Texas Bureau of Vital Statistics, Austin, Travis County, Texas.

Sims, Charley Edward, Sr. File Number 45961. Texas Bureau of Vital Statistics, Austin, Travis County, Texas.

Sims, Joseph, Rev. File Number 84422. Texas Bureau of Vital Statistics, Austin, Travis County, Texas.

Sims, Malinda Elizabeth. Local File Number 6691. Grayson County Clerk's Office, Sherman, Texas.

Sims, Rebecca Walton. File Number 34087. Texas Bureau of Vital Statistics, Austin, Travis County, Texas.

Vaughn, Sallie (Sarah) Weaver White. File Number 52103. Texas Bureau of Vital Statistics, Austin, Travis County, Texas.

Weaver, Ann. File Number 6805. Texas Bureau of Vital Statistics, Austin, Travis County, Texas.

Weaver, Malinda Norris. Local File Number 226, Page 118. Marion County Clerk's Office, Jefferson, Texas.

Weaver, Richard. File Number 43904. Texas Bureau of Vital Statistics, Austin, Travis County, Texas.

Weaver, Richard. Local File Number 203. Marion County Clerk's Office, Jefferson, Texas.

White, Mary Lou Bryant. File Number 74-053067. California Department of Health Services, Sacramento, Sacramento County, California.

DEEDS

Bill of Sale from Richard "Dick" Norris to Granville Martin Jones, Agent. 29 August 1891. Marion County Deed Record V, page 640. County Clerk's Office, Jefferson, Texas.

Bill of Sale from Berry Sims to Frederica Fox. 14 May 1881. Marion County Deed Record O, page 462. County Clerk's Office, Jefferson, Texas.

Bill of Sale from Berry Sims to Max Simmons. 17 February 1893. Marion County, Deed Record W, pages 589-590. County Clerk's Office, Jefferson, Texas.

Deed from William Martin Dunn, Martin Homer Wurtsbaugh, and Edwin Jacob Rand to Berry Sims. 26 November 1892. Marion County Deed Record W, pages 456-457. County Clerk's Office, Jefferson, Texas.

Deed from Sylvanus Grady Echols, Agent for heirs of Ann Virginia Allen Ward Bynum to Grandison W. Weaver. 20 October 1899. Marion County Deed Record A-2, pages 531-533. County Clerk's Office, Jefferson, Texas.

Deed from Ambrose Fitzgerald to Berry Sims. 27 October 1888. Marion County Deed Record T, pages 116-117. County Clerk's Office, Jefferson, Texas.

Deed from Albert Kines to Peter Perry. 16 August 1877. Marion County Deed Record J, page 577. County Clerk's Office, Jefferson, Texas.

Deed from Minerva Lewis and Monroe Lewis to Walter P. Schluter. 26 February 1889. Marion County Deed Record T, pages 437 and 485. County Clerk's Office, Jefferson, Texas.

Deed from Enoch Love and wife Jennie to Felix Lewis. 01 January 1904. Marion County Deed Record, pages 625-626. County Clerk's Office, Jefferson, Texas.

Deed from Elizabeth (Eliza) Ellen Sharp Matthews (Mathis) to Peter Perry and Albert Kines. 01 January 1875. Marion County Deed Record J, page 599. County Clerk's Office, Jefferson, Texas.

Deed from Elizabeth (Eliza) Ellen Sharp Matthews (Mathis) to Peter Perry. 01 January 1878. Marion County Deed Record N, pages 248-249. County Clerk's Office, Jefferson, Texas.

Deed from Elizabeth (Eliza) Ellen Sharp Matthews (Mathis) to Peter
     Perry. 16 August 1877. Marion County Deed Record M, page
     77. County Clerk's Office, Jefferson, Texas.
Deed from Joe D. Mercer and wife Sallie Liverman to Felix Lewis. 22
     November 1900. Marion County Deed Record C-1, pages 156-
     158. County Clerk's Office, Jefferson, Texas.
Deed from Richard "Dick" Norris and wife Sarah Norris to Harrison
     Williams, Joe Smith, and Edmund Norris. 11 November 1891.
     Marion County Deed Record W, pages 47-49. County Clerk's
     Office, Jefferson, Texas.
Deed from Sarah Norris to Betty Pattillo. 27 July 1901. Marion County
     Deed Record Y, page 216. County Clerk's Office, Jefferson,
     Texas.
Deed from Benjamin F. Orr and Whitmill "Whit" Phillips to Richard
     "Dick" Norris. 01 January 1887. Marion County Deed Record
     S, pages 104-106. County Clerk's Office, Jefferson, Texas.
Deed from Benjamin. F. Orr and Whitmill "Whit" Phillips to Sarah
     Norris. 21 February 1893. Marion County Deed Record C-1,
     pages 412-413. County Clerk's Office, Jefferson, Texas.
Deed from W. P. Schluter to Grandison W. Weaver and Richard Weaver
     Sr. 17 May 1913. Marion County Deed Record L-1, pages 84-
     85. County Clerk's Office, Jefferson, Texas.
Deed from Marion DeKalb Taylor to Felix Lewis. 26 December 1888.
     Marion County Deed Record T, pages 338-339. County Clerk's
     Office, Jefferson, Texas.
Deed from Marion DeKalb Taylor to Helon Lewis and wife Elizabeth C.
     Moore Lewis. 30 November 1892. Marion County Deed
     Record W, page 525-526. County Clerk's Office, Jefferson,
     Texas.
Deed from Ward Taylor, et al. to Minerva Lewis and Monroe Lewis. 08
     November 1886. Marion County Deed Record T, page 91.
     County Clerk's Office, Jefferson, Texas.
Deed from Grandison W. Weaver and wife Malinda Norris Weaver to
     Richard Weaver, Sr. and wife Mary Lee Etta Williams Weaver.
     06 October 1917. Marion County Deed Record O-1, pages 268-
     269. County Clerk's Office, Jefferson, Texas.
Deed from Richard Weaver, Sr. and wife Mary Lee Etta Williams
     Weaver to Grandison W. Weaver and wife Malinda Norris
     Weaver. 06 October 1917. Marion County Deed Record O-1,
     pages 269-270. County Clerk's Office, Jefferson, Texas.
Oscar Perry Affidavit of Heirship. 27 April 1920. Marion County Deed

Record S-1, pages 140-141. County Clerk's Office, Jefferson, Texas.

Oil and Gas Lease from Grandison W. Weaver and wife Malinda Norris Weaver to George S. Niedermeir, Trustee. 01 August 1925. Marion County Deed of Trust S, pages 398-399. County Clerk's Office, Jefferson, Texas.

Oil and Gas Lease from Grandison W. Weaver and wife Malinda Norris Weaver to J. M. Singleton. 07 October 1930. Marion County Deed Record I-2, pages 592-594. County Clerk's Office, Jefferson, Texas.

Warranty Deed from Tom Belcher to Berry Sims. 25 January 1907. Marion County Deed Record I-1, page 284. County Clerk's Office, Jefferson, Texas.

Warranty Deed from Melvin Calhoun and Ada Calhoun descendants to the Brooks Farms, a partnership [to include] Brooks descendants and the Estate of Rebecca Willis Brooks, deceased. 18 August 1986. Marion County Deed Record Volume 491, page 890.

Warranty Deed from Ada Calhoun descendant to the Brooks Farms, a partnership [to include] Brooks descendants and the Estate of Rebecca Willis Brooks, deceased. 05 December 1986. Marion County Deed Record Volume 494, pages 775-776.

Warranty Deed from Nancy Sims Sharp Bryant descendant to the Brooks Farms, a partnership [to include] Brooks descendants and the Estate of Rebecca Willis Brooks, deceased. 21 December 1986. Marion County Deed Record Volume 494, pages 773-774.

Warranty Deed from Raymond Calhoun to the Brooks Farms, a partnership [to include] Brooks descendants and the Estate of Rebecca Willis Brooks, deceased. 01 October 1986. Marion County Deed Record Volume 491, page 492.

Warranty Deed from Berry Sims and wife Rebecca Sims to M. M. Fitzgerald. 16 February 1907. Marion County Deed Record H-1, page 324. County Clerk's Office, Jefferson, Texas.

Warranty Deed from Berry Sims and wife Rebecca Sims to J. H. Matthews. 11 August 1913. Marion County Deed Record L-1, page 173. County Clerk's Office, Jefferson, Texas.

Warranty Deed from F. P. Walker and H. R. Walker to Milus Sims. 01 October 1894. Cass County Deed Record, page 452. County Clerk's Office, Linden, Texas.

DIALOGS and DOCUMENTS

Note:

All transcripts made of personal communications and documents received with/from these 120 persons or more were not previously published and have been retained by book author unless otherwise specified. The majority of whom are now deceased.

Allen, Bobbie Smith. Texas. Interview by book author. April 1999, August 1999.

Allen, Odelle Hodge (deceased). Texas. Interview by book author. 1988, July 2003, August 2003, October 2003.

Allen, Sammy. Texas. Interview by book author. July 2003, November 2004.

Armstrong, Mattie D. Sims (deceased). Louisiana. Interview by book author. December 1992, July 1994, August 1994, September 1996, December 1996, July 1997, November 1998, June 2003.

Beard, Jennie V. Calhoun (deceased). Alabama. Interview by book author. 1992, December 1996, October 2003.

Bonner, Larry D. Texas. Interview by book author. June 1993, March 1995, January 1996, February 1996.

Bonner, Mildred Sims. Texas. Interview by book author. July 1994, October 2003.

Brooks, Margaret Ruth Allen. Nevada. Interview by book author. 2000, September 2001.

Brown, Hattie Wallace, (deceased). Texas. Interview by book author. September 1998.

Brown, Luise Sims. Texas. Interview by book author. December 1992, April 1997, August 1999.

Calhoun, Allen (deceased). Louisiana. Interview by book author. February 1999.

Calhoun, Ezzie Jones. Louisiana. Interview by book author. December 1992.

Calhoun, Oscar (deceased). Texas. Interview by book author. 1993.

Canada, Gertrude Elizabeth Norris (deceased). California. Interview by book author. August 1999, October 2003.

Cawthon Juanita D. Louisiana. Query by book author. November 1998, November 1999.

Chadwick, Ruby Calhoun. California. Interview by book author. November 1992, January 1996, December 1996.

Charlot, Edie. Texas. Query by book author. November 2003, January

2005.

Cheatham, Bellzora Brown. Illinois. Interview by book author. September 1998, October 1998, November 1998, January 1999, February 1999, March 1999, May/June 1999, July 1999, August 1999, March 2000, July 2000, November 2002, March 2003, October 2003.

Clancy, Imogene Dixon (deceased). Louisiana. Interview by book author. May 1999.

Cole, Azzie Lee Rose (deceased). Texas. Interview by book author. November 2003, October 2004.

Cooper, Paulette. Texas. Interview by book author. 2000, September 2001, November 2002, November 2003.

Coverson, Lobis Ray. Texas. Interview by book author. July 2003.

Coverson, Pearly Mae. Texas. Interview by book author. November 2002.

Criss, Constance F. California. Interview by book author. August 2003.

Criss, M. C., Jr. California. Interview by book author. August 2003.

Davis, Ethel Raye Weaver (deceased). Texas. Interview by book author. February 1999, May 1999, November 2002.

Davis, Sammie Lois Fitzpatrick (deceased). Texas. Interview by book author. November 2002, July 2003.

Dillard, Irene Mable Lewis (deceased). Texas. Interview by book author. December 1998, October 2003.

Dixon, John. Maryland. Interview by book author. May 1999.

Dixon, Norman. Michigan. Interview by book author. May 1999, July 1999.

Doutherd, Cyrille. California. Interview by book author. February 2003, March 2003, June 2003, July 2003, November 2004, December 2004.

Eaton, Rebecca Bryant Ball Lawson (deceased). California. Interview by book author. December 1992, December 1996, September 1998.

Edwards, Mary Lou Wilson. California. Interview by book author. August 1994, December 1996, September 1998, February 1999, May 1999, June 1999, October 1999, March 2000.

Fennoy, Thelma Rand (deceased). Texas. Interview by book author. August 1999.

Gabriel, Herman. Texas. Interview by book author. November 1996, 2005.

Gaines, Cheryl, Dr. Illinois. Interview by book author. October 1998, November 1998, December 1998, January 1999, July 1999,

September 2001, March 2002, October 2002, November 2002, May 2003, June 2003, July 2003, October 2003, December 2004, 2005.

Giles, Darlene. Texas. Interview by book author. May 1999.

Gilham, James Vaughn (deceased). Texas. Interview by book author. October 1998, November 1998.

Goins, Delena Graham. Texas. Interview by book author. November 2003.

Gulley, Cynthia. Texas. Interview by book author. January 2005, February 2005.

Hawkins, Ester W. Sims Cole (deceased) and James A. Hawkins (deceased). Texas. Interview by book author. 1989, August 1992, April/June, 1993, June 1994, August 1994, 1995, November 1996, December 1996, September 1998, October 1998, February 1999, April 1999, September 1999, September 2000, November 2002, July 2003, October 2003, December 2003, April 2004, July 2004, 2005.

High, Lucille Jefferson (deceased). Texas. Interview by book author. August 1999.

High, Oris Luther, Rev. (deceased). Interview by book author. April 1999.

High, Robert. Texas. Interview by book author. December 1998, February 1999, August 1999, August 2000.

Hobbs, Yolanda R. Perry. Texas. Interview by book author. November 1992.

Jackson, Gloria. California. Interview by book author. August 2003.

Jefferson, Della Rowell (deceased). Texas. Interview by book author. August 1999.

Jefferson, Ima V. Sims (deceased). Texas. Interview by book author. 1989, August 1992, November 1992, January 1993, March 1996, December 1996, October 1998, March 1999, August 1999, February 2001.

Jefferson, James E. Texas (deceased). Interview by book author. June 1994.

Jefferson, Lafayette, Sr. (deceased). Interview by book author. January 1993, December 1996.

Jefferson, Thomas Earl. Texas. Interview by book author. March 1997.

Johnson, Chantelle (Perry). Texas. Interview by book author. July 2003.

Johnson, Louise Zackery Heath. Louisiana. Interview by book author. October 2003.

Jones, Christine. Texas. Interview by book author. February 1999, March

1999.

Lewis, Bertran A., Jr., Dr. North Carolina. Interview by book author. November 2003.

Lewis, Carl Lee (deceased). Interview by book author. November 1998, December 1998, October 2003.

Lewis, Fred Edward, Dr. (deceased). Interview by book author. April 1999, August 1999, November 2002.

Lewis, Lillian Delia McAllister (deceased). Texas. Interview by book author. July 2003, November 2003.

Lewis, Roscoe, Jr. Texas. Interview by book author. October 2003.

Lindsay, Sarah Lee Anderson Weaver Jennings Clark (deceased). Georgia. Interview by book author. June 1999.

Mason, Mildred (deceased). Texas. Interview by book author. April 1999, March 2005.

McDade, Willie Mae Hodge. Alabama. Interview by book author. June 2003, July 2003, September 2003.

McKee, Rose (deceased). Texas. Interview by book author. December 1996.

McKenzie, Fred. Texas. Query by book author. October 1999.

Morrow, Beatrice (deceased). Texas. Correspondences by book author.

Neblett, Pauline (deceased). Texas. Interview by book author. December 1996.

Nelson, Doris Smith (deceased). Texas. Interview by book author. April 1999, July 2003, January 2005.

Newton, Mae Dean Norris (deceased). Louisiana. Interview by book author. May 1999.

Norris, Curtis, Rev. (deceased) Texas. Interview by book author. October 2003.

Norris, Ethel (deceased). California. Interview by book author. April 1999 and July 2003.

Norris, Freddy. Kansas. Interview by book author. October 2003.

Norris, Homer. Louisiana. Interview by book author. April 1999 and August 1999.

Norris, Marzella Heath (deceased). Texas. Interview by book author. September 1999.

Oaks, Sylvia Sharp. Texas. Interview by book author.

Parker, Myrtis McAlister. Texas. Interview by book author. January, May 1999, July 1999, July 2003, August 2003.

Perkins, Janice Hodge. Texas. Interview by book author. November 2003.

Perry, Claude (deceased). New Jersey. Interview by book author.

November 2002.

Phillips, Vida Calhoun. California. Interview by book author. March 1999.

Pickens, Peggy. Texas. Interview by book author. April 1991, August 1992, January 1996, May 1996, July 1997, March 1999, February 2003, August 2003.

Rand, Earl W., Dr. (deceased). Interview by book author. August 1999.

Reeder, Shirley C. Sims (deceased). Texas. Interview by book author. November 1992, July 1994, February 1996.

Rice, Edgar Lorenzo, III. (deceased). Texas. Interview by book author. April 1999.

Roberts, Margaret Dixon. California. Interview by book author. May 1999.

Roberts, Lekita S. Smith. Texas. Interview by book author. April 1996.

Sanders, Myrtle Jefferson. Texas. Interview by book author. January 1993, July 1994.

Sanders, William Lawrence, Jr. Texas. Interview by book author. December 1992, July 1994.

Scott, Gloria Jefferson. Texas. Interview by book author. December 1992, August 1994.

Sharpe, Herman. California. Interview by book author. July 2003.

Sims, Addie Mae Darty. Texas. Interview by book author. 1988, November 1992, December 1994.

Sims, Alice Pauline Williams, Rev. Texas. Interview by book author. February 1993, February 1995, January 1996, July 2003.

Sims, Charles Edward (deceased). Interview by book author. April 1988.

Sims, Charley Edward, Jr. (deceased). Interview by book author. August 1992.

Sims, Chester, Arnold (deceased). Interview by book author.

Sims, Clinton (deceased). Interview by book author. August 1992, April 1999.

Sims, Ernest, Jr. Texas. Interview by book author. November 1992.

Sims, Jewerl Elaine (Bibbs/Crosby). Texas. Interview by book author. June 1994.

Sims, Johnny Wesley (Love) (deceased). Interview by book author. December 1996, September 1998, October 1998.

Sims, Leslie White Lyons Harmon. Washington. Interview by book author. June 1993, July 1993, February 1994, April 1994, September 1994, October 1994, December 1994, May 1996, December 1996, September 1998, October 1998, July 2003, January 2004.

Sims, Loyd Edward (deceased). Interview by book author. August 1992 and December 1996.

Sims, Malinda Elizabeth (deceased). Interview by book author. March 1888, July 1992, August 1994.

Sims, Noris. (deceased) Texas. Interview by book author. November 2004.

Sims, Sammie Lee Harper (deceased). Texas. Interview by book author. December 1996, November 1998, May 1999, and 2000. Transcripts retained by book author and documents returned to interviewee.

Sims, William Lee. Texas. Interview by book author. July 1994.

Smith, Sandra E. Texas. Interview by book author. January 1993, November 2004.

Smith, Zelpha Lee Jefferson. Texas. Interview by book author. July 1994.

Spencer, Jewel Singleton. Michigan. Interview by book author. November 2004.

Stansell, Linda McCain. Texas. Query by book author.

Tyson, Hattie Mae Sims (deceased). Texas. Interview by book author. August 1992, July 1993, April 1994, August 1994, May 1996, November 1996, April 1999, August 1999, March 2000.

Ward, Christine Tyler. California. Interview by book author. March 1999, October 1999.

Watson, Roosevelt. Texas. Interview by book author. September 1998, December 1998.

Weaver, Aaron (deceased). Texas. Interview by book author. October 1998, December 1998.

Weaver, Christine Hodge. Texas. Interview by book author. August 1999.

Weaver, Clarence (deceased). Texas. Interview by book author. October 1998.

Weaver, Lois. Georgia. Interview by book author. May 1999.

Weaver, Ruby. Texas. Interview by book author. October 1998.

Williams, Bobbie Matthews Smith. Texas. Interview by book author. December 1996.

Williams, Dorothy. Texas. Interview by book author. October 2003.

Williams, Lee Willow Zackery (deceased). Interview by book author. August 1994, September 1994.

Williams, Willy Alvin. Texas. Interview by book author. March 1999, April 1999, July 1999, January 2000, March 2001.

Windom, Homer (deceased). Texas. Interview by book author. October 2003.

DISSERTATION

McGhee, Fred Lee. "The Black Crop: Slavery And Slave Trading In
    Nineteenth Century Texas." PhD dissertation, University of
    Texas, Austin, 2000, page 1. Quoting Lanker, Brian. I
    Dream A World: Portraits Of Black Women Who Changed
    America. New York: Stewart, Tabori, and Chang, 1989.
    [Barbara Jordan].

FEDERAL FREE CENSUS

Berry. 1880 U.S. Federal Census, Population Schedule, Jefferson,
    Marion County, Texas. Precinct 4, ED 87, Sheet 3, Page Stamp
    405, Dwelling 28, Family 29. National Archives Microfilm
    Publication T9, Roll 1318. Accessed National Archives
    Building, Washington, D.C. and Marietta Public Library, Cobb
    County, Georgia.
Brown, Ranie. 1920 U.S. Federal Census, Population Schedule,
    Jefferson, Marion County, Texas. Precinct 2, ED 126, Sheet
    16B, Page Stamp 162B, Dwelling 291, Family 308. National
    Archives Microfilm Publication T625, Roll 1832. Accessed
    National Archives Building, Washington, D.C.
Brown, Ranie. 1930 U.S. Federal Census, Population Schedule,
    Jefferson, Marion County, Texas. Justice Precinct 2, ED 158-2,
    Sheet 6A, Page Stamp 141A, Dwelling Number illegible, Family
    Number illegible. National Archives Microfilm Publication
    T626, Roll 2375. Accessed National Archives Building,
    Washington, D.C.
Calhoun, Oscar. 1930 U.S. Federal Census, Population Schedule,
    Shreveport, Caddo Parish, Louisiana. District 5, ED 9-45, Sheet
    13A, Page Stamp 26A, Dwelling 267, Family 215. National
    Archives Microfilm Publication T626, Roll 787. Accessed
    National Archives Building, Washington, D.C.
Clark, Coleman. 1870 U.S. Federal Census, Population Schedule,
    Jefferson, Marion County, Texas. Ward 2, Sheet unknown,
    Page Stamp unknown, Dwelling 299, Family 302. National
    Archives Microfilm Publication M593, Roll 1597. Accessed
    National Archives Building, Washington, D.C. and Marietta
    Public Library, Cobb County, Georgia.

Cole, Aboliva. 1910 U.S. Federal Census, Population Schedule, Jefferson, Marion County, Texas. Precinct 4, ED 106, Sheet 1A, Page Stamp 213A, Dwelling 2, Family 2. National Archives Microfilm Publication T624, Roll 1576. Accessed National Archives Building, Washington, D.C. and Marietta Public Library, Cobb County, Georgia.

Cole, Aboliva. 1920 U.S. Federal Census, Population Schedule, Jefferson, Marion County, Texas. Precinct 4, ED 130, Sheet 12A, Page Stamp 229A, Dwelling 188, Family 199. National Archives Microfilm Publication T625, Roll 1832. Accessed National Archives Building, Washington, D.C.

Cole, Aboliva. 1930 U.S. Federal Census, Population Schedule, Jefferson, Marion County, Texas. Justice Precinct 4, ED 158-5, Sheet 1A, Page Stamp 196A, Dwelling 3, Family 4. National Archives Microfilm Publication T626, Roll 2375. Accessed National Archives Building, Washington, D.C.

Cooper, Thomas. 1870 U.S. Federal Census, Population Schedule, Jefferson, Marion County, Texas. Beat 2, Sheet 31, Page Stamp unknown, Dwelling 232, Family 247. National Archives Microfilm Publication M593, Roll 1597. Accessed National Archives Building, Washington, D.C. and Marietta Public Library, Cobb County, Georgia.

Crawford, Moses "M. K.". 1880 U.S. Federal Census, Population Schedule, Jefferson, Marion County, Texas. Ward 2, Precinct 4, ED 91, SD 2, Sheet 7, Dwelling 65, Family 65. National Archives Microfilm Publication T9, Roll 1319. Accessed National Archives Building, Washington, D.C. and Marietta Public Library, Cobb County, Georgia.

Davis, Tobe. 1930 U.S. Federal Census, Population Schedule, Jefferson, Marion County, Texas. Justice Precinct 4, ED 158-5, Sheet 7A, Page Stamp 202A, Dwelling 131, Family 136. National Archives Microfilm Publication T626, Roll 2375. Accessed National Archives Building, Washington, D.C.

Dixon. 1900 U.S. Federal Census, Population Schedule, Jefferson, Marion County, Texas. Precinct 4, ED 93, Sheet 2B, Page Stamp 202B, Dwelling 33, Family 33. National Archives Microfilm Publication T623, Roll 1658. Accessed National Archives Building, Washington, D.C. and Marietta Public Library, Cobb County, Georgia.

Dixon, Moscoe. 1930 U.S. Federal Census, Population Schedule, Jefferson, Marion County, Texas. Justice Precinct 4, ED 158-5,

Sheet 7A, Page Stamp 202A, Dwelling 132, Family 137. National Archives Microfilm Publication T626, Roll 2375. Accessed National Archives Building, Washington, D.C.

Emory. 1880 U.S. Federal Census, Population Schedule, Jefferson, Marion County, Texas. Precinct 4, ED 87, Sheet 9, Page Stamp 408A, Dwelling 79, Family 85. National Archives Microfilm Publication T9, Roll 1318. Accessed National Archives Building, Washington, D.C. and Marietta Public Library, Cobb County, Georgia.

Fitzgerald, Ambrose. 1850 U.S. Federal Census, Population Schedule, Cass County, Texas. Precinct 7, Page 795, Dwelling 49, Family 50. National Archives Microfilm Publication M432, Roll 909. Accessed National Archives Building, Washington, D.C. and Marietta Public Library, Cobb County, Georgia.

Ford, John V. 1860 U.S. Federal Census, Population Schedule, Monterey, Marion County, Texas. Beat 5, Dwelling 208, Family 223. National Archives Microfilm Publication M653, Roll 1300. Accessed National Archives Building, Washington, D.C. and Marietta Public Library, Cobb County, Georgia.

Ford, Robert. 1920 U.S. Federal Census, Population Schedule, Paris, Lamar County, Texas. Justice, Precinct 1, ED 99, Sheet 4B, Page Stamp 229B, Dwelling 90, Family 90. National Archives Microfilm Publication T625, Roll 1827. Accessed National Archives Building, Washington, D.C.

Ford, Robert. 1930 U.S. Federal Census, Population Schedule, Paris, Lamar County, Texas. Ward 4, District 9, ED 139-9, Sheet 3B, Page Stamp 174, Dwelling 79, Family 98. National Archives Microfilm Publication T626, Roll 2367. Accessed National Archives Building, Washington, D.C.

Ford, Spencer. 1900 U.S. Federal Census, Population Schedule, Jefferson, Marion County, Texas. Precinct 4, ED 93, Sheet 17B, Page Stamp 217B, Dwelling 298, Family 299. National Archives Microfilm Publication T623, Roll 1658. Accessed National Archives Building, Washington, D.C. and Marietta Public Library, Cobb County, Georgia.

Ford, Spencer. 1920 U.S. Federal Census, Population Schedule, Jefferson, Marion County, Texas. Precinct 4, ED 130, Sheet 2A, Page Stamp 210A, Dwelling 18, Family 20. National Archives Microfilm Publication T625, Roll 1832. Accessed National Archives Building, Washington, D.C.

Ford, William S. 1920 U.S. Federal Census, Population Schedule,

Jefferson, Marion County, Texas. Precinct 4, ED 130, Sheet 4B, Page Stamp 212B, Dwelling 51, Family 57. National Archives Microfilm Publication T625, Roll 1832. Accessed National Archives Building, Washington, D.C.

Ford, William Thompson. 1860 U.S. Federal Census, Population Schedule, Jefferson, Marion County, Texas. Beat 3, Dwelling 159, Family 168. National Archives Microfilm Publication M653, Roll 1300. Accessed National Archives Building, Washington, D.C. and Marietta Public Library, Cobb County, Georgia.

Freeman, William M. 1860 U.S. Federal Census, Population Schedule, Jefferson, Marion County, Texas. Beat unknown, Dwelling 301, Family 329. National Archives Microfilm Publication M653, Roll 1300. Accessed National Archives Building, Washington, D.C. and Marietta Public Library, Cobb County, Georgia.

Glover, William "Bill" Mack. 1930 U.S. Federal Census, Population Schedule, Fort Worth, Tarrant County, Texas. Precinct 6, District 121, ED 220-121, Sheet 13A, Page Stamp 30, Dwelling 312, Family 330. National Archives Microfilm Publication T626, Roll 2399. Accessed National Archives Building, Washington, D.C.

Graham. 1920 U.S. Federal Census, Population Schedule, Jefferson, Marion County, Texas. Precinct 4, ED 130, Sheet 12B, Page Stamp 229B, Dwelling 189, Family 200. National Archives Microfilm Publication T625, Roll 1832. Accessed National Archives Building, Washington, D.C.

Graham. 1930 U.S. Federal Census, Population Schedule, Jefferson, Marion County, Texas. Justice Precinct 4, ED 158-5, Sheet 8A, Page Stamp 203A, Dwelling 145, Family 151. National Archives Microfilm Publication T626, Roll 2375. Accessed National Archives Building, Washington, D.C.

Hagerty, Rebecca McIntosh Hawkins. 1860 U.S. Federal Census, Population Schedule, Jefferson, Marion County, Texas. Beat 3, Dwelling 174, Family 183. National Archives Microfilm Publication M653, Roll 1300. Accessed National Archives Building, Washington, D.C. and Marietta Public Library, Cobb County, Georgia.

Hoddin, Jesse. 1870 U.S. Federal Census, Population Schedule, Jefferson, Marion County, Texas. Ward 2, Sheet unknown, Page Stamp unknown, Dwelling 237, Family 240. National Archives Microfilm Publication M593, Roll 1597. Accessed

National Archives Building, Washington, D.C. and Marietta
Public Library, Cobb County, Georgia.

Hodge, Isom. 1910 U.S. Federal Census, Population Schedule, Cass
County, Texas. Precinct 1, Part 4, ED 26, Sheet 27B, Page
Stamp 37B, Dwelling 514, Family 516. National Archives
Microfilm Publication T624, Roll 1537. Accessed National
Archives Building, Washington, D.C. and Marietta Public
Library, Cobb County, Georgia.

Hodge, Isom. 1920 U.S. Federal Census, Population Schedule, Cass
County, Texas. Justice, Precinct 1, ED 32, Sheet 16B, Page
Stamp 73B, Dwelling 287, Family 296. National Archives
Microfilm Publication T625, Roll 1785. Accessed National
Archives Building, Washington, D.C.

Hodge, Isom. 1930 U.S. Federal Census, Population Schedule, Cass
County, Texas. Precinct 1, ED 34-6, Sheet 9B, Page Stamp 60B,
Dwelling 182, Family 187. National Archives Microfilm
Publication T626, Roll 2306. Accessed National Archives
Building, Washington, D.C.

Johnson, Henry. 1870 U.S. Federal Census, Population Schedule,
Jefferson, Marion County, Texas. Ward 2, Sheet unknown,
Page Stamp unknown, Dwelling 303, Family 306. National
Archives Microfilm Publication M593, Roll 1597. Accessed
National Archives Building, Washington, D.C. and Marietta
Public Library, Cobb County, Georgia.

Johnson, Hezekiah, Sr. 1910 U.S. Federal Census, Population Schedule,
Jefferson, Marion County, Texas. Precinct 4, ED 106, Sheet
1A, Page Stamp 213A, Dwelling 5, Family 5. National Archives
Microfilm Publication T624, Roll 1576. Accessed National
Archives Building, Washington, D.C. and Marietta Public
Library, Cobb County, Georgia.

Johnson, Hezekiah, Sr. 1920 U.S. Federal Census, Population Schedule,
Jefferson, Marion County, Texas. Precinct 4, ED 130, Sheet
13A, Page Stamp 221A, Dwelling 198, Family 210. National
Archives Microfilm Publication T625, Roll 1832. Accessed
National Archives Building, Washington, D.C.

Johnson, Hezekiah, Sr. 1930 U.S. Federal Census, Population Schedule,
Jefferson, Marion County, Texas. Justice Precinct 4, ED 158-5,
Sheet 1A, Page Stamp 196A, Dwelling 10, Family 11. National
Archives Microfilm Publication T626, Roll 2375. Accessed
National Archives Building, Washington, D.C.

Jones, John M. 1860 U.S. Federal Census, Population Schedule,

Jefferson, Marion County, Texas. Beat 3, Dwelling 105, Family 114. National Archives Microfilm Publication M653, Roll 1300. Accessed National Archives Building, Washington, D.C. and Marietta Public Library, Cobb County, Georgia.

Jones, John M. 1870 U.S. Federal Census, Population Schedule, Jefferson, Marion County, Texas. Beat 2, Sheet 37, Page Stamp 368, Dwelling 287, Family 305. National Archives Microfilm Publication M593, Roll 1597. Accessed National Archives Building, Washington, D.C. and Marietta Public Library, Cobb County, Georgia.

Jordan. 1920 U.S. Federal Census, Population Schedule, Jefferson, Marion County, Texas. Precinct 4, ED 130, Sheet 4B, Page Stamp 212B, Dwelling 54, Family 60. National Archives Microfilm Publication T625, Roll 1832. Accessed National Archives Building, Washington, D.C.

Kines, Albert. 1880 U.S. Federal Census, Population Schedule, Jefferson, Marion County, Texas. Precinct 4, ED 87, SD 2, Sheet 5, Dwelling 43, Family 45. National Archives Microfilm Publication T9, Roll 1318. Accessed National Archives Building, Washington, D.C. and Marietta Public Library, Cobb County, Georgia.

Lee. 1870 U.S. Federal Census, Population Schedule, Jefferson, Marion County, Texas. Beat 4, Sheet 16, Page Stamp 377, Dwelling 116, Family 120. National Archives Microfilm Publication M593, Roll 1597. Accessed National Archives Building, Washington, D.C. and Marietta Public Library, Cobb County, Georgia.

Lewis, Andrew J. 1860 U.S. Federal Census, Population Schedule, Hickory Hill, Cass County, Texas. Sheet 51, Dwelling 347, Family 355. National Archives Microfilm Publication M653, Roll 1290. Accessed National Archives Building, Washington, D.C. and Marietta Public Library, Cobb County, Georgia.

Lewis, Charles Monroe, Dr. 1910 U.S. Federal Census, Population Schedule, Hope, Hempstead County, Arkansas. Ward 1, ED 76, Sheet 19 A, Page Stamp 83B, Dwelling 56, Family 53. National Archives Microfilm Publication T624, Roll 52. Accessed National Archives Building, Washington, D.C. and Marietta Public Library, Cobb County, Georgia.

Lewis, Charles Monroe, Dr. 1930 U.S. Federal Census, Population Schedule, Hope, Hempstead County, Arkansas. District 5, ED 29-5, Sheet 19A, Page Stamp 61, Dwelling 381, Family 456.

National Archives Microfilm Publication T626, Roll 76. Accessed National Archives Building, Washington, D.C.

Lewis, Felix, Sr. 1880 U.S. Federal Census, Population Schedule, Jefferson, Marion County, Texas; Precinct 4, ED 87, Sheet 2, Page Stamp 404, Dwelling 17, Family 18. National Archives Microfilm Publication T9, Roll 1318. Accessed National Archives Building, Washington, D.C. and Marietta Public Library, Cobb County, Georgia.

Lewis, Felix, Sr. 1900 U.S. Federal Census, Population Schedule, Jefferson, Marion County, Texas. Precinct 4, ED 93, Sheet 1B, Page Stamp 201B, Dwelling 13, Family 13. National Archives Microfilm Publication T623, Roll 1658. Accessed National Archives Building, Washington, D.C. and Marietta Public Library, Cobb County, Georgia.

Lewis, Felix, Sr. 1910 U.S. Federal Census, Population Schedule, Jefferson, Marion County, Texas. Precinct 4, ED 106, Sheet 1B, Page Stamp 213B, Dwelling 11, Family 12. National Archives Microfilm Publication T624, Roll 1576. Accessed National Archives Building, Washington, D.C. and Marietta Public Library, Cobb County, Georgia.

Lewis, Felix, Sr. 1920 U.S. Federal Census, Population Schedule, Jefferson, Marion County, Texas Precinct 4, ED 130, Sheet 13A, Page Stamp 221A, Dwelling 199, Family 211. National Archives Microfilm Publication T625, Roll 1832. Accessed National Archives Building, Washington, D.C.

Lewis, Helon. 1900 U.S. Federal Census, Population Schedule, Jefferson, Marion County, Texas. Precinct 4, ED 93, Sheet 1B, Page Stamp 201B, Dwelling 12, Family 12. National Archives Microfilm Publication T623, Roll 1658. Accessed National Archives Building, Washington, D.C. and Marietta Public Library, Cobb County, Georgia.

Lewis, Helon. 1910 U.S. Federal Census, Population Schedule, Jefferson, Marion County, Texas. Precinct 4, ED 106, Sheet 2A, Page Stamp 214A, Dwelling 14, Family 17. National Archives Microfilm Publication T624, Roll 1576. Accessed National Archives Building, Washington, D.C. and Marietta Public Library, Cobb County, Georgia.

Lewis, Helon. 1920 U.S. Federal Census, Population Schedule, Jefferson, Marion County, Texas. Precinct 4, ED 130, Sheet 13A, Page Stamp 221A, Dwelling 203, Family 215. National Archives Microfilm Publication T625, Roll 1832. Accessed

National Archives Building, Washington, D.C.

Lewis, Isaac. 1910 U.S. Federal Census, Population Schedule, Jefferson, Marion County, Texas. Precinct 4, ED 106, Sheet 1B, Page Stamp 213B, Dwelling 10, Family 11. National Archives Microfilm Publication T624, Roll 1576. Accessed National Archives Building, Washington, D.C. and Marietta Public Library, Cobb County, Georgia.

Lewis, Isaac. 1920 U.S. Federal Census, Population Schedule, Jefferson, Marion County, Texas. Precinct 4, ED 130, Sheet 13A, Page Stamp 221A, Dwelling 201, Family 213. National Archives Microfilm Publication T625, Roll 1832. Accessed National Archives Building, Washington, D.C.

Lewis, Isaac. 1930 U.S. Federal Census, Population Schedule, Jefferson, Marion County, Texas. Justice Precinct 4, ED 158-5, Sheet 1B, Page Stamp 196B, Dwelling 15, Family 16. National Archives Microfilm Publication T626, Roll 2375. Accessed National Archives Building, Washington, D.C.

Lewis, Minerva. 1870 U.S. Federal Census, Population Schedule, Jefferson, Marion County, Texas. Beat 4, Sheet 15, Page Stamp 377, Dwelling 110, Family 114. National Archives Microfilm Publication M593, Roll 1597. Accessed National Archives Building, Washington, D.C. and Marietta Public Library, Cobb County, Georgia.

Lewis, Minerva. 1880 U.S. Federal Census, Population Schedule, Jefferson, Marion County, Texas. Precinct 4, ED 87, Sheet 3, Page Stamp 405, Dwelling 29, Family 30. National Archives Microfilm Publication T9, Roll 1318. Accessed National Archives Building, Washington, D.C. and Marietta Public Library, Cobb County, Georgia.

Lewis, Minerva. 1900 U.S. Federal Census, Population Schedule, Jefferson, Marion County, Texas. Precinct 4, ED 93, Sheet 2B, Page Stamp 202B, Dwelling 32, Family 32. National Archives Microfilm Publication T623, Roll 1658. Accessed National Archives Building, Washington, D.C. and Marietta Public Library, Cobb County, Georgia.

Lewis, Monroe. 1900 U.S. Federal Census, Population Schedule, Jefferson, Marion County, Texas. Precinct 4, ED 93, Sheet 2A, Page Stamp 202A, Dwelling 27, Family 27. National Archives Microfilm Publication T623, Roll 1658. Accessed National Archives Building, Washington, D.C. and Marietta Public Library, Cobb County, Georgia.

Lewis, Monroe. 1910 U.S. Federal Census, Population Schedule,
Jefferson, Marion County, Texas. Precinct 4, ED 106, Sheet
1A, Page Stamp 213A, Dwelling 7, Family 7. National Archives
Microfilm Publication T624, Roll 1576. Accessed National
Archives Building, Washington, D.C. and Marietta Public
Library, Cobb County, Georgia.

Martin, Solomon. 1900 U.S. Federal Census, Population Schedule,
Jefferson, Marion County, Texas. Precinct 4, ED 93, Sheet 13B,
Page Stamp 212B, Dwelling 230, Family 231. National Archives
Microfilm Publication T623, Roll 1658. Accessed National
Archives Building, Washington, D.C. and Marietta Public
Library, Cobb County, Georgia.

Martin, Solomon, Jr. 1910 U.S. Federal Census, Population Schedule,
Jefferson, Marion County, Texas. ED 104, Sheet 1A, Page
Stamp 189A, Dwelling 112, Family 115. National Archives
Microfilm Publication T624, Roll 1576. Accessed National
Archives Building, Washington, D.C. and Marietta Public
Library, Cobb County, Georgia.

Martin, Tom. 1880 U.S. Federal Census, Population Schedule,
Jefferson, Marion County, Texas. Precinct 4, ED 87, Sheet 28,
Page Stamp 417D, Dwelling 263, Family 279. National
Archives Microfilm Publication T9, Roll 1318. Accessed
National Archives Building, Washington, D.C. and Marietta
Public Library, Cobb County, Georgia.

Martin, Tom. 1900 U.S. Federal Census, Population Schedule,
Jefferson, Marion County, Texas. Precinct 4, ED 93, Sheet 9B,
Page Stamp 209B, Dwelling 165, Family 166. National Archives
Microfilm Publication T623, Roll 1658. Accessed National
Archives Building, Washington, D.C. and Marietta Public
Library, Cobb County, Georgia.

Matthews, Elizabeth (Eliza) Ellen Sharp. 1860 U.S. Federal Census,
Population Schedule, Monterey, Marion County, Texas. Beat 5,
Dwelling 214, Family 229. National Archives Microfilm
Publication M653, Roll 1300. Accessed National Archives
Building, Washington, D.C. and Marietta Public Library, Cobb
County, Georgia.

McCoy. 1870 U.S. Federal Census, Population Schedule, Jefferson,
Marion County, Texas. Ward 2, Sheet unknown, Page Stamp
unknown, Dwelling 244, Family 247. National Archives
Microfilm Publication M593, Roll 1597. Accessed National
Archives Building, Washington, D.C. and Marietta Public

Library, Cobb County, Georgia.

Norris, Alex "Alec". 1920 U.S. Federal Census, Population Schedule, Cass County, Texas. Justice, Precinct 2, ED 33, SD 1, Sheet 15?, Page Stamp 92, Dwelling 270, Family 270. National Archives Microfilm Publication T625, Roll 1785. Accessed National Archives Building, Washington, D.C. [Alec/Alex Norris resided as a boarder in the John Davis household].

Norris, Ben. 1920 U.S. Federal Census, Population Schedule, Jefferson, Marion County, Texas. Precinct 2, ED 126, Sheet 16B, Page Stamp 162B, Dwelling 290, Family 307. National Archives Microfilm Publication T625, Roll 1832. Accessed National Archives Building, Washington, D.C.

Norris, Ben. 1930 U.S. Federal Census, Population Schedule, Jefferson, Marion County, Texas. Justice Precinct 2, ED 158-2, Sheet 6A, Page Stamp 141A, Dwelling Number illegible, Family Number illegible. National Archives Microfilm Publication T626, Roll 2375. Accessed National Archives Building, Washington, D.C.

Norris, Edmund. 1900 U.S. Federal Census, Population Schedule, Jefferson, Marion County, Texas. Justice Precinct 2, ED 89, Sheet 6A, Page Stamp 140A, Dwelling 117, Family 121. National Archives Microfilm Publication T623, Roll 1658. Accessed National Archives Building, Washington, D.C. and Marietta Public Library, Cobb County, Georgia.

Norris, Edmund. 1910 U.S. Federal Census, Population Schedule, Jefferson, Marion County, Texas. Precinct 2, ED 102, Sheet 7A, Page Stamp 151A, Dwelling 12, Family 12. National Archives Microfilm Publication T624, Roll 1576. Accessed National Archives Building, Washington, D.C. and Marietta Public Library, Cobb County, Georgia.

Norris, Edmund. 1920 U.S. Federal Census, Population Schedule, Jefferson, Marion County, Texas. Precinct 2, ED 126, Sheet 16B, Page Stamp 162B, Dwelling 289, Family 306. National Archives Microfilm Publication T625, Roll 1832. Accessed National Archives Building, Washington, D.C.

Norris, Edmund. 1930 U.S. Federal Census, Population Schedule, Jefferson, Marion County, Texas. Justice Precinct 2, ED 158-2, Sheet 6A, Page Stamp 141A, Dwelling Number illegible, Family Number illegible. National Archives Microfilm Publication T626, Roll 2375. Accessed National Archives Building, Washington, D.C.

Norris, Edward. 1930 U.S. Federal Census, Population Schedule,

Beaumont, Jefferson County, Texas. District 7, ED 123-7, Sheet 9B, Page Stamp 95B, Dwelling 203, Family 204. National Archives Microfilm Publication T626, Roll 361. Accessed National Archives Building, Washington, D.C.

Norris, Richard "Dick". 1870 U.S. Federal Census, Population Schedule, Jefferson, Marion County, Texas. Beat 2, Sheet 38, Page Stamp 368, Dwelling 296, Family 314. National Archives Microfilm Publication M593, Roll 1597. Accessed National Archives Building, Washington, D.C. and Marietta Public Library, Cobb County, Georgia.

Norris, Richard "Dick". 1880 U.S. Federal Census, Population Schedule, Jefferson, Marion County, Texas. Precinct 3, ED 86, Sheet 3, Page Stamp 381C, Dwelling 27, Family 27. National Archives Microfilm Publication T9, Roll 1318. Accessed National Archives Building, Washington, D.C. and Marietta Public Library, Cobb County, Georgia.

Norris, Robert. 1930 U.S. Federal Census, Population Schedule, Jefferson, Marion County, Texas. Justice Precinct 2, ED 158-2, Sheet 7A, Page Stamp 142A, Dwelling 120, Family 120. National Archives Microfilm Publication T626, Roll 2375. Accessed National Archives Building, Washington, D.C.

Norris, Sam. 1930 U.S. Federal Census, Population Schedule, Jefferson, Marion County, Texas. Justice Precinct 2, ED 158-2, Sheet 6A, Page Stamp 141A, Dwelling 111, Family Number 111. National Archives Microfilm Publication T626, Roll 2375. Accessed National Archives Building, Washington, D.C.

Norris, Samuel. 1920 U.S. Federal Census, Population Schedule, Jefferson, Marion County, Texas. Precinct 2, ED 126, Sheet 13A, Page Stamp 159A, Dwelling 220, Family 232. National Archives Microfilm Publication T625, Roll 1832. Accessed National Archives Building, Washington, D.C.

Norris, Sanford. 1900 U.S. Federal Census, Population Schedule, Jefferson, Marion County, Texas. Justice Precinct 3, ED 90, Sheet 19, Page Stamp 167, Dwelling 340, Family 341. National Archives Microfilm Publication T623, Roll 1658. Accessed National Archives Building, Washington, D.C. and Marietta Public Library, Cobb County, Georgia.

Norris, Sanford. 1910 U.S. Federal Census, Population Schedule, Jefferson, Marion County, Texas. Precinct 2, ED 102, Sheet 1B, Page Stamp 151B, Dwelling 16, Family 16. National Archives Microfilm Publication T624, Roll 1576. Accessed National

Archives Building, Washington, D.C. and Marietta Public Library, Cobb County, Georgia.

Norris, Sanford. 1920 U.S. Federal Census, Population Schedule, Jefferson, Marion County, Texas. Precinct 2, ED 126, Sheet 16A, Page Stamp 162A, Dwelling 279, Family 295. National Archives Microfilm Publication T625, Roll 1832. Accessed National Archives Building, Washington, D.C.

Norris, Will, Sr. 1930 U.S. Federal Census, Population Schedule, Texarkana, Bowie County, Texas. District 7, ED 19-7, Sheet 3A, Page Stamp 139, Dwelling 54, Family 56. National Archives Microfilm Publication T626, Roll 2300. Accessed National Archives Building, Washington, D.C.

Pattillo, Lewis Alexander. 1860 U.S. Federal Census, Population Schedule, Hickory Hill, Marion County, Texas. Beat 2, Dwelling 65, Family 71. National Archives Microfilm Publication M653, Roll 1300. Accessed National Archives Building, Washington, D.C. and Marietta Public Library, Cobb County, Georgia.

Phillips. 1860 U.S. Federal Census, Population Schedule, Jefferson City, Marion County, Texas. Beat 3, Dwelling 94, Family 103. National Archives Microfilm Publication M653, Roll 1300. Accessed National Archives Building, Washington, D.C. and Marietta Public Library, Cobb County, Georgia.

Perry, Oscar. 1910 U.S. Federal Census, Population Schedule, Jefferson, Marion County, Texas. Precinct 4, ED 106, Sheet 9B, Page Stamp 221B, Dwelling 136, Family 138. National Archives Microfilm Publication T624, Roll 1576. Accessed National Archives Building, Washington, D.C. and Marietta Public Library, Cobb County, Georgia.

Perry, Oscar. 1920 U.S. Federal Census, Population Schedule, Jefferson, Marion County, Texas. Precinct 4, ED 130, Sheet 4A, Page Stamp 212A, Dwelling 48, Family 54. National Archives Microfilm Publication T625, Roll 1832. Accessed National Archives Building, Washington, D.C.

Perry, Oscar. 1930 U.S. Federal Census, Population Schedule, Jefferson, Marion County, Texas. Justice Precinct 4, ED 158-5, Sheets 17A and 17B, Page Stamps 212A and 212B, Dwelling 332, Family 381. National Archives Microfilm Publication T626, Roll 2375. Accessed National Archives Building, Washington, D.C.

Perry, Peter. 1870 U.S. Federal Census, Population Schedule, Jefferson,

Marion County, Texas. Beat 4, Sheet 6, Page Stamp 372, Dwelling 44, Family 44. National Archives Microfilm Publication M593, Roll 1597. Accessed National Archives Building, Washington, D.C. and Marietta Public Library, Cobb County, Georgia.

Perry, Peter. 1880 U.S. Federal Census, Population Schedule, Jefferson, Marion County, Texas. Precinct 4, ED 87, Sheet 4, Page Stamp 405D, Dwelling 42, Family 43. National Archives Microfilm Publication T9, Roll 1318. Accessed National Archives Building, Washington, D.C. and Marietta Public Library, Cobb County, Georgia.

Perry, Peter. 1900 U.S. Federal Census, Population Schedule, Jefferson, Marion County, Texas. Precinct 4, ED 93, Sheet 9A, Page Stamp 209A, Dwelling 155, Family 156. National Archives Microfilm Publication T623, Roll 1658. Accessed National Archives Building, Washington, D.C. and Marietta Public Library, Cobb County, Georgia.

Perry, Peter. 1910 U.S. Federal Census, Population Schedule, Jefferson, Marion County, Texas. Precinct 4, ED 106, Sheet 9B, Page Stamp 221B, Dwelling 141, Family 143. National Archives Microfilm Publication T624, Roll 1576. Accessed National Archives Building, Washington, D.C. and Marietta Public Library, Cobb County, Georgia.

Powell, Rebecca. 1870 U.S. Federal Census, Population Schedule, Jefferson, Marion County, Texas. Ward 2, Sheet unknown, Page Stamp unknown, Dwelling 286, Family 290. National Archives Microfilm Publication M593, Roll 1597. Accessed National Archives Building, Washington, D.C. and Marietta Public Library, Cobb County, Georgia.

Rice, Edgar. 1920 U.S. Federal Census, Population Schedule, Little Rock City, Pulaski County, Arkansas. Big Rocks Township, ED 141, Sheet 8A, Page Stamp 26A, Dwelling 169, Family 198. National Archives Microfilm Publication T625, Roll 79. Accessed National Archives Building, Washington, D.C.

Rice, Edgar. 1930 U.S. Federal Census, Population Schedule, Little Rock, Pulaski County, Arkansas. District 38, ED 60-38, Sheet 12A, Page Stamp 204A, Dwelling 9, Family 10. National Archives Microfilm Publication T626, Roll 92. Accessed National Archives Building, Washington, D.C.

Roberts, Sallie. 1870 U.S. Federal Census, Population Schedule, Jefferson, Marion County, Texas. Ward 2, Sheet unknown,

Page Stamp unknown, Dwelling 257, Family 261. National Archives Microfilm Publication M593, Roll 1597. Accessed National Archives Building, Washington, D.C. and Marietta Public Library, Cobb County, Georgia.

Schluter, Walter P. 1860 U.S. Federal Census, Population Schedule, Jefferson, Marion County, Texas. Jefferson City, Dwelling 266, Family 286. National Archives Microfilm Publication M653, Roll 1300. Accessed National Archives Building, Washington, D.C. and Marietta Public Library, Cobb County, Georgia.

Sims, Berry. 1880 U.S. Federal Census, Population Schedule, Jefferson, Marion County, Texas. Precinct 4, ED 87, Sheet 11, Page Stamp 409C, Dwelling 102, Family 108. National Archives Microfilm Publication T9, Roll 1318. Accessed National Archives Building, Washington, D.C. and Marietta Public Library, Cobb County, Georgia.

Sims, Berry. 1900 U.S. Federal Census, Population Schedule, Jefferson, Marion County, Texas. Precinct 4, ED 93, Sheet 9B, Page Stamp 209B, Dwelling 159, Family 160. National Archives Microfilm Publication T623, Roll 1658. Accessed National Archives Building, Washington, D.C. and Marietta Public Library, Cobb County, Georgia.

Sims, Berry. 1910 U.S. Federal Census, Population Schedule, Jefferson, Marion County, Texas. Precinct 4, ED 106, Sheet 12A, Page Stamp 224A, Dwelling 175. Family 177, National Archives Microfilm Publication T624, Roll 1576. Accessed National Archives Building, Washington, D.C. and Marietta Public Library, Cobb County, Georgia.

Sims, Berry. 1920 U.S. Federal Census, Population Schedule, Jefferson, Marion County, Texas. Precinct 4, ED 130, Sheet 4B, Page Stamp 212B, Dwelling 53, Family 59. National Archives Microfilm Publication T625, Roll 1832. Accessed National Archives Building, Washington, D.C.

Sims, Charley Edward, Sr. 1910 U.S. Federal Census, Population Schedule, Jefferson, Marion County, Texas. Precinct 4, ED 106, Sheet 12A, Page Stamp 224A, Dwelling 174, Family 176. National Archives Microfilm Publication T624, Roll 1576. Accessed National Archives Building, Washington, D.C. and Marietta Public Library, Cobb County, Georgia.

Sims, Charley Edward, Sr. 1920 U.S. Federal Census, Population Schedule, Jefferson, Marion County, Texas. Precinct 4, ED 130, Sheet 4B, Page Stamp 212B, Dwelling 52, Family 58.

National Archives Microfilm Publication T625, Roll 1832. Accessed National Archives Building, Washington, D.C.

Sims, Charley Edward, Sr. 1930 U.S. Federal Census, Population Schedule, Jefferson, Marion County, Texas. Justice Precinct 4, ED 158-5, Sheet 13B, Page Stamp 208B, Dwelling 262, Family 269. National Archives Microfilm Publication T626, Roll 2375. Accessed National Archives Building, Washington, D.C.

Sims, Joseph. 1930 U.S. Federal Census, Population Schedule, Jefferson, Marion County, Texas. Justice Precinct 4, ED 158-5, Sheets 16 A and 16B, Page Stamps 211A and 211B, Dwelling 309, Family 318. National Archives Microfilm Publication T626, Roll 2375. Accessed National Archives Building, Washington, D.C.

Sims, Milus. 1880 U.S. Federal Census, Population Schedule, Jefferson, Marion County, Texas. Precinct 4, ED 87, Sheet 17, Page Stamp 412A, Dwelling 164, Family 174. National Archives Microfilm Publication T9, Roll 1318. Accessed National Archives Building, Washington, D.C. and Marietta Public Library, Cobb County, Georgia.

Sims, Milus. 1900 U.S. Federal Census, Population Schedule, Cass County, Texas. Precinct 5, ED 27, Sheet 4B, Page Stamp 267B, Dwelling 69, Family 74. National Archives Microfilm Publication T623, Roll 1618. Accessed National Archives Building, Washington, D.C. and Marietta Public Library, Cobb County, Georgia.

Sims, Milus. 1910 U.S. Federal Census, Population Schedule, Cass County, Texas. Precinct 5, ED 35, Sheet 12B, Page Stamp illegible, Dwelling 233, Family 233. National Archives Microfilm Publication T624, Roll 1537. Accessed National Archives Building, Washington, D.C. and Marietta Public Library, Cobb County, Georgia.

Sims, Rebecca. 1930 U.S. Federal Census, Population Schedule, Jefferson, Marion County, Texas. Justice Precinct 4, ED 158-5, Sheet 16B, Page Stamp 211B, Dwelling 312, Family 321. National Archives Microfilm Publication T626, Roll 2375. Accessed National Archives Building, Washington, D.C.

Slaughter, Marion Try. 1860 U.S. Federal Census, Population Schedule, Jefferson, Marion County, Texas. Beat 3, Dwelling 119, Family 128. National Archives Microfilm Publication M653, Roll 1300. Accessed National Archives Building, Washington, D.C. and Marietta Public Library, Cobb County, Georgia.

Slaughter, Marion Try. 1880 U.S. Federal Census, Population Schedule,

Jefferson, Marion County, Texas. Precinct 3, ED 86, Sheet 40D, Dwelling 395, Family 403. National Archives Microfilm Publication T9, Roll 1318. Accessed National Archives Building, Washington, D.C. and Marietta Public Library, Cobb County, Georgia.

Smith, John. 1900 U.S. Federal Census, Population Schedule, Jefferson, Marion County, Texas. Justice Precinct 3, ED 90, Sheet 19, Page Stamp 167B, Dwelling 357/335, Family 358/336. National Archives Microfilm Publication T623, Roll 1658. Accessed National Archives Building, Washington, D.C. and Marietta Public Library, Cobb County, Georgia.

Smith, Susan Ann Cocke. 1860 U.S. Federal Census, Population Schedule, Smithland, Marion County, Texas. Beat 4, Dwelling 186, Family 197. National Archives Microfilm Publication M653, Roll 1300. Accessed National Archives Building, Washington, D.C. and Marietta Public Library, Cobb County, Georgia.

Taylor, Marion DeKalb. 1860 U.S. Federal Census, Population Schedule, Smithland, Marion County, Texas. Beat 4, Dwelling 186, Family 200. National Archives Microfilm Publication M653, Roll 1300. Accessed National Archives Building, Washington, D.C. and Marietta Public Library, Cobb County, Georgia.

Thompson, W. B. 1930 U.S. Federal Census, Population Schedule, Shreveport, Caddo Parish, Louisiana. District 45, ED 9-45, Sheet 16A, Page Stamp 29A, Dwelling 341, Family 391. National Archives Microfilm Publication T626, Roll 787. Accessed National Archives Building, Washington, D.C.

Tullis, Aaron Duke. 1860 U.S. Federal Census, Population Schedule, Jefferson, Marion County, Texas. Jefferson City, Dwelling 254, Family 272. National Archives Microfilm Publication M653, Roll 1300. Accessed National Archives Building, Washington, D.C. and Marietta Public Library, Cobb County, Georgia.

Vaughn. 1900 U.S. Federal Census, Population Schedule, Sherman, Grayson County, Texas. ED 87, Sheet 17B, Page Stamp 72B, Dwelling 376, Family 387. National Archives Microfilm Publication T623, Roll 1639. Accessed National Archives Building, Washington, D.C. and Marietta Public Library, Cobb County, Georgia.

Vaughn. 1910 U.S. Federal Census, Population Schedule, Sherman, Grayson County, Texas. ED 65, Sheet 8B, Page Stamp 82B,

Dwelling 159, Family 172. National Archives Microfilm Publication T624, Roll 1556. Accessed National Archives Building, Washington, D.C. and Marietta Public Library, Cobb County, Georgia.

Vaughn. 1920 U.S. Federal Census, Population Schedule, Sherman, Grayson County, Texas. ED 69, Sheet 9A, Page Stamp 81A, Dwelling 199, Family 207. National Archives Microfilm Publication T625, Roll 1808. Accessed National Archives Building, Washington, D.C.

Vaughn. 1930 U.S. Federal Census, Population Schedule, Sherman, Grayson County, Texas. ED 91-1, Sheet, 4B, Page Stamp 4B, Dwelling 92, Family 104. National Archives Microfilm Publication T626, Roll 2337. Accessed National Archives Building, Washington, D.C.

Walton, Squire. 1870 U.S. Federal Census, Population Schedule, Jefferson, Marion County, Texas. Beat 4, Sheet 32, Page Stamp 385, Dwelling 242, Family 255. National Archives Microfilm Publication M593, Roll 1597. Accessed National Archives Building, Washington, D.C. and Marietta Public Library, Cobb County, Georgia.

Weaver, Ann. 1900, U.S. Federal Census, Population Schedule, Jefferson, Marion County, Texas. Precinct 4, ED 93, Sheet 2B, Page Stamp 202B, Dwelling 31, Family 31. National Archives Microfilm Publication T623, Roll 1658. Accessed National Archives Building, Washington, D.C. and Marietta Public Library, Cobb County, Georgia.

Weaver, Grandison. 1900 U.S. Federal Census, Population Schedule, Jefferson, Marion County, Texas. Precinct 4, ED 93, Sheet 2B, Page Stamp 202B, Dwelling 30, Family 30. National Archives Microfilm Publication T623, Roll 1658. Accessed National Archives Building, Washington, D.C. and Marietta Public Library, Cobb County, Georgia.

Weaver, Grandison. 1910 U.S. Federal Census, Population Schedule, Jefferson, Marion County, Texas. Precinct 4, ED 106, Sheet 1A, Page Stamp 213A, Dwelling 3, Family 3. National Archives Microfilm Publication T624, Roll 1576. Accessed National Archives Building, Washington, D.C. and Marietta Public Library, Cobb County, Georgia.

Weaver, Grandison. 1920 U.S. Federal Census, Population Schedule, Jefferson, Marion County, Texas. Precinct 4, ED 130, Sheet 12B, Page Stamp 229B, Dwelling 193, Family 204. National

Archives Microfilm Publication T625, Roll 1832. Accessed National Archives Building, Washington, D.C.

Weaver, Grandison. 1930 U.S. Federal Census, Population Schedule, Jefferson, Marion County, Texas. Justice Precinct 4, ED 158-5, Sheet 1A, Page Stamp 196A, Dwelling 6, Family 8A. National Archives Microfilm Publication T626, Roll 2375. Accessed National Archives Building, Washington, D.C.

Weaver, Henry Lee. 1920 U.S. Federal Census, Population Schedule, Jefferson, Marion County, Texas. Precinct 4, ED 130, Sheet 12B, Page Stamp 229B, Dwelling 193, Family 205. National Archives Microfilm Publication T625, Roll 1832. Accessed National Archives Building, Washington, D.C.

Weaver, Henry Lee. 1930 U.S. Federal Census, Population Schedule, Jefferson, Marion County, Texas. Justice Precinct 4, ED 158-5, Sheet 1A, Page Stamp 196A, Dwelling 7, Family 8. National Archives Microfilm Publication T626, Roll 2375. Accessed National Archives Building, Washington, D.C.

Weaver, Richard, Sr. 1900 U.S. Federal Census, Population Schedule, Jefferson, Marion County, Texas. Precinct 4, ED 93, Sheets 2A and 2B, Page Stamps 202A and 202B, Dwelling 28, Family 28. National Archives Microfilm Publication T623, Roll 1658. Accessed National Archives Building, Washington, D.C. and Marietta Public Library, Cobb County, Georgia.

Weaver, Richard, Sr. 1910 U.S. Federal Census, Population Schedule, Jefferson, Marion County, Texas. Precinct 4, ED 106, Sheet 1A, Page Stamp 213A, Dwelling 4, Family 4. National Archives Microfilm Publication T624, Roll 1576. Accessed National Archives Building, Washington, D.C. and Marietta Public Library, Cobb County, Georgia.

Weaver, Richard, Sr. 1920 U.S. Federal Census, Population Schedule, Jefferson, Marion County, Texas. Precinct 4, ED 130, Sheet 12B, Page Stamp 229B, Dwelling 194, Family 206. National Archives Microfilm Publication T625, Roll 1832. Accessed National Archives Building, Washington, D.C.

Weaver, Richard, Sr. 1930 U.S. Federal Census, Population Schedule, Jefferson, Marion County, Texas. Justice Precinct 4, ED 158-5, Sheet 1A, Page Stamp 196A, Dwelling 8, Family 9. National Archives Microfilm Publication T626, Roll 2375. Accessed National Archives Building, Washington, D.C.

Weaver, Richard M., Rev. 1930 U.S. Federal Census, Population Schedule, Fort Worth, Tarrant County, Texas. District 69, ED

220-69, Sheet 101A, Page Stamp 101, Dwelling 866, Family
866. National Archives Microfilm Publication T626, Roll 2396.
Accessed National Archives Building, Washington, D.C.
Weaver, Robert. 1870 U.S. Federal Census, Population Schedule,
Jefferson, Marion County, Texas. Beat 4, Sheet 16, Page Stamp
377, Dwelling 117, Family 121. National Archives Microfilm
Publication M593, Roll 1597. Accessed National Archives
Building, Washington, D.C. and Marietta Public Library, Cobb
County, Georgia.
Weaver, Robert. 1880 U.S. Federal Census, Population Schedule,
Jefferson, Marion County, Texas. Precinct 4, ED 87, Sheet 25,
Page Stamp 416A, Dwelling 239, Family 255. National
Archives Microfilm Publication T9, Roll 1318. Accessed
National Archives Building, Washington, D.C. and Marietta
Public Library, Cobb County, Georgia.
Wiggins, Green. 1880 U.S. Federal Census, Population Schedule,
Jefferson, Marion County, Texas. Precinct 3, ED blank, SD
blank, Sheet 17, Dwelling 150, Family 153. National Archives
Microfilm Publication T9, Roll 1318. Accessed National
Archives Building, Washington, D.C. and Marietta Public
Library, Cobb County, Georgia.
Williams, Harrison. 1880 U.S. Federal Census, Population Schedule,
Jefferson, Marion County, Texas. Precinct 3, ED 86, SD 2,
Sheet 46, Dwelling 470, Family 477. National Archives
Microfilm Publication T9, Roll 1318. Accessed National
Archives Building, Washington, D.C. and Marietta Public
Library, Cobb County, Georgia.
Williams, Wash. 1880 U.S. Federal Census, Population Schedule,
Jefferson, Marion County, Texas. Precinct 5, ED 88, SD 2,
Sheet 23, Dwelling illegible, Family illegible. National Archives
Microfilm Publication T9, Roll 1319. Accessed National
Archives Building, Washington, D.C. and Marietta Public
Library, Cobb County, Georgia. [Wash Williams staying with a
Scott family as a stepson].

FREEMAN BUREAU RECORDS

Ford, Mr. Records of the Assistant Commissioner for the State of Texas,
Bureau of Refugees, Freedmen, and Abandoned Lands 1865-
1869 (National Archives Microfilm Publication M821, Roll 21);
Registered Reports of Operations and Conditions, June-Aug.

1867. Accessed at the National Archives and Records
Administration—Southeast Region, East Point, Georgia.

Freedmen Conditions. Records of the Assistant Commissioner for the
State of Texas, Bureau of Refugees, Freedmen, and Abandoned
Lands 1865-1869 (National Archives Microfilm Publication
M821, Roll 20); Registered Reports of Operations and
Conditions, December 1866-May 1867. Accessed at the
National Archives and Records Administration—Southeast
Region, East Point, Georgia.

Perry, Peter. Records of the Assistant Commissioner for the State of
Texas, Bureau of Refugees, Freedmen, and Abandoned Lands
1865-1869 (National Archives Microfilm Publication M821,
Roll 21); Registered Reports of Operations and Conditions,
June-Aug. 1867. Accessed at the National Archives and Records
Administration—Southeast Region, East Point, Georgia.

FUNERAL PROGRAMS and/or OBITUARIES

Benson, Veria Mae Jefferson. Publicly distributed at funeral, Berea Baptist
Church, Fort Worth, Tarrant County, Texas, 31 December 1996.

Black, Nancy Mae Sims. Publicly distributed at funeral, Saint Luke
Christian Methodist Episcopal Church, Shreveport, Caddo
Parish, Louisiana, 24 August 1985.

Cole, Azzie Lee Rose. Publicly distributed at funeral, Hayward Stanmore
Chapel, Marshall, Harrison County, Texas, 17 September 2011.

Cole, James "Jack" Calvin. Publicly distributed at funeral, Shady Grove
Church of Christ, Jefferson, Marion County, Texas, 10 April
1993.

Davis, Ada Lewis Dixon. Publicly distributed at funeral, Logan Chapel
MC, Jefferson, Marion County, Texas, 08 August 1961.

Davis, Ethel Raye Weaver. Publicly distributed at funeral, Saint Andrews
UMC, Fort Worth, Tarrant County, Texas, 15 May 2015.

Dilliard, Irene Mable Lewis. Publicly distributed at funeral, Mount
Vernon UMC, Houston, Harris County, Texas, 28 July 2011.

Donelson, Earline Weaver. Publicly distributed at funeral, Chicago,
Cook County, Illinois, 02 April 1987.

Eaton, Rebecca Bryant Ball Lawson. Publicly distributed at funeral, San
Diego, San Diego County, California, 05 May 2006.

Fitzpatrick, Maggie Martin. Publicly distributed at funeral, Union
Missionary Baptist Church, Jefferson, Marion County, Texas, 27
March 1993.

Gaines, Mazel Norris. Publicly distributed at funeral, The Church of Saint Paul and the Redeemer Episcopal, Chicago, Cook County, Illinois, 29 June 1990.

Hawkins, Ester Weaver Sims Cole. Publicly distributed at funeral, Lewis Chapel UMC, Jefferson, Marion County, Texas, 23 December 2016.

High, Lucille Jefferson. Publicly distributed at funeral, Texas and Louisiana Baptist Association Building, Marshall, Harrison County, Texas, 17 August 2015.

High, Oris Luther, Rev. Publicly distributed at funeral, New Bethel Missionary Baptist Church, Marshall, Harrison County, Texas, 17 February 2001.

Hodge, Clarence. Publicly distributed at funeral, New Light Missionary Baptist Church, Linden, Cass County, Texas, 29 September 2004.

Hodge, Eleanor Dixon. Publicly distributed at funeral, Logan Chapel UMC, Jefferson, Marion County, Texas, 15 August 1987.

Hodge, Hattie Mae Sims. Publicly distributed at funeral, Salem Missionary Baptist Church, Linden, Cass County, Texas, 20 February 1988.

Hodge, Oscar Douglas. Publicly distributed at funeral, February 1997 and obituary-in-part donated by Willie Mae Hodge McDade.

Hodge, Zettie Mae. Obituary transcripts donated by Willie Mae Hodge McDade, June 2003.

Jackson, Novelle Hodge Richardson. Publicly distributed at funeral November 1996 and obituary-in-part donated by Willie Mae Hodge McDade, June 2003.

Jefferson, Ima Viola Sims. Publicly distributed at funeral, Mount Olive Missionary Baptist Church, Fort Worth, Tarrant County, Texas, 02 November 2007.

Jefferson, James Edward. Publicly distributed at funeral, Jefferson Middle School, Jefferson, Marion County, Texas, 28 January 1995.

Johnson, Hezekiah, Jr. Publicly distributed at funeral, Logan Chapel UMC, Jefferson, Marion County, Texas, 23 August 1986.

Jones, Thelma Lois Norris. Publicly distributed at funeral, Saint Paul UMC, Texarkana, Bowie County, Texas, 06 June 1988.

Lewis, Carl Lee. Publicly distributed at funeral, Logan Chapel UMC, Jefferson, Marion County, Texas, 11 December 2004.

Lewis, Fred Edward, Dr. Publicly distributed at funeral, Ebenezer UMC, Marshall, Harrison County, Texas, 19 March 2005 and donated by Mildred Mason, March 2005.

Martin, Bruce Edward. Publicly distributed at funeral, Los Angeles (city and county), California, 02 February 1996.

Norris, Ed Lee. Publicly distributed at funeral, Saint Thomas Episcopal Church, Chicago, Cook County, Illinois, 02 December 1999.

Norris, Edmond. Publicly distributed at funeral, Saint Paul UMC, Jefferson, Marion County, Texas, 02 March 1989.

Norris, Hazel Pearl Smith. Publicly distributed at funeral, Saint Thomas Episcopal Church, Chicago, Cook County, Illinois, 24 August 1994.

Norris, Theodore Lorenzo. Publicly distributed at funeral, Chapel of Griffin Funeral Home, Chicago, Cook County, Illinois, 04 March 1975.

Norris, Will. Publicly distributed at funeral, Saint Paul UMC, Texarkana, Bowie County, Texas, 25 September 1982.

Reeder, Shirley C. Sims. Publicly distributed at funeral, Cullen Missionary Baptist Church, Houston, Harris County, Texas, 07 January 2006.

Reeves, Inez Weaver. Publicly distributed at funeral, Saint Paul UMC, Jefferson, Marion County, Texas, 14 September 1985.

Rhynes, Bessie Mae Martin Williams. Publicly distributed at funeral, Star Light Church of God, Marion County, Texas, 16 January 1982.

Rice, Edgar Lorenzo, III. Publicly distributed at funeral, Miles Memorial CME Church, Marshall, Harrison County, Texas, 13 April 2013.

Richardson, Valerie Sims. Publicly distributed at funeral, Johnson Memorial Christian Methodist Episcopal Church, Shreveport, Caddo Parish, Louisiana, 03 June 1993.

Sims, Carrie Jane Weaver. Publicly distributed at funeral, Lewis Chapel UMC, Jefferson, Marion County, Texas, 11 April 1970.

Sims, Charles Edward. Publicly distributed at funeral, Cullen Missionary Baptist Church, Houston, Harris County, Texas, 14 June 2003.

Sims, Charley Edward, Jr. Publicly distributed at funeral, Campus Drive UMC, Fort Worth, Tarrant County, Texas, 24 September 1992.

Sims, Charley Ray. Publicly distributed at funeral, Lewis Chapel UMC, Jefferson, Marion County, Texas, 30 April 2011.

Sims, Chester. Publicly distributed at funeral, Greater Sweet Home Baptist Church, Fort Worth, Tarrant Count, Texas, 01 July 2004.

Sims, Clarence. Publicly distributed at funeral, Greater Jerusalem Baptist Church, Houston, Harris County, Texas, 27 June 2015.

317

Sims, Clifton Earl. Publicly distributed at funeral, Lewis Chapel UMC, Jefferson, Marion County, Texas, 29 October 1988.

Sims, Clinton. Publicly distributed at funeral, Lewis Chapel UMC, Jefferson, Marion County, Texas, 26 April 2003.

Sims, Cloria Goodman McKinney. Publicly distributed at funeral, Greater New Hope Church, Sherman, Grayson County, Texas, 27 July 2016.

Sims, Howard Cleveland. Publicly distributed at funeral, Saint James UMC, Sherman, Grayson County, Texas, 11 December 1969.

Sims, Johnny Wesley (Love). Publicly distributed at funeral, New Creation UMC, Shreveport, Caddo Parish, Louisiana, 24 January 2003.

Sims, Joseph, Rev. Publicly distributed at funeral, Lewis Chapel MC, Jefferson, Marion County, Texas, 09 December 1968.

Sims, Loyd Edward. Publicly distributed at funeral, Saint James UMC, Sherman, Grayson County, Texas, 06 March 2004.

Sims, Malinda Elizabeth. Publicly distributed at funeral, Saint James UMC, Sherman, Grayson County, Texas, 26 November 1996.

Sims, Milton. Publicly distributed at funeral, McGee Chapel Baptist Church, Houston, Harris County, Texas, 22 February 1989.

Sims, Willy Taylor, Sr. Publicly distributed at funeral, Lewis Chapel UMC, Jefferson, Marion County, Texas, 12 December 1998.

Singleton, Gertie Mae Hodge. Publicly distributed at funeral, Mount Olive Baptist Church, Orange, Orange County, Texas, 31 August 1996.

Taylor, Mattie Sims (Crawford) Jordan Heard. Publicly distributed at funeral, Johnson Chapel UMC, Shreveport, Caddo Parish, Louisiana, 04 November 1973.

Tyson, Hattie Mae Sims. Publicly distributed at funeral, Mount Ira Baptist Church, Jefferson, Marion County, Texas, 03 January 2009.

Warren, Verna Mae Rice Sedberry. Publicly distributed at funeral at the city and county of Los Angeles, California, 12 July 1995.

Weaver, Asa "Acie". Publicly distributed at funeral, Saint Paul UMC, Jefferson, Marion County, Texas, 22 November 1980.

Weaver, Curtis Martin, Jr. Publicly distributed at funeral, Saint Mary's UMC, Houston, Harris County, Texas, 07 January 1978.

Weaver, Curtis Shedwell, Rev. Publicly distributed at funeral, Mount Vernon UMC, Houston, Harris County, Texas, 23 May 1992.

Weaver, Grandison "Grant" W., Jr. Publicly distributed at funeral, Faith Temple Church of God In Christ, Chicago, Cook County, Illinois, 09 November 1968.

Weaver, Isaac "Ike" Gilham. Publicly distributed at funeral, Saint Andrew's UMC, Fort Worth, Tarrant County, Texas, 22 June 1995.

Weaver, Morris Wellington. Publicly distributed at funeral, Saint Andrew's UMC, Fort Worth, Tarrant County, Texas, 30 January 1978.

Weaver, Richard McCallihan, Rev. Publicly distributed at funeral, Mallalieu MC Marshall, Harrison County, Texas, 13 July 1961.

Weaver, Spencer. Publicly distributed at funeral, Lewis Chapel UMC, Jefferson, Marion County, Texas, 30 July 1989.

Weaver, Verna Burns. Publicly distributed at funeral, Judea Baptist Church, Jefferson, Marion County, Texas, 30 July 1967.

Weaver, Walter. Publicly distributed at funeral, Siloam Presbyterian Church, Brooklyn, New York, 31 January 1980.

Whaley, Ivory Pearl Hodge Sims. Publicly distributed at funeral, Salem Missionary Baptist Church, Linden, Cass County, Texas, 15 June 1991.

HEAD RIGHT CERTIFICATES

Grayson, Charles. First Class Head Right Certificate 193 (abstract 164). 09 May 1854. File Red-1-538. Archives and Records Division, Texas General Land Office, Austin, Texas. [acres 4,428].

Hagerty, Rebecca McIntosh Hawkins. First Class Head Right Certification 216 (abstract 451). 08 February 1838. File Bow-1-39. Archives and Records Division, Texas General Land Office, Austin, Texas. [acres 3,965].

INTERNET

Albrecht, Theodore. "Handbook of Texas Online: Scott Joplin." University of Texas, Austin. http://www.tsha.utexas.edu/handbook/online/articles/view/ (accessed January 2005).

Anderson, H. Allen. "Handbook of Texas Online: Marion Try Slaughter II." University of Texas, Austin. http://www.tsha.utexas.edu/handbook/online/ articles/view/ (accessed January 2003).

Atkins, Mark Howard. "Handbook of Texas Online: Marion County." University of Texas, Austin.

http://www.tsha.utexas.edu/handbook/online/articles/ view/ (accessed January 2005).

Barber, E. Susan. "One Hundred Years Toward Suffrage: An Overview." National American Woman Suffrage Association. http://lcweb2.loc.gov/ammem/naw/nawstime.html (accessed July 2005).

Bryan, Jami L. "FIGHTING FOR RESPECT: African-American Soldiers in WWI." The Army Historical Foundation. https://armyhistory.org/fighting-for-respect-african-american-soldiers-in-wwi/ (accessed December 2022).

Christian, Garna L. "Handbook of Texas Online: Brownsville Raid of 1906." University of Texas, Austin. http://www.tsha.utexas.edu/handbook/online/articles/view/ (accessed January 2005).

CNN.com. "Four U.S. Sailors Killed in Navy Ship Blast in Yemen." CNN.com, 12 October 2000. http://www.cnn.com/ (accessed January 2003).

CNN.com. "Massive Bomb Rocks U.S. Military Complex." CNN.com, 26 June 1996. http://www.cnn.com/ (accessed January 2003).

CNN.com. "Oprah: 'Free Speech Rocks.'" CNN.com, 26 February 1998. http://www.cnn.com/US/9802/oprah.verdict/ (accessed July 2005).

CNN.com. "Remains Thought to be From Columbia Crew." CNN.com, 01 February 2003. http//www.cnn.com/2003/TECH/space/02/01/shuttle.colu mbia/ (accessed July 2005).

Conger, Roger N. "Handbook of Texas Online: Waco, Texas." University of Texas, Austin. http://www.tsha.utexas.edu/handbook/online/articles/view/ (accessed March 2005).

Crouch, Barry A. "Handbook of Texas Online: Cullen Montgomery Baker." University of Texas, Austin. http://www.tsha.utexas.edu/handbook/ online/articles/view/ (accessed January 2005).

Decision. Thomas Jordan, Inc., et al., Appellants, vs. Skelly Oil Company et al., Appellees, Number 6886, Court of Civil Appeals of Texas, Texarkana, 296 SW 2nd 279, 08 November 1956. (accessed online 2001–web site discontinued).

Durham, Ken. "Handbook of Texas Online: Longview Race Riot of 1919." University of Texas, Austin.

http://www.tsha.utexas.edu/handbook/online/articles/view/ (accessed January 2005).

FiftyStates.com. "Texas State Flower Bluebonnet." 50states.com. http://www.50states.com/flower/321over.htm (accessed January 2005).

Fry, Hank. "Chapter History." Houston and Texas Area, Region Eight, Heating Ventilation, Air Conditioning and Refrigeration Industry (American Society of Heating, Refrigeration, and Air Conditioning Engineers, Inc). http://www.ashrae-houston.org/pages/history.html (accessed January 2003).

Gale. "John Downing Weaver." *Contemporary Authors Online* (2005). Reproduced in Biography Resource Center. Farmington Hills, Michigan: Thomson Gale, 2005. http://galenet.galegroup.com/servlet/BioRC (accessed January 2005). [Brownsville].

Gale Group. "Lonnie H. Norris." *Who's Who Among African Americans, 17th Edition* (2004). Reproduced in Biography Resource Center. Farmington Hills, Michigan: Thomas Gale, 2005. http://galenet.galegroup.com/servlet/BioRC (accessed January 2005).

Gale Research. "Louis E. Martin." *Contemporary Black Biography* volume 16 (1997). Reproduced in Biography Resource Center. Farmington Hills, Michigan: Thomson Gale, 2005. http://galenet.galegroup.com/servlet/BioRC (accessed January 2005).

Graham, Don B. "Handbook of Texas Online: Literature." University of Texas, Austin. http://www.tsha.utexas.edu/handbook/online/articles/view/ (accessed January 2005).

Green, George N. "Handbook of Texas Online: Mansfield School Desegregation Incident." University of Texas, Austin. http://www.tsha.utexas.edu/ handbook/online/articles/view/ (accessed January 2005).

Hamm, Christine. "Handbook of Texas Online: Huddie Ledbetter." University of Texas, Austin. http://www.tsha.utexas.edu/handbook/online/articles/view/ (accessed January 2005).

"Handbook of Texas Online: Marion DeKalb Taylor." University of Texas, Austin.

http://www.tsha.utexas.edu/handbook/online/ articles/view/ (accessed January 2005). [no author].

Harper, Cecil, Jr. "Handbook of Texas Online: Hughes Springs, Texas." University of Texas, Austin. http://www.tsha.utexas.edu/handbook/online/articles/view/ (accessed January 2005).

History.com Editors. "Army major kills 13 people in Fort Hood shooting spree." https://www.history.com/this-day-in-history/army-major-kills-13-people-in-fort-hood-shooting-spree (accessed January 2023).

Huddleston, John D. "Handbook of Texas Online: Texas Department of Transportation." University of Texas, Austin. http://www.tsha.utexas.edu/ handbook/online/articles/view/ (accessed January 2005).

Jones, G. William. "Handbook of Texas Online: Black Filmmaking." University of Texas, Austin. http://www.tsha.utexas.edu/handbook/online/articles/view/ (accessed January 2005).

Kramer, Kari. "Cullen Baker Country Fair." *Country World News*. 04 November 2004. http://www.countryworldnews.com/ (accessed January 2005).

Lale, Max S. "Handbook of Texas Online: Stockade Case." University of Texas, Austin. http://www.tsha.utexas.edu/handbook/online/articles/view/ (accessed December 2002).

Leatherwood, Art. "Handbook of Texas Online: Red River Campaign." University of Texas, Austin. http://www.tsha.utexas.edu/handbook/online/ articles/view/ (accessed January 2003).

Library of Congress. "Historic American Buildings Survey/Historic American Engineering Record Excelsior Hotel." The Library of Congress. http://memory.loc.gov/cgibin/ampage?collId=hhdatapage&fileName=tx/tx0400/ (accessed January 2005).

Library of Congress. "Historic American Buildings Survey/Historic American Engineering Record Old Jefferson Courthouse." The Library of Congress. http://memory.loc.gov/cgi-bin/ampage?collId=hhsupp&322overnor=tx/ tx0400/tx0488/supp/ (accessed February 2003).

Library of Congress. "Historic American Buildings Survey/Historic

American Engineering Record William M. Freeman House."
The Library of Congress.
http://memory.loc.gov/cgibin/ampage?collId=hhdatapage&file
Name=tx/tx0400/tx0485/data/_(accessed February 2003).

Long, Christopher. "Handbook of Texas Online: Jefferson, Texas."
University of Texas, Austin.
http://www.tsha.utexas.edu/handbook/online/articles/view/
(accessed January 2005). [Handbook Jefferson article cites
population at 4,180, not 4,190; population at 3,800 citizens
and 150 businesses at 1940; and 3,203 citizens and seventy-five
businesses].

Long, Christopher. "Handbook of Texas Online: Willis Whitaker, Sr."
University of Texas, Austin.
http://www.tsha.utexas.edu/handbook/online/articles/view/
(accessed January 2005).

Louisiana Legislature Joint Committee on Conduct of Elections.
"Supplemental Report of Joint Committee of the General
Assembly of Louisiana on the Conduct of the Late Elections,
and the Conditions of Peace and Good Order in the State."
New Orleans, Louisiana: A. L. Lee, State Printer, 1869, pages
75-76. http://moa.umdl.umich.edu/cgi-bin/moa/sgml/moa-
idx?notisid=AEW6809. (accessed 1998).

Morales, Roni. "Handbook of Texas Online: Bessie Coleman."
University of Texas, Austin.
http://www.tsha.utexas.edu/handbook/online/articles/view/
(accessed January 2005).

National Baseball Hall of Fame. "Joseph Williams." National Baseball
Hall of Fame. http://www.baseballhalloffame.org/ (accessed
January 2005).

National Book Foundation. "1999 Young People's Literature." National
Book Award Winners.
http://www.nationalbook.org/nbawinners1990.html
(accessed January 2005).

National Climatic Data Center. "Event Record Details." National
Oceanic and Atmospheric Administration.
http://www.4.ncdc.noaa.gov/cgi/win/wwcgidll?wwevent~Show
Event (accessed January 2005).

National Climatic Data Center. "Query Output." National Oceanic and
Atmospheric Administration.
http://www.4.ncdc.noaa.gov/cgiwin/wwcgidll?wwevent~storms
(accessed January 2005).

National Climatic Data Center. "Record Lowest Temperatures By State Texas." National Oceanic and Atmospheric Administration. http://www.ncdc.noaa.gov/oa/pub/data/special/ (accessed January 2005).

National Weather Service. "April 29, 2017 East Texas Tornado Event." National Oceanic and Atmospheric Administration. https://www.weather.gov/fwd/tornadoes-29apr2017 (accessed January 2023).

National Weather Service. "Major Hurricane Harvey - August 25-29, 2017." National Oceanic and Atmospheric Administration. https://www.weather.gov/crp/hurricane_harvey (accessed January 2023).

National Organization for Women. "Equal Rights Amendment." NOW.org. http://www.now.org/issues/economic/eratext.html (accessed July 2005).

Nobelprize.org. "The Discovery Of Penicillin." Nobel Prize Organization. http://nobelprize.org/medicine/educational/penicillin/ readmore.html (accessed July 2005).

Odintz, Mark. "Handbook of Texas Online: Lewis Chapel, Texas." University of Texas, Austin. http://www.tsha.utexas.edu/handbook/online/articles/view/ (accessed January 2005).

—— "Handbook of Texas Online: Union, Texas." University of Texas, Austin. http://www.tsha.utexas.edu/handbook/online/articles/view/ (accessed January 2005).

PBS.org. "The American Experience Fly Girls People and Events Bessie Coleman." PBS.org. http://www.pbs.org/wgbh/amex/flygirls/peopleevents/ pandeAMEX02.html (accessed January 2005).

PBS.org. "The American Experience Reagan People and Events The Iran-Contra Affair." PBS.org. http://www.pbs.org/wgbh/amex/324overn/peopleevents/pan de08.html (accessed July 2005).

PBS.org. "Frontline The Gulf War." PBS.org. http/www.pbs.org/wgbh/pages/frontline/gulf/ (accessed July 2005).

PBS.org. "Frontline Target America: Terrorist Attacks on Americans,

1979-1988." PBS.org. http/www.pbs.org/wgbh/pages/frontline/shows/target/etc/cron.html (accessed July 2005).

PBS.org. "Frontline Waco The Inside Story Chronology of the Siege." PBS.org. http/www.pbs.org/wgbh/pages/frontline/325ove/timeline.html (accessed November 2003).

PBS.org. "Online NewsHour: The '87 Crash Revisiting The Crash Site 17 October 1997." PBS.org. http://www.pbs.org/newshour/bb/economy/july-dec97/ (accessed July 2005).

PBS.org. "The Rise and Fall of Jim Crow Jim Crow Stories Jessie Daniel Ames." PBS.org. http://www/pbs.org/325ove/jimcrow/stories_people_ames.html (accessed January 2005).

Pitre, Merline. "Handbook of Texas Online: David Abner, Sr." University of Texas, Austin. http://www.tsha.utexas.edu/handbook/online/articles/view/ (accessed January 2005).

Pulitzer.org. "The Pulitzer Prize Winners 1980 Journalism Feature Photography Erwin H. Hagler." Pulitzer Prize Organization. http://www.pulitzer.org/cgi-bin/ (accessed January 2005).

Pulitzer.org. "The Pulitzer Prize Winners 1988 Journalism Spot News Photography Scott Shaw." Pulitzer Prize Organization. http://www.pulitzer.org/cgi/-bin/ (accessed January 2005).

Pulitzer.org. "The Pulitzer Prize Winners 1981 Journalism Spot News Photography Larry C. Price." Pulitzer Prize Organization. http://www.pulitzer.org/cgi/-bin/ (accessed January 200).

Pulitzer.org. "The Pulitzer Prize Winners 1986 Journalism National Reporting Craig Flournoy and George Rodrigue." Pulitzer Prize Organization. http://www.pulitzer.org/cgi-bin/ (accessed January 2005).

Pulitzer.org. "The Pulitzer Prize Winners 1993 Journalism Spot News Photography Ken Geiger and William Snyder." Pulitzer Prize Organization. http://www.pulitzer.org/cgi-bin/ (accessed January 2005).

Pulitzer.org. "The Pulitzer Prize Winners 1977 Special Citations and Awards Letters Alex Haley." Pulitzer Prize Organization. http://www.pulitzer.org/cgi-bin/ (accessed January 2005).

Pulitzer.org. "The Pulitzer Prize Winners 1976 Special Citations and

Awards Music Scott Joplin." Pulitzer Prize Organization.
http://www.pulitzer.org/cgi-bin/ (accessed January 2005).

Pulitzer.org. "The Pulitzer Prize Winners 1964 Journalism Photography
Robert H. Jackson." Pulitzer Prize Organization.
http://www.pulitzer.org/cgi-bin/ (accessed January 2005).

Pulitzer.org. "The Pulitzer Prize Winners 1931 Journalism Reporting A.
B. MacDonald." Pulitzer Prize Organization.
http://www.pulitzer.org/cgi-bin/ (accessed January 2005).

Rempfer, Kyle. "The mass shooting at Fort Hood was 10 years ago, on
Nov. 5, 2009." Army Times.
https://www.armytimes.com/news/your-
army/2019/11/05/the-mass-shooting-at-fort-hood-was-10-years-
ago-on-nov-5-2009/. (accessed January 2023).

Saint James Press. "(Mary) Edmonia Lewis." *Saint James Guide to Black
Artists* (1997). Reproduced in Biography Resource Center.
Farmington Hills, Michigan: Thomson Gale, 2005.
http://galenet.galegroup.com/servlet/BioRC (accessed January
2005).

Scott, Tom III. "Handbook of Texas Online: William Thomas Scott."
University of Texas, Austin.
http://www.tsha.utexas.edu/handbook/online/ articles/view/
(accessed January 2005).

Slaughter, John Etta and Gary W. Houston. "Handbook of Texas
Online: Myra Lillian Davis Hemmings." University of Texas,
Austin.
http://www.tsha.utexas.edu/ handbook/online/articles/view/
(accessed January 2005).

Southern Region Headquarters National Oceanic and Atmospheric
Administration. "Texas Weather Extremes TEX-tremes."
SRH.NOAA.GOV.
http://srh.noaa.gov/fwd/CLIMO/textremes.html
(accessed July 2005).

Tarpley, Fred. "A Guide to Literary East Texas." Texas A and M
University-Commerce.
http://www.humanities-interactive.org/literature/east_texas/
essay.html (accessed January 2005).

Texas Almanac–Texas History. "The Deadly Visitor Yellow Fever."
Texasalmanac.com. http://texasalmanac.com/texasfever.html
(accessed January 2005).

Texas Book Festival. "Texas Book Festival Library Award Winners." Texas
Book Festival.

http://www.texasbookfestival.org/library_grants/allawards.pdf (accessed January 2005).

Texas Department of State Health Services. "West Nile Virus In Texas, 2003." Zoonosis Control Division. http://www.tdh.state.tx.us/zoonosis/327overnor/Arboviral/westNile/statistics/stats.asp?year=2003 (accessed November 2003).

Texas Department of State Health Services. "West Nile Virus In Texas, 2002." Zoonosis Control Division. http://www.tdh.state.tx.us/zoonosis/327overnor/Arboviral/westNile/statistics/stats.asp?year=2002 (accessed November 2003).

Texas Historical Commission. "Texas Historic Sites Atlas Brooks House (Burned)." Texas Historical Commission. http://atlas.the.state.tx.us/scripts/viewform.cgi?atlas_num (accessed January 2005).

Texas Historical Commission. "Texas Historic Sites Atlas Captain William Perry." Texas Historical Commission. http://atlas.the.state.tx.us/scripts/viewform.cgi?atlas_num (accessed January 2005).

Texas Historical Commission. "Texas Historic Sites Atlas Dalhart, Vernon." Texas Historical Commission. http://atlas.the.state.tx.us/scripts/viewform.cgi?atlas_num (accessed January 2005). [Notes Dalhart's birth year as 1881].

Texas Historical Commission. "Texas Historic Sites Atlas Dunn, Wurtzbaugh, Rand." Texas Historical Commission. http://atlas.the.state.tx.us/scripts/viewform.cgi?atlas_num (accessed September 2002).

Texas Historical Commission. "Texas Historic Sites Atlas Excelsior Hotel." Texas Historical Commission. http://atlas.the.state.tx.us/scripts/viewform.cgi?atlas_num (accessed January 2005).

Texas Historical Commission. "Texas Historic Sites Atlas First National Bank of Jefferson." Texas Historical Commission. http://atlas.the.state.tx.us/scripts/viewform.cgi?atlas_num (accessed January 2005).

Texas Historical Commission. "Texas Historic Sites Atlas First Texas Artificial Gas Plant." Texas Historical Commission. http://atlas.the.state.tx.us/scripts/viewform.cgi?atlas_num (accessed September 2002).

Texas Historical Commission. "Texas Historic Sites Atlas Freeman Plantation House." Texas Historical Commission. http://atlas.the.state.tx.us/scripts/viewform.cgi?atlas_num

(accessed September 2002).

Texas Historical Commission. "Texas Historic Sites Atlas Hughes
    Springs." Texas Historical Commission.
    http://atlas.the.state.tx.us/scripts/viewform.cgi?atlas_num
    (accessed January 2005).

Texas Historical Commission. "Texas Historic Sites Atlas International
    Paper Company." Texas Historical Commission.
    http://atlas.the.state.tx.us/scripts/viewform.cgi?atlas_num
    (accessed January 2005).

Texas Historical Commission. "Texas Historic Sites Atlas Jefferson."
    Texas Historical Commission.
    http://atlas.the.state.tx.us/scripts/viewform.cgi?atlas_num
    (accessed January 2005).

Texas Historical Commission. "Texas Historic Sites Atlas The Jefferson
    Jimplecute." Texas Historical Commission.
    http://atlas.the.state.tx.us/scripts/viewform.cgi?atlas_num
    (accessed January 2005).

Texas Historical Commission. "Texas Historic Sites Atlas Jefferson
    Public Library." Texas Historical Commission.
    http://atlas.the.state.tx.us/scripts/viewform.cgi?atlas_num
    (accessed January 2005).

Texas Historical Commission. "Texas Historic Sites Atlas Law Office –
    Gulf Station." Texas Historical Commission.
    http://atlas.the.state.tx.us/scripts/viewform.cgi?atlas_num
    (accessed January 2005).

Texas Historical Commission. "Texas Historic Sites Atlas M. H.
    Wurtsbaugh Lumber Company." Texas Historical Commission.
    http://atlas.the.state.tx.us/scripts/viewform.cgi?atlas_num
    (accessed September 2002).

Texas Historical Commission. "Texas Historic Sites Atlas." Perry,
    Captain William, House. Texas Historical Commission.
    http://atlas.the.state.tx.us/scripts/viewform.cgi?atlas_num
    (accessed January 2005).

Texas Historical Commission. "Texas Historic Sites Atlas Orr and
    Phillips." Texas Historical Commission.
    http://atlas.the.state.tx.us/scripts/viewform.cgi?atlas_num
    (accessed September 2002).

Texas Historical Commission. "Texas Historic Sites Atlas Stone's Texaco
    Station." Texas Historical Commission.
    http://atlas.the.state.tx.us/scripts/viewform.cgi?atlas_num
    (accessed January 2005).

Texas Historical Commission. "Texas Historic Sites Atlas Taylor, Dr. M.
  D., K. Texas Confederate Legislator (Civil War)." Texas
  Historical Commission.
  http://atlas.the.state.tx.us/scripts/viewform.cgi?atlas_num
  (accessed September 2002).

Texas Historical Commission. "Texas Historic Sites Atlas Whitaker
  Memorial Cemetery." Texas Historical Commission.
  http://atlas.the.state.tx.us/scripts/viewform.cgi?atlas_num
  (accessed September 2002).

Texas Rangers Organization. "Texas Ranger History." Texas Ranger
  Research Center. http://texasranger.org/ReCenter/
  (accessed March 2005).

Texas State Library and Archives Commission. "Portraits of Texas
  Governors Chronological List." Texas State Library and
  Archives Commission.
  http://www.tsl.state.tx.us/governors/chron.html
  (accessed November 2003).

Texas State Library Association. "Previous Bluebonnet Winners." Texas
  State Library Association.
  http://www.txla.org/groups/tba/winners.html
  (accessed January 2005).

TravelTex.com. "Carnegie Library." The Official Site of Texas Tourism.
  http://www.traveltex.com/pg.asp?PN=5199&SN=7749590&L
  S (accessed July 2005).

U.S. Census Bureau. "Fact Sheet Jefferson City, Texas." U.S. Census
  Bureau.
  http://factfinder.census.gov/servlet/SAFFFacts?event=Search&
  geo_id=&_geoC (accessed January 2005).

U.S. Census Bureau. "Fact Sheet Marion County, Texas." U.S. Census
  Bureau.
  http://factfinder.census.gov/servlet/SAFFFacts?_event=Search
  &geo_id=&_geoC (accessed January 2005).

U.S. Census Bureau. "Marion County, Texas-DP-1 General Population
  and Housing Characteristics 1990." U.S. Census Bureau.
  http://factfinder.census.gov/servlet/QTTable?_bm=
  (accessed January 2005).

U.S. Census Bureau. "Texas Population of Counties by Decennial
  Census 1900 to 1990." U.S. Census Bureau.
  http://www.census.gov/population/cencounts/tx190090.txt
  (accessed January 2005).

U.S. Census Bureau. "Texas Quick Facts Texas." U.S. Census Bureau.

http://quickfacts.census.gov/qfd/states/4800.html
(accessed January 2005).

United States Mint. "Press Releases and Public Statements The Eyes of
Texas and the Nation Are on Austin as the U.S. Mint Launches
the New Texas Quarter." United States Mint Pressroom.
http://www.usmint.gov/pressroom/ (accessed January 2005).

United States Postal Service. "Folk Musicians Press Release." United
States Postal Service. http://shop.usps.com/
(accessed January 2005).

USA Track and Field. "Hall of Fame Carl Lewis." USA Track and Field.
http://www.usatf.org/HallOfFame/TfshowBio.asp?HOFIDs=9
6 (accessed January 2005).

Wes Smith. "Our History Year By Year: Twentieth Century Historical
Factoids About Jefferson and Marion County."
http://www.texoma.com/~wessmith/page11.htm
(accessed between 1997 and 1999; site has not been updated
since 1997; owner deceased).

Wiley, Nancy. "Handbook of Texas Online: State Fair of Texas."
University of Texas, Austin.
http://www.tsha.utexas.edu/handbook/online/articles/view/
(accessed March 2005).

JOURNALS

Addington, Wendell G. "Slave Insurrections in Texas." The Journal of
Negro History volume 35, number 4 (October 1950): page 420.

Bargo, Michael. "Women's Occupations in the West in 1870." Journal of
the West volume 32, number 1 (January 1993): pages 39, 40.

Hornsby, Alton, Jr. "The Freedmen's Bureau Schools in Texas 1865-
1870." Southwestern Historical Quarterly volume 76, number 4
(April 1973): pages 397-398, 403, 405.

Lale, Max S. "Stagecoach Roads to Marshall." East Texas Historical
Association volume 17, number 2, (1979): pages 20, 25.

Ledbetter, Bill. "Slave Unrest and White Panic: The Impact of Black
Republicanism in Ante-Bellum Texas." Texana 10 (1972): pages
337, 342.

Lentz, Sallie M. "Highlights of Early Harrison County." Southwestern
Historical Quarterly volume 61, number 2 (October 1957): pages
249, 251, 254.

Means, Emilia Gay. "East Texas and the Transcontinental Railroad."

East Texas Historical Association volume 25, number 2 (Fall 1987): pages 49-50.

O'Neal, Bill. "The Country School in East Texas: 1 Room + 3 R's." *East Texas Historical Association* volume 26, number 1 (Spring 1988): page 50.

Smyrl, Frank H. "Texans in the Union Army, 1861-1865." *Southwestern Historical Quarterly* volume 65, number 2 (1961): page 235.

Wooster, Ralph A. "East of the Trinity: Glimpses of Life in East Texas in the Early 1850s." *East Texas Historical Association* volume 13, number 2 (Fall 1975): pages 3, 6.

Wooster, Ralph A. "Notes on Texas' Largest Slaveholders, 1860." *Southwestern Historical Quarterly* volume 65, number 1 (1961): page 76, fn12.

MAGAZINES

Browning, Jennifer. "Turn of the Century Timeline." *Ancestry* volume 17, number 6 (November/December 1999): pages 16, 18, 20-21.

Editors. "Sweet Seventy." *Jet* volume 93, number 23 (04 May 1998), page 30.

Elliott, Lawrence. "The Place That Wouldn't Die." *Reader's Digest* (May 1997): pages 124-126.

England, Nelson. "Urban Indians Trails of Hope." *Texas Highways* (October 1995): page 32.

Martin, Paul. "The Little Town That Could." *National Geographic Traveler* (March/April 1997): pages 30, 32.

Peacock, Howard. "Marshall City With Star Quality." *Texas Highways* (October 1996): page 42.

MARRIAGE CERTIFICATES

Allen, George E. to Odelle Hodge. Cass County Marriage Record Book 16, page 426. County Clerk's Office, Atlanta, Texas.

Berry, Aaron to Ann (Anna) Lewis Berry. Marion County Marriage Record C 1872-1882, page 427. County Clerk's Office, Jefferson, Texas.

Brown, Ranie to Mary Norris Brown. Marion County Marriage Record H 1913-1920, page 192. County Clerk's Office, Jefferson, Texas.

Bryant, James "Jim", Rev. to Nancy Sims Sharp Bryant. Marion County

Marriage Record G 1906-1914, page 527. County Clerk's Office, Jefferson, Texas.

Bryant, S. B. [BROWN] to Ethel Proctor Bryant. Caddo Parish Marriage Record Volume 62, page 378. Parish Clerk's Office, Shreveport, Louisiana.

Calhoun, Oscar to Ada [BROWN] Sharp Calhoun. Caddo Parish Marriage Record Volume 52, page 429. Parish Clerk's Office, Shreveport, Louisiana.

Fitzpatrick, Samuel to Maggie Martin Fitzpatrick. Marion County Marriage Record M 1942-1949, page 178. County Clerk's Office, Jefferson, Texas.

Green, James to Mary Weaver Green. Marion County Marriage Record D 1882-1891, page 245. County Clerk's Office, Jefferson, Texas.

Heard, James "Jim" to Mattie Sims Crawford Jordan Heard Taylor. Caddo Parish Marriage Record Volume 68, page 103. Parish Clerk's Office, Shreveport, Louisiana.

Hodge, Isom, Jr. to Hattie Mae Sims Hodge. Cass County Marriage Record Book 9, page 531. County Clerk's Office, Linden, Texas.

Jackson, Elvis to Novelle Hodge Richardson Jackson. Cass County Marriage Record Book 18, page 509. County Clerk's Office, Linden, Texas.

Jefferson, Layfayette, Sr. to Ima Viola Sims Jefferson. Marion County Marriage Record Book J 1926 – 1931, page 222. County Clerk's Office, Jefferson, Texas.

Lewis, Babe to Miss Ida Peppers Lewis. Marion County Marriage Record Book unknown, page 544. County Clerk's Office, Jefferson, Texas.

Lewis, Carl Lee to Lillian Delia McAlister Lewis. Marion County Marriage Record Book M 1942 – 1049, page 14. County Clerk's Office, Jefferson, Texas.

Lewis, Charles Monroe, Sr., Dr. to Birdie Mae Washington Lewis. Marion County Marriage Record F 1900-1906, page unknown. County Clerk's Office, Jefferson, Texas.

Lewis, Felix, Jr. to Mabel Moore Lewis Isaac. Marion County Marriage Record G 1906-1914, page 183. County Clerk's Office, Jefferson, Texas.

Lewis, Felix, Sr. to Eliza (Liza) Luster Lewis. Marion County Marriage Record H 1913-1920, page 447. County Clerk's Office, Jefferson, Texas.

Lewis, Felix, Sr. to Emaline (Emiline) Spencer Lewis. Marion County
    Marriage Record C 1872-1882, page 24. County Clerk's Office,
    Jefferson, Texas.
Lewis, Isaac to Mary Lou Jackson Lewis. Marion County Marriage Record
    F 1900-1906, page unknown. County Clerk's Office, Jefferson,
    Texas.
Lewis, Monroe to Adeline (Addie) King Lewis. Marion County Marriage
    Record D 1882-1891, page 373. County Clerk's Office,
    Jefferson, Texas.
Lucky, Chappell "J. C." to Mary Walton Martin Lucky. Marion County
    Marriage Record I 1920-1926, page 37. County Clerk's Office,
    Jefferson, Texas.
Martin, John Wesley, Sr. to Mary Exter Moon Martin Hawkins Rockwell
    Davis. Marion County Marriage Record G 1906-1914, page
    unknown. County Clerk's Office, Jefferson, Texas.
Martin, Solomon, Sr. to Mary Walton Martin Lucky. Marion County
    Marriage Record D 1882-1891, page 218. County Clerk's
    Office, Jefferson, Texas.
Norris, Ben Louis to Frances Jane Royal Norris. Marion County Marriage
    Record H 1913-1920, page 342. County Clerk's Office,
    Jefferson, Texas.
Norris, Edmund to Emma Smith Norris. Marion County Marriage
    Record D 1882-1891, page 270. County Clerk's Office,
    Jefferson, Texas.
Norris, Edward to Addie Lee Smith Norris. Vernon Parish Marriage
    Records Volume 5, page 193. Parish Clerk's Office, Louisiana.
Norris, Robert William to Mattie Lee Pitts Norris. Marion County
    Marriage Record H 1913-1920, page 454. County Clerk's Office,
    Jefferson, Texas.
Norris, Sanford to Adaline (Ada, Addie) M. Weaver Norris. Marion
    County Marriage Record Book unknown, page 399. County
    Clerk's Office, Jefferson, Texas.
Norris, Sanford to Luella (Ella) Gallou. Marion County Marriage Record G
    1906-1914, page 295. County Clerk's Office, Jefferson, Texas.
Norris, Will to Wilhelmina Hawkins Norris. Marion County Marriage
    Record I 1920-1926, page 222. County Clerk's Office, Jefferson,
    Texas.
Perry, Oscar to Addie Houston Perry. Marion County Marriage Record F
    1900-1906, page 169. County Clerk's Office, Jefferson, Texas.
Perry, Peter to Winnie Kines. Marion County Marriage Record D 1882-
    1891, page 459. County Clerk's Office, Jefferson, Texas.

Rhynes, Jimmy to Bessie Mae Martin Williams Rhynes. Marion County
    Marriage Record Book unknown, page 213. County Clerk's
    Office, Jefferson, Texas.

Richardson, Oscar to Novelle Hodge Richardson Jackson. Cass County
    Marriage Record Book 16, page 27. County Clerk's Office,
    Linden, Texas.

Sharp, Charley "Jim Bo" Henry to Lillie B. Freeman Sharp. Caddo Parish
    Marriage Record Volume 59, page 504. Parish Clerk's Office,
    Shreveport, Louisiana.

Sharp, John Henry to Nancy Sims Sharp Bryant. Marion County
    Marriage Record E 1891-1900, page 530. County Clerk's
    Office, Jefferson, Texas.

Sims, Berry to Rebecca (Becky) Walton Sims. Marion County Marriage
    Record C 1872-1882, page 201. County Clerk's Office, Jefferson,
    Texas.

Sims, Charley Edward, Sr. and Carrie Jane Weaver Sims. Marion
    County Marriage Record G, 1906-1914, page 18. County
    Clerk's Office, Jefferson, Texas.

Sims, Ernest, Rev. to Ollie Mae Bennett Perry Sims. Marion County
    Marriage Record K 1931-1937, page 118. County Clerk's
    Office, Jefferson, Texas.

Sims, Ernest, Rev. to Leola White Sims. Cass County Marriage Record
    Book 18, page 474. County Clerk's Office, Linden, Texas.

Sims, Howard Cleveland to Corrie Lee Moss Sims Manuel. Marion
    County Marriage Record J 1926-1931, page 517. County
    Clerk's Office, Jefferson, Texas.

Sims, Johnny Wesley (Love) to Annie Mae Ruffin Sims. Marion County
    Marriage Record K 1931-1937, page 490. County Clerk's
    Office, Jefferson, Texas.

Sims, Joseph, Rev. to Willie B. Crawford Sims. Marion County Marriage
    Record H 1913-1920, page 489. County Clerk's Office,
    Jefferson, Texas.

Sims, Loyd Edward to LeVelma Smith. Marion County Marriage Record
    L 1937-1942, page 536. County Clerk's Office, Jefferson, Texas.

Sims, Milton married. Marion County Marriage Record M 1942-1949,
    page 361. County Clerk's Office, Jefferson, Texas.

Sims, Milus to Angeline (Angelina) Love Sims. Marion County
    Marriage Record C 1872-1882, page 91. County Clerk's Office,
    Jefferson, Texas.

Singleton, Lester B. to Gertie Mae Hodge Singleton. Marion County
    Marriage Record K 1931-1937, page 381. County Clerk's Office,

Jefferson, Texas.

Smith, Joseph "Joe" to Patsey Norris Smith. Marion County Marriage
Record D 1882-1891, page 26. County Clerk's Office, Jefferson,
Texas.

Stevenson, Dan to Sallie B. Lewis Cole Stevenson. Marion County
Marriage Record L 1937-1942, page 574. County Clerk's
Office, Jefferson, Texas.

Taylor, Theodore "Ted" R., Rev. to Mattie Sims Crawford Jordan Heard
Taylor. Caddo Parish Marriage Record Volume 76, page 285.
Parish Clerk's Office, Shreveport, Louisiana.

Thompson, W. B. to Ruby Lee Sharp Thompson. Caddo Parish Marriage
Record Volume 74, page 243. Parish Clerk's Office, Shreveport,
Louisiana.

Tyson, Ed to Hattie Mae Sims Tyson. Marion County Marriage
Record Book L 1927 – 1942, page 11. County Clerk's Office,
Jefferson, Texas.

Weaver, Grandison to Malinda Norris Weaver. Marion County Marriage
Record Book unknown, page 317. County Clerk's Office,
Jefferson, Texas.

Weaver, Henry Lee to Betty Smith Weaver. Marion County Marriage
Record H 1913-1920, page 499. County Clerk's Office,
Jefferson, Texas.

Weaver, Henry Lee to Edith Smith Weaver. Marion County Marriage
Record H 1913-1920, page 175. County Clerk's Office,
Jefferson, Texas.

Weaver, Isaac "Ike" Gilham to Etta Mae McKie Yeldell Weaver. Tarrant
County Marriage Records, Local File Number 35954. County
Clerk's Office, Fort Worth, Texas.

Weaver, Milton to Bessie Dixon Weaver. Marion County Marriage
Record H 1913-1920, page 400. County Clerk's Office,
Jefferson, Texas.

Weaver, Richard to Mary Williams Weaver. Marion County Marriage
Record Book unknown, page 277. County Clerk's Office,
Jefferson, Texas.

Weaver, Spencer to Murrie Greenwood Weaver. Marion County
Marriage Record K 1931-1937, page 54. County Clerk's Office,
Jefferson, Texas.

White, Leslie to Mary Lou [BROWN] Bryant White. Caddo Parish,
Marriage Record Volume 138, page 423. Parish Clerk's Office,
Shreveport, Louisiana.

White, Sydney J. to Sallie (Sarah) Weaver White Vaughn. Marion County

Marriage Record D 1882-1891, page 251. County Clerk's Office, Jefferson, Texas.

MILITARY SERVICE RECORDS

Norris, Will. WWI Draft Registration Cards. 20 April 1999. National Archives and Records Administration—Southeast Region, East Point, Georgia.

Sims, Milton. Military Personnel Record. 13 May 1999. Military Personnel Records Center, Saint Louis, Missouri. [Public Information Releasable Under the Freedom of Information Act].

Weaver, Morris Wellington. Military Personnel Record. 29 July 1999. Military Personnel Records Center, Saint Louis, Missouri. [Public Information Releasable Under the Freedom of Information Act].

Weaver, Richard McCallihan, Rev. WWI Draft Registration Cards. 09 March 1999. National Archives and Records Administration—Southeast Region, East Point, Georgia.

MINISTERIAL RECORDS

Weaver, Curtis Shedwell, Rev. Minister Obituary. 1992. Journal of the Texas Annual Conference of the United Methodist Church, South Central Jurisdiction. General Commission on Archives and History. The United Methodist Church, Madison, New Jersey.

Weaver, Richard McCallihan, Rev. Minister Mentions in Conference Minutes. 1962. General Minutes of the Methodist Church, Texas Conference, Central Jurisdiction. General Commission on Archives and History. The United Methodist Church, Madison, New Jersey.

NEWSPAPERS

"Actor Makes Quick Trip to Jefferson." *Jefferson Jimplecute* (16 September 2004): page 8, columns 1-4.

"Administrator's Notice." *Jefferson Jimplecute* (24 February 1911): page and column number unknown. *Jefferson Jimplecute* from 06 January 1911 to 18 December 1913, Microfilm Publication 6050-1, Southwest Micropublishing, Inc., El Paso, Texas.

"Barbecue and Picnic at Lover's Leap." *Jefferson Jimplecute* (07 July 1911): page and column number unknown. *Jefferson Jimplecute* from 06 January 1911 to 18 December 1913, Microfilm Publication 6050-1, Southwest Micropublishing, Inc., El Paso, Texas.

"A Call To Arms." *Jefferson Jimplecute* (16 June 1911): page number unknown, column 5. *Jefferson Jimplecute* from 06 January 1911 to 18 December 1913, Microfilm Publication 6050-1, Southwest Micropublishing, Inc., El Paso, Texas.

"Civil Conservation Corps Reunion." *Jefferson Jimplecute* (29 July 2004): page 3, columns 4-6.

"Closing Down." *Jefferson Jimplecute* (04 March 1999): page 8, columns 1-3.

"Death Notice Marvis Wilson "Bill" McGuffin." *Jefferson Jimplecute* (20 May 2004): page 4, column 1.

"Death Notice Inez Weaver Reeves." *Jefferson Jimplecute* (19 September 1985): page and column numbers unknown; newspaper death notice contributed by Ester W. Sims Cole Hawkins, newspaper death notice in possession of book author.

"Death Notices Carrie Jane Weaver Sims." *Jefferson Jimplecute* (publication date unknown): page and column numbers unknown; photocopy of newspaper death notice contributed by Ester W. Sims Cole Hawkins, original newspaper death notice in possession of Ester W. Sims Cole Hawkins.

"Death Notice Malinda Elizabeth Sims." *Sherman Herald Democrat* (24 November 1996): page A8, column 4.

"Death Notice Ann Weaver." *Jefferson Jimplecute* volume 45, number 39 (13 March 1913): page unknown. *Jefferson Jimplecute* from 06 January 1911 to 18 December 1913, Microfilm Publication 6050-1, Southwest Micropublishing, Inc., El Paso, Texas.

"Death Notice Clipping Rev. Curtis Shedwell Weaver." Newspaper name unknown (date of publication unknown): page number unknown; newspaper death notice clipping contributed by Ester W. Sims Cole Hawkins, newspaper death notice clipping in possession of book author.

"District Court Notice Sharp." *Jefferson Jimplecute* (28 April 1911) page number unknown, column 4. *Jefferson Jimplecute* from 06 January 1911 to 18 December 1913, Microfilm Publication 6050-1, Southwest Micropublishing, Inc., El Paso, Texas.

"The First History of Jefferson." *Jeffersonian* volume 17, number 1 Spring/Summer 1997): page 4, columns 1-5.

"Jeffersonian to be Honored in Brochure." *Jefferson Jimplecute* (04

November 1999) page 11, columns 1-2.

"Juneteenth Celebration." *Jefferson Jimplecute* (16 June 1911) page
number unknown, column 2. *Jefferson Jimplecute* from 06
January 1911 to 18 December 1913, Microfilm Publication
6050-1, Southwest Micropublishing, Inc., El Paso, Texas.

"Legislature Designates Jefferson as Bed and Breakfast Capital."
Jeffersonian volume 17, number 1 (Spring/Summer 1997): page
1.

"Local Churches." *Jefferson Jimplecute* 52nd Pilgrimage Supplement (29
April 1999): page 33, column 2.

"Long-lost Indian Village Found in Marion County." *Jefferson Jimplecute*
(11 February 1999): pages 1, 3, columns 2-6, 1-6.

"Marion County Cotton." *Jefferson Jimplecute* (23 June 1911): page
number unknown, column 4. *Jefferson Jimplecute* from 06
January 1911 to 18 December 1913, Microfilm Publication
6050-1, Southwest Micropublishing, Inc., El Paso, Texas.

"Marion County Veterans Memorial Dedicated." *Jefferson Jimplecute* 52nd
Pilgrimage Supplement (29 April 1999) page 35, column 5.

"Methodist Army Schedules Local Rehab Efforts." *Jefferson Jimplecute* (17
June 2004) page 12, columns 1-4.

"Obituaries Azzie Lee Rose Cole." *Marshall News Messenger.* (?
September 2011) page ?, column 3.

"Personal Mention Wurtsbaugh." *Jefferson Jimplecute* (06 January 1911):
page number unknown, column 4. *Jefferson Jimplecute* from 06
January 1911 to 18 December 1913, Microfilm Publication
6050-1, Southwest Micropublishing, Inc., El Paso, Texas.

"Prohibition Rally." *Jefferson Jimplecute* (09 June 1911): page number and
column unknown. *Jefferson Jimplecute* from 06 January 1911 to
18 December 1913, Microfilm Publication 6050-1, Southwest
Micropublishing, Inc., El Paso, Texas.

"Sims Professional Building." *Texas Times* (12 August 1982): pages 3, 10,
columns 1-6; article contributed by Ester W. Sims Cole
Hawkins, article in possession of book author.

"Texaco Station." *Jefferson Jimplecute* (12 August 2004): page 1, columns
1-6.

PROPERTY TAX ASSESSMENTS

Ford, John V. 1860 Marion County, Texas, Tax Rolls. Texas Secretary
of State, Archives and Information Services Division, Texas

State Library and Archives Commission Microfilm Reel 115501 and Reel 115502. Accessed Marietta, Cobb County, Georgia, Public Library and O'Fallon, Saint Clare County, Illinois, Public Library.

Freeman, William M. 1860 Marion County, Texas, Tax Rolls. Texas Secretary of State, Archives and Information Services Division, Texas State Library and Archives Commission Microfilm Reel 115501 and Reel 115502. Accessed Marietta, Cobb County, Georgia, Public Library and O'Fallon, Saint Clare County, Illinois, Public Library.

Hagerty, Rebecca McIntosh Hawkins. 1860 Marion County, Texas, Tax Rolls. Texas Secretary of State, Archives and Information Services Division, Texas State Library and Archives Commission Microfilm Reel 115501 and Reel 115502. Accessed Marietta Public Library, Cobb County, Georgia and O'Fallon Public Library, Saint Clare County, Illinois.

Jones, John M. 1860 Marion County, Texas, Tax Rolls. Texas Secretary of State, Archives and Information Services Division, Texas State Library and Archives Commission Microfilm Reel 115501 and Reel 115502. Accessed Marietta Public Library, Cobb County, Georgia and O'Fallon Public Library, Saint Clare County, Illinois.

Lewis, Felix. 1870-1900, Marion County, Texas, Tax Rolls. Texas Secretary of State, Archives and Information Services Division, Texas State Library and Archives Commission Microfilm Reel 115501 and Reel 115502. Accessed Marietta Public Library, Cobb County, Georgia and O'Fallon Public Library, Saint Clare County, Illinois.

Martin, Solomon. 1892 Marion County, Texas, Tax Rolls. Texas Secretary of State, Archives and Information Services Division, Texas State Library and Archives Commission Microfilm Reel 115501 and Reel 115502. Accessed Marietta Public Library, Cobb County, Georgia and O'Fallon Public Library, Saint Clare County, Illinois.

Norris, Richard "Dick". 1870-1897, Marion County, Texas, Tax Rolls. Texas Secretary of State, Archives and Information Services Division, Texas State Library and Archives Commission Microfilm Reel 115501 and Reel 115502. Accessed Marietta Public Library, Cobb County, Georgia and O'Fallon Public Library, Saint Clare County, Illinois.

Pattillo, Lewis Alexander. 1860 Marion County, Texas, Tax Rolls. Texas

Secretary of State, Archives and Information Services Division, Texas State Library and Archives Commission Microfilm Reel 115501 and Reel 115502. Accessed Marietta, Cobb County, Georgia, Public Library and O'Fallon, Saint Clare County, Illinois, Public Library.

Perry, Peter. 1870-1900, Marion County, Texas, Tax Rolls. Texas Secretary of State, Archives and Information Services Division, Texas State Library and Archives Commission Microfilm Reel 115501 and Reel 115502. Accessed Marietta Public Library, Cobb County, Georgia and O'Fallon Public Library, Saint Clare County, Illinois.

Sims, Berry. 1875-1897, Marion County, Texas, Tax Rolls. Texas Secretary of State, Archives and Information Services Division, Texas State Library and Archives Commission Microfilm Reel 115501 and Reel 115502. Accessed Marietta Public Library, Cobb County, Georgia and O'Fallon Public Library, Saint Clare County, Illinois.

Sims, Milus. 1878, 1884, Marion County, Texas, Tax Rolls. Texas Secretary of State, Archives and Information Services Division, Texas State Library and Archives Commission Microfilm Reel 115501 and Reel 115502. Accessed Marietta Public Library, Cobb County, Georgia and O'Fallon Public Library, Saint Clare County, Illinois.

Slaughter, Marion Try, Agent for wife. 1860 Marion County, Texas, Tax Rolls. Texas Secretary of State, Archives and Information Services Division, Texas State Library and Archives Commission Microfilm Reel 115501 and Reel 115502. Accessed Marietta Public Library, Cobb County, Georgia and O'Fallon Public Library, Saint Clare County, Illinois.

Walton, Peter W. 1860 Marion County, Texas, Tax Rolls. Texas Secretary of State, Archives and Information Services Division, Texas State Library and Archives Commission Microfilm Reel 115501 and Reel 115502. Accessed Marietta Public Library, Cobb County, Georgia and O'Fallon Public Library, Saint Clare County, Illinois.

SCHOOL RECORDS

Cole, Aboliva Household. Scholastic Census 1930-1931, Office of the Superintendent of School; Union School District, Marion County, Texas, School Census Card, 10 March 1931. Archives and Information Services Division, Texas State Library and Archives Commission Microfilm Reel 1503063. Accessed O'Fallon Public Library, Saint Clare County, Illinois.

Johnson, Hezekiah, Sr. Household. Scholastic Census 1930-1931, Office of the Superintendent of School; Union School District, Marion County, Texas, School Census Card, 10 March 1931. Archives and Information Services Division, Texas State Library and Archives Commission Microfilm Reel 1503063. Accessed O'Fallon Public Library, Saint Clare County, Illinois.

Lewis, Charles Monroe, Jr. School Attendance and Graduation Record Verification. Wiley College, Marshall, Harrison, County, Texas,

Lewis, Isaac Household. Scholastic Census 1930-1931, Office of the Superintendent of School; Jefferson School District, Marion County, Texas, School Census Card, 16 March 1931. Archives and Information Services Division, Texas State Library and Archives Commission Microfilm Reel 1503063. Accessed O'Fallon Public Library, Saint Clare County, Illinois.

Norris, Ben Household. Scholastic Census 1930-1931, Office of the Superintendent of School; blank School District, Marion County, Texas, School Census Card, 11 March 1931. Archives and Information Services Division, Texas State Library and Archives Commission Microfilm Reel 1503063. Accessed O'Fallon, Saint Clare County, Illinois, Public Library.

Norris, Robert Household. Scholastic Census 1930-1931, Office of the Superintendent of School; blank School District, Marion County, Texas, School Census Card, 11 March 1931. Archives and Information Services Division, Texas State Library and Archives Commission Microfilm Reel 1503063. Accessed O'Fallon Public Library, Saint Clare County, Illinois.

Norris, Sam Household. Scholastic Census 1930-1931, Office of the Superintendent of School; blank School District, Marion County, Texas, School Census Card, 11 March 1931. Archives and Information Services Division, Texas State Library and Archives Commission Microfilm Reel 1503063. Accessed O'Fallon Public Library, Saint Clare County, Illinois.

Perry, Oscar Household. Scholastic Census 1930-1931, Office of the Superintendent of School; Lewis Chapel School District, Marion County, Texas, School Census Card, 05 March 1931. Archives and Information Services Division, Texas State Library and Archives Commission Microfilm Reel 1503063. Accessed O'Fallon Public Library, Saint Clare County, Illinois.

Porter, Hattie Weaver Household. Scholastic Census 1930-1931, Office of the Superintendent of School; Bethlehem School District, Marion County, Texas, School Census Card, 19 March 1931. Archives and Information Services Division, Texas State Library and Archives Commission Microfilm Reel 1503063. Accessed O'Fallon Public Library, Saint Clare County, Illinois.

Sims, Charley Edward, Sr. Household. Scholastic Census 1930-1931, Office of the Superintendent of School; Lewis Chapel School District, Marion County, Texas, School Census Card, 05 March 1931. Archives and Information Services Division, Texas State Library and Archives Commission Microfilm Reel 1503063. Accessed O'Fallon Public Library, Saint Clare County, Illinois.

Sims, Joseph, Rev. Household. Scholastic Census 1930-1931, Office of the Superintendent of School; Lewis Chapel School District, Marion County, Texas, School Census Card, 05 March 1931. Archives and Information Services Division, Texas State Library and Archives Commission Microfilm Reel 1503063. Accessed O'Fallon Public Library, Saint Clare County, Illinois.

Sims, Milton. Grammar Grades Certificate. Lewis Chapel School, Jefferson, Texas, 1940. [Certificate permitted Milton to enter high school].

Warren, Verna Mae Rice Sedberry Warren. School Attendance and Graduation Record Verification. Prairie View A and M University, Prairie View, Waller County, Texas.

SLAVE SCHEDULES

Ford, John V. 1860 U.S. Slave Schedule, Jefferson, Marion County, Texas. Beat 4, 20 August 1860, page 126. National Archives Microfilm Publication M653, Roll 1311. Microfilm reproduced by Heritage Quest Genealogical Services, Bountiful, Utah.

Freeman, William M., Agent for wife. 1860 U.S. Slave Schedule, Jefferson, Marion County, Texas. Beat 4, [Date not legible] August 1860, page unknown. National Archives Microfilm Publication M653, Roll 1311. Microfilm reproduced by Heritage Quest Genealogical Services, Bountiful, Utah.

Hagerty, Rebecca McIntosh Hawkins. 1860 U.S. Slave Schedule, Jefferson, Marion County, Texas. Beat 4, 24 August 1860, pages 129-130. National Archives Microfilm Publication M653, Roll 1311. Microfilm reproduced by Heritage Quest

Genealogical Services, Bountiful, Utah.

Hughes, Reese. 1860 U.S. Slave Schedule, Cass County, Texas. Beat 2, 12 October 1860, page unknown. National Archives Microfilm Publication M653, Roll 1309. Microfilm reproduced by Heritage Quest Genealogical Services, Bountiful, Utah.

Jones, John M. 1860 U.S. Slave Schedule, Jefferson, Marion County, Texas. Beat 3, 16 July 1860, pages unknown. National Archives Microfilm Publication M653, Roll 1311. Microfilm reproduced by Heritage Quest Genealogical Services, Bountiful, Utah.

Kelly, George Addison. 1860 U.S. Slave Schedule, Jefferson, Marion County, Texas. Beat 2, 10 July 1860, page 122. National Archives Microfilm Publication M653, Roll 1311. Microfilm reproduced by Heritage Quest Genealogical Services, Bountiful, Utah.

Lewis, Andrew J. 1860 U.S. Slave Schedule, Cass County, Texas. Beat 2, 15 October 1860, page unknown. National Archives Microfilm Publication M653, Roll 1309. Microfilm reproduced by Heritage Quest Genealogical Services, Bountiful, Utah.

Matthews, Elizabeth (Eliza) Ellen Sharp 1860 U.S. Slave Schedule, Jefferson, Marion County, Texas. Beat 4, 24 August 1860, page unknown. National Archives Microfilm Publication M653, Roll 1311. Microfilm reproduced by Heritage Quest Genealogical Services, Bountiful, Utah.

Pattillo, Lewis Alexander. 1860 U.S. Slave Schedule, Jefferson, Marion County, Texas. Beat 1, 05 July 1860, page 121. National Archives Microfilm Publication M653, Roll 1311. Microfilm reproduced by Heritage Quest Genealogical Services, Bountiful, Utah.

Perry slaveholders, various. 1850 U.S. Slave Schedule, Port Caddo, Harrison County, Texas, 13 December 1850, page 377; 14 December 1850, pages 384-385; and 15 December 1850, pages 379-380. National Archives Microfilm Publication M432, Roll 917. CD-ROM reproduced by Heritage Quest Genealogical Services, Bountiful, Utah.

Rogers, Thomas Jefferson. 1860 U.S. Slave Schedule, Jefferson, Marion County, Texas. Beat unknown, 25 August 1860, page unknown. National Archives Microfilm Publication M653, Roll 1311. Microfilm reproduced by Heritage Quest Genealogical Services, Bountiful, Utah.

Slaughter, Marion Try, Agent for wife. 1860 U.S. Slave Schedule, Jefferson, Marion County, Texas. Beat 3, 16 July 1860, page unknown. National Archives Microfilm Publication M653, Roll 1311. Microfilm reproduced by Heritage Quest Genealogical Services, Bountiful, Utah.

Smith, Susan Ann Cocke, Agent for heirs. 1860 U.S. Slave Schedule, Jefferson, Marion County, Texas. Beat 4, 17 August 1860, page unknown. National Archives Microfilm Publication M653, Roll 1311. Microfilm reproduced by Heritage Quest Genealogical Services, Bountiful, Utah.

Taylor, Marion DeKalb. 1860 U.S. Slave Schedule, Jefferson, Marion County, Texas. Beat 4, 17 August 1860, page unknown. National Archives Microfilm Publication M653, Roll 1311. Microfilm reproduced by Heritage Quest Genealogical Services, Bountiful, Utah.

Tullis, Aaron Duke, Agent for wife. 1860 U.S. Slave Schedule, Jefferson, Marion County, Texas. Beat unknown, 25 August 1860, page unknown. National Archives Microfilm Publication M653, Roll 1311. Microfilm reproduced by Heritage Quest Genealogical Services, Bountiful, Utah.

Walton, Peter W. 1860 U.S. Slave Schedule, Jefferson, Marion County, Texas. Beat 4, 17 August 1860, page unknown. National Archives Microfilm Publication M653, Roll 1311. Microfilm reproduced by Heritage Quest Genealogical Services, Bountiful, Utah.

Whitaker, Willis, Sr. 1860 U.S. Slave Schedule, Cass County, Texas. Beat 1, 11 October 1860, page unknown. National Archives Microfilm Publication M653, Roll 1309. Microfilm reproduced by Heritage Quest Genealogical Services, Bountiful, Utah.

SOCIAL SECURITY NUMBER APPLICATIONS

Bryant, S. B. Social Security Number Application. Number 5487. Social Security Administration, Washington, D.C.

Hill, Sallie Gray Weaver. Social Security Number Application. Number 2250. Social Security Administration, Washington, D.C.

Hodge, Hattie Mae Sims. Social Security Number Application. Number 5170. Social Security Administration, Washington, D.C.

Jackson, Novelle Hodge Richardson. Social Security Number Application. Number 0660. Social Security Administration, Washington, D.C.

Lewis, Roscoe Conklin, Dr. Social Security Number Application. Number 2180. Social Security Administration, Washington,

D.C.

Martin, Bruce Edward. Social Security Number Application. Number 4940. Social Security Administration, Washington, D.C.

Norris, Ben Louis. Social Security Number Application. Number 6385. Social Security Administration, Washington, D.C.

Norris, Edmund. Social Security Number Application. Number 7174. Social Security Administration, Washington, D.C.

Norris, Edward. Social Security Number Application. Number 7885. Social Security Administration, Washington, D.C.

Norris, Sanford. Rev. Social Security Number Application. Number 0724. Social Security Administration, Washington, D.C.

Norris, Will. Social Security Number Application. Number 9852. Social Security Administration, Washington, D.C.

Perry, Oscar. Request for E/R Action. Number 3892. Social Security Administration, Washington, D.C.

Reeves, Inez Weaver. Social Security Number Application. Number 5862. Social Security Administration, Washington, D.C.

Rice, Eula V. Weaver. Social Security Number Application. Number 2928. Social Security Administration, Washington, D.C.

Rose, Adene (Addline) (Addine) Dixon Graham. Social Security Number Application. Number 8550. Social Security Administration, Washington, D.C.

Sharp, Charley "Jim Bo" Henry. Social Security Number Application. Number 1960. Social Security Administration, Washington, D.C.

Sims, Carrie Jane Weaver. Social Security Number Application. Number 1592. Social Security Administration, Washington, D.C.

Sims, Charley Edward, Jr. Social Security Number Application. Number 4388. Social Security Administration, Washington, D.C.

Sims, Clinton. Social Security Number Application. Number 0896. Social Security Administration, Washington, D.C.

Sims, Joseph, Rev. Social Security Number Application. Number 3116. Social Security Administration, Washington, D.C.

Sims, Malinda Elizabeth. Social Security Number Application. Number 7686. Social Security Administration, Washington, D.C.

Sims, Milton. Social Security Number Application. Number 0809. Social Security Administration, Washington, D.C.

Singleton, Gertie Mae Hodge. Social Security Number Application. Number 5887. Social Security Administration, Washington, D.C.

Weaver, Asa "Acie". Social Security Number Application. Number 7050.

Social Security Administration, Washington, D.C.

Weaver, Curtis Martin, Jr. Social Security Number Application. Number 7881. Social Security Administration, Washington, D.C.

Weaver, Curtis Shedwell, Rev. Social Security Number Applications. Number 2318. Social Security Administration, Washington, D.C.

Weaver, Etta Mae McKie Yeldell. Social Security Number Application. Number 7227. Social Security Administration, Washington, D.C.

Weaver, Grandison "Grant" W., Jr. Social Security Number Application. Number 8166. Social Security Administration, Washington, D.C.

Weaver, Henry Lee. Social Security Number Application. Number 5453. Social Security Administration, Washington, D.C.

Weaver, Isaac "Ike" Gilham. Social Security Number Application. Number 3639. Social Security Administration, Washington, D.C.

Weaver, Morris Wellington. Social Security Number Application. Number 2236. Social Security Administration, Washington, D.C.

Weaver, Murrie Greenwood. Social Security Number Application. Number 9905. Social Security Administration, Washington, D.C.

Weaver, Patsey Charleston Jones. Social Security Number Application. Number 6123. Social Security Administration, Washington, D.C.

Weaver, Spencer. Social Security Number Application. Number 7055. Social Security Administration, Washington, D.C.

Weaver, Walter. Social Security Number Application. Number 0864. Social Security Administration, Washington, D.C.

Whaley, Ivory Pearl Hodge Sims. Social Security Number Application. Number 9508. Social Security Administration, Washington, D.C.

Williams, Zena (Zennie) Arvesta Lewis. Social Security Number Application. Number 4731. Social Security Administration, Washington, D.C.

TOMBSTONE TRANSCRIPTS

Note:

Headstones may be absent for any number of reasons: vandalism, inclement weather, financial, and/or burial overlapping. Some birth and death dates may be innocently inaccurate, attributable to informant and/or tombstone engraver's unintentional error. The book's author walked these three cemeteries in 1998 on a cold day in the sleet and rain; however, only the names that pertain to bloodlines within four generations appear here in this recording. Additional interments are noted per obituaries or death certificates. Lewis Chapel Cemetery is located on Lewis Chapel Road, Jefferson, Marion County, Texas. Union Chapel Cemetery is located on Union Chapel Road, Jefferson, Marion County, Texas. Valley Plain Cemetery is located off Highway 49, Kellyville, Marion County, Texas.

Bryant, Nancy. 1 Jun 1879 30 Oct 1927 Age 48. At Rest. Lewis Chapel Cemetery, Jefferson, Marion County, Texas.

Calhoun, Ada. 10 May 1941 Age 40. J. S. Williams and Sons, Inc., Shreveport, LA. Lewis Chapel Cemetery, Jefferson, Marion County, Texas.

Cole, James "Jack" Calvin. Additional interment, per obituary. Union Chapel Cemetery, Jefferson, Marion County, Texas.

Dixon, Moscoe. 27 Mar 06 20 Aug 45 Age 39. Union Chapel Cemetery, Jefferson, Marion County, Texas.

Hawkins, Zuma. 9 Mar 19?12/13? H May Burton FH Jefferson Texas. Union Chapel Cemetery, Jefferson, Marion County, Texas.

High, Oris Luther, Rev. Additional interment, per obituary. Union Chapel Cemetery, Jefferson, Marion County, Texas.

Lewis, Carl Lee. Additional interment, per obituary. Union Chapel Cemetery, Jefferson, Marion County, Texas.

Lewis, Charles M., Dr. 1874 1936 Union Chapel Cemetery, Jefferson, Marion County, Texas.

Lewis, Erbie. 14 Sep 1903 30 Nov 1945. Union Chapel Cemetery, Jefferson, Marion County, Texas.

Lewis, Felix, Jr. Additional interment, per death certificate. Union Chapel Cemetery, Jefferson, Marion County, Texas.

Lewis, Helon. 1862 1925. Union Chapel Cemetery, Jefferson, Marion County, Texas.

Lewis, Helon, Rev. 5 Oct 1905 21 Dec 1994. Hayes Mortuary Texarkana Texas. Union Chapel Cemetery, Jefferson, Marion County, Texas.

Lewis, Isaac. 8 Apr 1883 13 Oct 1951 Age 68. GBNF In Memory Of. Union Chapel Cemetery, Jefferson, Marion County, Texas.

Lucky, Mary. 1852 1929 At Rest. Lewis Chapel Cemetery, Jefferson, Marion County, Texas.

Johnson, Hezekiah, Sr. Feb 1876 April 18? Age 78. Union Chapel Cemetery, Jefferson, Marion County, Texas.

Johnson, Hezekiah, Jr. 11 Jun 1919 8 Aug 1986. CPL U.S. Army WWII. Atlanta FH. Union Chapel Cemetery, Jefferson, Marion County, Texas.

Norris, Alex "Alec". Additional interment, per death certificate. Valley Plain Cemetery, Kellyville, Marion County, Texas.

Norris, Edmund. Additional interment, per death certificate. Valley Plain Cemetery, Kellyville, Marion County, Texas.

Norris, Maggie W. 6 Jan 1894 27 Jun 1959. OES 128. Valley Plain Cemetery, Kellyville, Marion County, Texas.

Norris, Sam. 30 Nov 1888 28 Dec 1940. In Memory. Valley Plain Cemetery, Kellyville, Marion County, Texas.

Norris, Sanford. Additional interment, per death certificate. Valley Plain Cemetery, Kellyville, Marion County, Texas.

Perry, Addie. Apr 1880 19 May 1946. Lewis Chapel Cemetery, Jefferson, Marion County, Texas.

Perry, Oscar. 1882 1969. Lewis Chapel Cemetery, Jefferson, Marion County, Texas.

Perry, Winnie. 22 Oct 1913. Member of ME Church Near my God to Thee Lilly of the Valley Household of Ruth Lodge 3171 GBNF. Lewis Chapel Cemetery, Jefferson, Marion County, Texas.

Reeves, Inez. 1907 1985. Lewis and Walker Jefferson Texas. Union Chapel Cemetery, Jefferson, Marion County, Texas.

Rice, Edgar. 1 Jan 1896 13 Feb 1986. PVT U.S. Army WWI. Lewis and Walker. Union Chapel Cemetery, Jefferson, Marion County, Texas.

Rice, Eula. 15 Feb 1898 27 Apr 1971. Union Chapel Cemetery, Jefferson, Marion County, Texas.

Rose, Addine D. G. 1892 1982. Atlanta FH. Union Chapel Cemetery, Jefferson, Marion County, Texas.

Sims, ?. 15 Jun 1904. Union Chapel Cemetery, Jefferson, Marion County, Texas.

Sims, Berry. 1858 27 Sep 1927. GBNF. Lewis Chapel Cemetery, Jefferson, Marion County, Texas.

Sims, Carrie J. 1899 1970. Mother. Lewis Chapel Cemetery, Jefferson, Marion County, Texas.

Sims, Charley, Sr. 1889 1954. Father. Lewis Chapel Cemetery,

Jefferson, Marion County, Texas.

Sims, Clinton. Additional interment per obituary. Lewis Chapel Cemetery, Jefferson, Marion County, Texas.

Sims, Howard Cleveland. Additional interment per obituary. Lewis Chapel Cemetery, Jefferson, Marion County, Texas.

Sims, J. S., Rev. 22 Feb 1897 4 Dec 1968. At Rest. Lewis Chapel Cemetery, Jefferson, Marion County, Texas.

Sims, Rebecca. 1881 22 Jul 1940. GBNF. Lewis Chapel Cemetery, Jefferson, Marion County, Texas.

Taylor, Mattie C. 18 May 1895 28 Oct 1973. At Rest. Lewis Chapel Cemetery, Jefferson, Marion County, Texas.

Weaver, Acie. 1898 1980. Union Chapel Cemetery, Jefferson, Marion County, Texas.

Weaver, Ann. Additional interment, per *Jefferson Jimplecute* newspaper death notice. Union Chapel Cemetery, Jefferson, Marion County, Texas.

Weaver, Henry L. 1898 1969. Lewis Walker. Union Chapel Cemetery, Jefferson, Marion County, Texas.

Weaver, Malinda Norris. Additional interment, per death certificate. Union Chapel Cemetery, Jefferson, Marion County, Texas.

Weaver, Milton. 6 Nov 1921. TEXAS PVT 368 INF 92nd DIV. Union Chapel Cemetery, Jefferson, Marion County, Texas.

Weaver, Richard. 20 Jan 1892 8 Jul 1961. Texas PVT U.S. Army WWI. Union Chapel Cemetery, Jefferson, Marion County, Texas.

Weaver, Richard. 1898 1944. Union Chapel Cemetery, Jefferson, Marion County, Texas.

Weaver, Richard, Jr. Additional interment, per death certificate. Union Chapel Cemetery, Jefferson, Marion County, Texas.

Weaver, Spencer. 20 Nov 190?8/9? 27 Jul 1989. Lewis Walker Jefferson Texas Union Chapel Cemetery, Jefferson, Marion County, Texas.

U.S. SPECIAL SCHEDULE

Norris, Sarah. 1890 U.S. Special Schedule Surviving Soldiers, Sailors, and Marines, and Widows, Etc., Marion County, Texas, Precinct 2, ED illegible, SD 151, Sheet 1, Page Stamp unknown, Dwelling 48, Family 48, Date June 1890. National Archives Microfilm Publication M123, Roll 99.

VOTING REGISTRATIONS

Browning, Albert. Voting Registration Lists 1867-1869, Marion County, Texas. Page 226, Registration 217, Date 04 July 1867. Texas Secretary of State, Archives and Information Services Division, Texas State Library and Archives Commission Microfilm, Reel VR-8. Accessed Marietta Public Library, Cobb County, Georgia.

Cooper, Thomas. Voting Registration Lists 1867-1869, Marion County, Texas. Page 222, Registration 47, Date 02 July 1867. Texas Secretary of State, Archives and Information Services Division, Texas State Library and Archives Commission Microfilm, Reel VR-8. Accessed Marietta Public Library, Cobb County, Georgia.

Crawford, Moses "M. K.". Voting Registration Lists 1867-1869, Marion County, Texas. Pages 226 and 262, Registrations 212 and 1669, Dates 04 July 1867 and 27 July 1869. Texas Secretary of State, Archives and Information Services Division, Texas State Library and Archives Commission Microfilm, Reel VR-8. Accessed Marietta Public Library, Cobb County, Georgia.

Fitzgerald, Ambrose. Voting Registration Lists 1867-1869, Marion County, Texas. Page 241, Registration 835, Date 16 July 1867. Texas Secretary of State, Archives and Information Services Division, Texas State Library and Archives Commission Microfilm, Reel VR-8. Accessed Marietta Public Library, Cobb County, Georgia.

Kelly, George Addison. Voting Registration Lists 1867-1869, Marion County, Texas. Page 228, Registration 297, Date 05 July 1867. Texas Secretary of State, Archives and Information Services Division, Texas State Library and Archives Commission Microfilm, Reel VR-8. Accessed Marietta Public Library, Cobb County, Georgia.

Kines, Albert. Voting Registration Lists 1867-1869, Marion County, Texas. Page 229, Registration 324, Date 06 July 1867. Texas Secretary of State, Archives and Information Services Division, Texas State Library and Archives Commission Microfilm, Reel VR-8. Accessed Marietta Public Library, Cobb County, Georgia.

McCoy, Nathaniel. Voting Registration Lists 1867-1869, Marion County, Texas. Page 272, Registration 2063, Date 26 November 1869. Texas Secretary of State, Archives and

Information Services Division, Texas State Library and Archives Commission Microfilm, Reel VR-8. Accessed Marietta Public Library, Cobb County, Georgia.

Norris, Richard "Dick". Voting Registration Lists 1867-1869, Marion County, Texas. Page 228, Registration 293, Date 05 July 1867. Texas Secretary of State, Archives and Information Services Division, Texas State Library and Archives Commission Microfilm, Reel VR-8. Accessed Marietta Public Library, Cobb County, Georgia.

Perry, Lawrence. Voting Registration Lists 1867-1869, Marion County, Texas. Page 242, Registration 846, Date 16 July 1867. Texas Secretary of State, Archives and Information Services Division, Texas State Library and Archives Commission Microfilm, Reel VR-8. Accessed Marietta Public Library, Cobb County, Georgia.

Perry, Peter. Voting Registration Lists 1867-1869, Marion County, Texas. Page 241, Registration 839, Date 16 July 1867. Texas Secretary of State, Archives and Information Services Division, Texas State Library and Archives Commission Microfilm, Reel VR-8. Accessed Marietta Public Library, Cobb County, Georgia.

Perry, William. Voting Registration Lists 1867-1869, Marion County, Texas. Page 223, Registration 88, Date 03 July 1867. Texas Secretary of State, Archives and Information Services Division, Texas State Library and Archives Commission Microfilm, Reel VR-8. Accessed Marietta Public Library, Cobb County, Georgia.

Phillips, Whitmill "Whit". Voting Registration Lists 1867-1869, Marion County, Texas. Page 250, Registration 1186, Date 20 August 1867. Texas Secretary of State, Archives and Information Services Division, Texas State Library and Archives Commission Microfilm, Reel VR-8. Accessed Marietta Public Library, Cobb County, Georgia.

Rogers, Thomas Jefferson. Voting Registration Lists 1867-1869, Marion County, Texas. Pages 227 and 259, Registrations 253 and 1559, Dates 05 July 1867 and 15 January 1869. Texas Secretary of State, Archives and Information Services Division, Texas State Library and Archives Commission Microfilm, Reel VR-8. Accessed Marietta Public Library, Cobb County, Georgia.

Schluter, Walter P. Voting Registration Lists 1867-1869, Marion County, Texas. Page 250, Registration 1190, Date 24 August

1867. Texas Secretary of State, Archives and Information Services Division, Texas State Library and Archives Commission Microfilm, Reel VR-8. Accessed Marietta Public Library, Cobb County, Georgia.

Smith, George Washington. Voting Registration Lists 1867-1869, Marion County, Texas. Page 221, Registration 2, Date 02 July 1867. Texas Secretary of State, Archives and Information Services Division, Texas State Library and Archives Commission Microfilm, Reel VR-8. Accessed Marietta Public Library, Cobb County, Georgia.

Stewart, Richard. Voting Registration Lists 1867-1869, Marion County, Texas. Page 221, Registration 20, Date 02 July 1867. Texas Secretary of State, Archives and Information Services Division, Texas State Library and Archives Commission Microfilm, Reel VR-8. Accessed Marietta Public Library, Cobb County, Georgia.

Tullis, Aaron Duke. Voting Registration Lists 1867-1869, Marion County, Texas. Page 223, Registration 119, Date 02 July 1867. Texas Secretary of State, Archives and Information Services Division, Texas State Library and Archives Commission Microfilm, Reel VR-8. Accessed Marietta Public Library, Cobb County, Georgia.

Younger, Thomas E. Voting Registration Lists 1867-1869, Marion County, Texas. Page 265, Registration 1792, Date 17 November 1869. Texas Secretary of State, Archives and Information Services Division, Texas State Library and Archives Commission Microfilm, Reel VR-8. Accessed Marietta Public Library, Cobb County, Georgia.

The Spirit itself beareth we are the children of God: And if children, then heirs; heirs of God, and joint-heirs with Christ; if so be that we suffer with him, that we may be also glorified together.

Romans 8:16-17 KJV

EVERY NAME INDEX

360

One generation passeth away, and another generation cometh: but the earth abideth for ever.

Ecclesiastes 1:4 KJV

EVERY PLACE INDEX

368

Henceforth I call you not servants: for the servant knoweth not what his lord doeth: but I have called you friends; for all things that I have heard of my Father I have made known unto you.

John 15:15 KJV

And It Came To Pass

Designed by Greta McKelvey

Typeset by Greta McKelvey

Printed and bound by outsourced commercial printing

Typeface: Goudy Old Style

Distributed by Amazon.

Made in the USA
Middletown, DE
26 October 2023

41409594R00205